Communications in Computer and Information Science 971

Commenced Publication in 2007
Founding and Former Series Editors:
Phoebe Chen, Alfredo Cuzzocrea, Xiaoyong Du, Orhun Kara, Ting Liu,
Dominik Ślęzak, and Xiaokang Yang

More information about this series at http://www.springer.com/series/7899

Ilsun You · Hsing-Chung Chen
Vishal Sharma · Igor Kotenko (Eds.)

Mobile Internet Security

Second International Symposium, MobiSec 2017
Jeju Island, Republic of Korea, October 19–22, 2017
Revised Selected Papers

 Springer

Editors
Ilsun You
Department of Information Security
Engineering
Soonchunhyang University
Choongchungnam-do, Korea (Republic of)

Hsing-Chung Chen
Asian University Taiwan
Taichung, Taiwan

Vishal Sharma
Department of Information Security
Soonchunhyang University
Seoul, Korea (Republic of)

Igor Kotenko
SPIIRAS
St. Petersburg, Russia

ISSN 1865-0929 ISSN 1865-0937 (electronic)
Communications in Computer and Information Science
ISBN 978-981-13-3731-4 ISBN 978-981-13-3732-1 (eBook)
https://doi.org/10.1007/978-981-13-3732-1

Library of Congress Control Number: 2018964132

This Springer imprint is published by the registered company Springer Nature Singapore Pte Ltd.
The registered company address is: 152 Beach Road, #21-01/04 Gateway East, Singapore 189721, Singapore

Preface

The emerging communication technologies leverage various solutions emphasizing communication efficiency, mobility, and low latency for the network devices. The 5G era is an adoption of such advantages, which aims to facilitate the services with a better connectivity and high quality of experience (QoS). Despite the revolutionary mobile technologies, the adoption of such technologies raises several issues such as security, privacy, and trust. There are certain challenges associated with communication entities that focus on 5G, including user identity management based on (U) subscriber identification module (SIM), mutual authentication between networks and users, securing the path between communicating parties, etc. Various facilities evolving in 5G, for example, Internet of Things (IoT), distributed mobility management (DMM), and network slicing require more secured and low latency procedures.

This volume contains revised and selected papers presented at the 2017 International Symposium on Mobile Internet Security held in Jeju Island, Republic of Korea, during October 19–22, 2017 and invited papers. The purpose of MobiSec 2017 was to bring together academia and industry working on different aspects to exchange ideas and explore new research directions for addressing the challenges in mobility Internet security. MobiSec 2017 focused on publishing high-quality papers, which are closely related to various theories and practical applications in mobility management to highlight state-of-the-art research.

MobiSec 2017 provided an international forum for sharing original research results among specialists in fundamental and applied problems of mobile Internet security. The symposium was organized by the Innovative Information Science and Technology Research Group, Laboratory of Mobile Internet Security at Soonchunhyang University, Elementary Education Research Institute of Jeju National University, STS Research Center of Jeju National University, and technically sponsored by the BK21 plus Team of Smart Internet-Based Fusion-Contents Technology at Chosun University, Korean Institute of Smart Media, in cooperation with Soonchunhyang University, Thunghai University, and Asia University.

A total of 38 papers related to significant aspects of the theory and applications of mobile security were accepted for presentation to MobiSec 2017. MobiSec 2017 was further enriched by the invited talks. Only 14 papers were selected for publication in CCIS. The success of the symposium was assured by the team effort of the sponsors, organizers, reviewers, and participants. We would like to acknowledge the contribution of the individual Program Committee members and thank the paper reviewers. Our sincere gratitude goes to the participants of the conference and all authors of the submitted papers.

We wish to express our gratitude to the team at Springer led by Alfred Hofmann for their help and cooperation.

October 2018

Ilsun You
Hsing-Chung Chen
Vishal Sharma
Igor Kotenko

Organization

General Co-chairs

Ilsun You   Soonchunhyang University, South Korea
Hsing-Chung Chen   Asia University, Taiwan

Program Co-chairs

Tianhan Gao   Northeastern University, China
Kangbin Yim   Soonchunhyang University, South Korea

Publication Co-chairs

Igor Kotenko   ITMO University and SPIIRAS, Russia
Xin Su   Hohai University, China

International Advisory Committee

Pankoo Kim   Chosun University, South Korea
Marek Ogiela   AGH University, Poland
Kyung-Hyune Rhee   Pukyong National University, South Korea

Program Committee

Ramon Alcarria   Technical University of Madrid, Spain
Hiroaki Anada   University of Nagasaki, Japan
Benjamin Aziz   University of Portsmouth, UK
Joonsang Baek   University of Wollongong, Australia
Andrey Chechulin   Bonch-Bruevich State University of Telecommications,
                              Russia
Seong-je Cho   Dankook University, South Korea
Luigi Coppolino   Epsilon Srl., Italy
Salvatore D'Antonio   Università degli Studi di Napoli Parthenope, Italy
Jianfeng Guan   BUPT, China
Hsu-Chun Hsiao   National Taiwan University, Taiwan
Antonio J. Jara   HES-SO University, Switzerland
Shinsaku Kiyomoto   KDDI, Japan
Kyung Ho Lee   Korea University, South Korea
Yong-Hwan Lee   Wonkwang University, South Korea
Alessio Merlo   University of Genoa, Italy
Evgenia Novikova   Electrotechnical University LETI, Russia
Vladimir A. Oleshchuk   University of Agder, Norway

Roland Rieke	Fraunhofer SIT, Germany
Igor Saenko	Signal Academy, Russia
Sang Uk Shin	Pukyong National University, South Korea
Kunwar Singh	National Institute of Technology, India
Fei Song	Beijing Jiaotong University, China
Chul Sur	Pusan University of Foreign Studies, South Korea
Chunhua Su	University of Aizu, Japan
Xin Su	Hohai University, China
Kunlin Tsai	ThungHai University, Taiwan
Isaac Woungang	Ryerson University, Canada
Toshihiro Yamauchi	Okayama University, Japan
Neil Yen	University of Aizu, Japan
Jeong Hyun Yi	Soongsil University, South Korea
Baokang Zhao	NUDT, China

Contents

Attack Detection in Mobile Internet and Networks Using the Graph-Based Schemes for Combining the Support Vector Machines

Alexander Branitskiy[1,2(✉)] (ID) and Igor Kotenko[1,2] (ID)

[1] St. Petersburg Institute for Informatics and Automation of the Russian Academy of Sciences (SPIIRAS), St. Petersburg, Russia
{branitskiy, ivkote}@comsec.spb.ru
[2] St. Petersburg National Research University of Information Technologies, Mechanics and Optics (ITMO University), St. Petersburg, Russia

Abstract. The paper presents a comparative analysis of two schemes for combining the binary classifiers. In the role of such classifiers we use well-known models—support vector machines (SVMs). For constructing the multiclass models we experimentally investigate two schemes for combining the SVMs, namely a classification binary tree (CBT) and a directed acyclic graph (DAG). Main application of considered models we demonstrate in the paper is attack detection and classification in mobile Internet and networks. The various performance indicators of classifiers are given. The results of experiments performed for to estimate these indicators and usage of time and system resources are presented.

Keywords: Network attack detection · Support vector machine
Classification binary tree · Directed acyclic graph
Principal component analysis

1 Introduction

Methods of machine learning are actively used in the research community for solving a lot of applied problems. Their popularity is largely due to the fact that such methods are able to perform a generalization of data when there are labeled training samples. This characteristic is especially useful when analyzing dynamically changing objects, e.g. the feature vectors of mobile network traffic. To detect anomalies in it the internal parameters of the intelligent classifiers are adjusted in such a way that they retain the ability to classify correctly most of the training elements as well as the earlier unseen elements.

To solve this problem SVMs are used in this paper, but their restriction is that a single SVM can be applied only for a binary classification of objects. Therefore to construct a multiclass model it is proposed to perform a comparative analysis of two approaches combining SVMs,—CBT and DAG. Both approaches are graph-based and designed for hierarchical placement of binary classifiers as node elements.

© Springer Nature Singapore Pte Ltd. 2019
I. You et al. (Eds.): MobiSec 2017, CCIS 971, pp. 1–16, 2019.
https://doi.org/10.1007/978-981-13-3732-1_1

The novelty of the paper is a comparative analysis of two graph-based schemes for combining the SVMs. Within this paper we introduce for each scheme several comparative characteristics which allow to estimate the complexity of constructing the scheme and training its elements. The contribution of the paper is a formal representation and experimental investigation of graph-based models for combining the SVMs and algorithms for classifying the objects on the basis of these models. In contrast to the other papers [1,2] of the authors, this paper is focused on theoretical and experimental analysis of schemes for combining the binary classifiers (SVMs) of the same type.

The rest of the paper is organized as follows. The Sect. 2 lists some relevant papers that consider the usage of SVMs for detecting the network attacks. The Sect. 3 presents the algorithm for training the SVM and several of its modified versions. In the Sect. 4 the proposed graph-based models for combining the SVMs are considered. The Sect. 5 contains the results of computational experiments aimed at calculating the performance indicators of each scheme using an open set of network dumps. The Sect. 6 summarizes the main results and reveals the direction of further research.

2   Related Work

In this section we present some papers devoted to applying the SVMs within the tackled problem.

In the paper [3] for describing the SVM-based multiclass model it is proposed to modify the basic classifier so that the elements of one class are located within the same area. For this purpose for each class a separate sphere is constructed which has the smallest radius and, if possible, accommodates all the training elements from the corresponding class. The resulting class of the test vector is that class for which the normalized distance from this vector to the decision boundary is maximum among all the other spheres. While the standard SVM is aimed at finding a hyperplane separating elements of two different classes, the approach proposed in this paper implies the application of SVM for isolation of elements of only one class within a minimal sphere and without regard to information about other classes.

The paper [4] presents an algorithm for training the SVM which is complemented by the introduction of a hierarchical clustering. The proposed optimization is aimed at reducing the SVM training time. For this purpose the hierarchical trees are constructed iteratively on the basis of training elements, then the SVM is trained on the nodes of these trees.

In the paper [5] authors propose to use two-step procedure for classifying the network connection records. The first stage is the reduction of redundancy in the analyzed vectors with the help of a principal component analysis (PCA). In the second stage the SVM is applied for detecting the network attacks. The advantage of this approach is to increase the speed of training the SVM as well as reduce the time of a vector analysis with the help of the SVM.

Combining the SVM with a genetic algorithm is presented in the paper [6]. The genetic algorithm is used for configuring the SVM parameters. Moreover, such a fusion allows to find the most acceptable set of network features. In another paper [7] the genetic algorithm is used for selection of certain fields from IP- and TCP-headers of network packets. Each field is assigned a coefficient (score) which reflects the frequency of occurrence of corresponding field in anomalous packets and indicates a flag of the change in the field. The vector formed from these fields is processed by the SVM.

Another population-based approach is employed in the paper [8]. However, compared with the papers [6,7], the paper [8] considers the particle swarm optimization which plays a dual role of stochastic algorithm designed both for setting the SVM parameters and selecting the features of network connection records. For this purpose two variants of particle swarm optimization are used: standard and binary.

The authors of the paper [9] use a combination of two approaches: the elements of rough set theory and fuzzy SVM. The purpose of the first component is to remove redundant attributes from the point of view of their non-informativity, as well as to speed up the operation of the following classifier. The second component is engaged in the detection of anomalous records.

In the paper [10] each SVM is trained in such a way that it is able to recognize instances of only one class among all the others (combination by the rule "one-vs-all"). The winner is the classifier, which possesses the highest confidence level, which in terms of SVM is expressed as the distance from the analyzed vector to the optimal separating hyperplane. The chi-square method is used as a procedure for preprocessing the analyzed vector (a set of attributes). Primarily for each attribute of the vector its chi-square metric value is calculated. Then on the basis of this value those attributes which are low priority in terms of their importance in the classification of this vector are removed from the initial set.

In the papers [11,12] for solving the task of network attack detection three classifiers are presented: decision tree, SVM and their combination. Functioning of the third hybrid classifier consists of two phases. First the test data are input for the decision tree which generated the node information (number of terminal node). Then the test data together with node information are processed by the SVM which output is a result of classification. In this approach it is assumed that additional information obtained from the decision tree will increase the efficiency of the SVM. In the case of a discrepancy of results obtained using these tree classifiers the ultimate result is based on weight voting.

The analysis of considered papers proves the relevance of the tackled problem and still requires a detailed investigation of methods for combining the SVMs.

3   Algorithm for Training the SVM

In this section we consider the standard algorithm for training the SVM and some of its improvements.

SVM is one of the most widespread approaches applicable for solving the tasks of classification [13], regression [14] and prediction [15]. The method has a simple geometric analogy which is associated with the assumption that the elements of various classes may be linearly separated as belonging to different subspaces. The set of such elements may be partitioned by several different hyperplanes which are described using the equation family $\left\{ \boldsymbol{W}^T \cdot \boldsymbol{Z} - b = 0 \right\}$. Such hyperplanes differ from each other by the normal vector $\boldsymbol{W}$ specifying a hyperplane inclination and bias parameter b, specifying an ascent/descent rate of the hyperplane. An optimal separating hyperplane is a hyperplane which provides a maximum and equal distance between the nearest elements from different classes, e.g. A and B.

Let such hyperplane H_O is described using the equation $\boldsymbol{W}_O^T \cdot \boldsymbol{Z} - b_O = 0$, where $\boldsymbol{W}_O^T = (w_{O1}, \ldots, w_{On})^T$, and separating hyperplanes H_A and H_B which are parallel to H_O pass through these nearest elements of classes A and B and are described using the equations $\boldsymbol{W}_O^T \cdot \boldsymbol{Z} - b_A = 0$ and $\boldsymbol{W}_O^T \cdot \boldsymbol{Z} - b_B = 0$ (Fig. 1). Then $b_A = b_O + \varepsilon$, $b_B = b_O - \varepsilon$, where $\varepsilon > 0$. Without loss of generality we can assume that $\varepsilon = 1$ (otherwise this can be achieved by dividing both parts of equations by ε). Thereby the equations of two hyperplanes H_A and H_B have the following form: $\boldsymbol{W}_O^T \cdot \boldsymbol{Z} - b_O = 1$ and $\boldsymbol{W}_O^T \cdot \boldsymbol{Z} - b_O = -1$, and classes A and B are presented as follows: $\left\{ \boldsymbol{Z} | \boldsymbol{W}_O^T \cdot \boldsymbol{Z} - b_O > 1 \right\}$, $\left\{ \boldsymbol{Z} | \boldsymbol{W}_O^T \cdot \boldsymbol{Z} - b_O < -1 \right\}$. Consequently the SVM model is described using the formula:

$$Y(\boldsymbol{Z}) = \text{sign}\left(\boldsymbol{W}_O^T \cdot \boldsymbol{Z} - b_O \right) = \text{sign}\left(\sum_{i=1}^{n} w_{Oi} \cdot z_i - b_O \right).$$

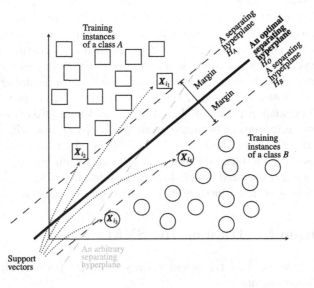

Fig. 1. Principle of constructing the optimal hyperplane in the SVM

Let us consider the training algorithm of the SVM upon the condition of existing the linear hyperplanes H_A and H_B which separate correctly all training instances (Listing 1).

Listing 1. SVM training

---

1 Prepare training data in the form $\mathcal{X} = \{(X_i, u_i)\}_{i=1}^{M}$, where $u_i = [X_i \in A] - [X_i \in B]$.

2 Calculate Lagrange multipliers $\left\{\lambda_i^{(O)}\right\}_{i=1}^{M}$ as a result of solving the

optimization task: $-\frac{1}{2} \cdot \sum_{i=1}^{M} \sum_{j=1}^{M} \lambda_i \cdot \lambda_j \cdot u_i \cdot u_j \cdot X_i^T \cdot X_j + \sum_{i=1}^{M} \lambda_i \to \max_{\lambda_1,\ldots,\lambda_M}$

with restrictions $\sum_{i=1}^{M} \lambda_i \cdot u_i = 0$ and $\lambda_i \geqslant 0$, where $i = 1, \ldots, M$ (e.g. using the sequential minimal optimization [16]).

3 Calculate the normal vector in the hyperplane equation:

$W_O = \sum_{i=1}^{M} \lambda_i^{(O)} \cdot u_i \cdot X_i = \sum_{j=1}^{M'} \lambda_{i_j}^{(O)} \cdot u_{i_j} \cdot X_{i_j}$, where

$\{i_1, \ldots, i_{M'}\} \subseteq \{1, \ldots, M\}$, and $\left\{X_{i_j}\right\}_{j=1}^{M'}$ — a set of support vectors with non-zero $\lambda_{i_j}^{(O)}$.

4 Calculate a free coefficient in the hyperplan equation: $b_O = W_O^T \cdot X_{i_j} - u_{i_j}$, where X_{i_j} — one of the support vectors.

5 Specify the SVM model: $Y(Z) = \text{sign}\left(\sum_{j=1}^{M'} w_{i_j} \cdot X_{i_j}^T \cdot Z - b_O\right)$, where

$w_{i_j} = \lambda_{i_j}^{(O)} \cdot u_{i_j}$, and summation operator is taken over the index subset of training sample, which corresponds only to support vectors $\left\{X_{i_j}\right\}_{j=1}^{M'} \subseteq \{X_i\}_{i=1}^{M}$.

When the objects from different classes cannot be separated linearly, two approaches may be used both of which are aimed at decreasing the following value: $\Omega(Y, \mathcal{X}) = \frac{1}{M} \cdot \# \{X_i \,|\, Y(X_i) \neq u_i\}_{i=1}^{M}$—an empirical risk functional on the elements of training set. The first approach is to apply special nonlinear transformations—kernels φ for transition to a new n'-dimensional space. It is assumed that in a new space, which is obtained as a result of the mapping $\varphi(Z) = (\varphi_1(Z), \ldots, \varphi_{n'}(Z))^T$, there is a hyperplane satisfying the previously specified criteria.

The second approach is based on introducing the penalty function so that to ignore some of false classified objects either on the basis of (I) total quantity or (II) summary distance to the separating hyperplane. The case I is to search such separating hyperplane which provides a minimum value of the following characteristic function $\sum_{i=1}^{M} [Y(X_i) \neq u_i]$. In the case II the objective function is $\sum_{i=1}^{M} \text{dist}(X_i, H_O) \cdot [Y(X_i) \neq u_i]$, where $\text{dist}(\cdot, \cdot)$ - the distance function between the indicated pair of arguments (vector, hyperplane) within a given metrics.

4   Graph-Based Schemes for Combining the SVMs

In this section we consider two graph-based schemes for combining the SVM into the multiclass model.

First we introduce the following notation:

- $\mathcal{C} = \{0, \ldots, m\}$—the set of class labels
  - 0—normal label
  - $\{1, \ldots, m\}$—attack labels
- $\mathcal{X}_{\mathcal{C}}^{(LS)} = \{(\boldsymbol{X}_i, c_i)\}_{i=1}^{M}$—the labeled training data set, where $c_i \in \mathcal{C}$
- $\mathcal{X}_{\mathcal{C}}^{(TS)} = \{(\boldsymbol{Z}_i, c_i)\}_{i=1}^{M^*}$—the labeled testing data set, where $c_i \in \mathcal{C}$
- $Y_{\mathcal{A}_1 \mathcal{B}_1}, \ldots, Y_{\mathcal{A}_K \mathcal{B}_K} : \mathbb{R}^n \to \{-1, 1\}$—the SVMs which are to be combined using CBT or DAG, where $\mathcal{A}_i \neq \varnothing$, $\mathcal{B}_i \neq \varnothing$, $\mathcal{A}_i \cap \mathcal{B}_i = \varnothing$, $\mathcal{A}_i \subsetneq \mathcal{C}$, $\mathcal{B}_i \subsetneq \mathcal{C}$.

Each i-th SVM $Y_{\mathcal{A}_i \mathcal{B}_i}$ can be considered as a mapping which transforms the n-dimensional real input vector to one-dimensional output value -1 or 1. Thus the SVM is intended only for binary classification, i.e. when there are elements belonging strictly to two classes. For the transition to the case of a larger number of classes we propose to consider two graph-based schemes—CBT and DAG which allow to combine several SVMs trained on different subsamples into the multiclass model.

CBT is defined recursively using the following formula in which each j-th node SVM $Y_{\mathcal{A}_j \mathcal{B}_j}$ is trained to recognize elements having the different labels from class sets $\mathcal{A}_j$ and $\mathcal{B}_j$:

$$CBT_{\mathcal{D}} = \begin{cases} \langle Y_{\mathcal{A}_j \mathcal{B}_j}, CBT_{\mathcal{A}_j}, CBT_{\mathcal{B}_j} \rangle, & \text{if } \#\mathcal{D} \geqslant 2, \text{ where } \mathcal{D} = \mathcal{A}_j \bigcup \mathcal{B}_j \\ \mathcal{D}, & \text{if } \#\mathcal{D} = 1. \end{cases}$$

Here $\mathcal{A}_j \subsetneq \mathcal{C}$ and $\mathcal{B}_j \subsetneq \mathcal{C}$—randomly generated or user specified subsets. $CBT_{\mathcal{A}_j}$ and $CBT_{\mathcal{B}_j}$—left and right CBT respectively. Each j-th SVM located in the nodes of such structure is trained on the elements of two class subsets $\mathcal{A}_j$ and $\mathcal{B}_j$: $\{(\boldsymbol{X}_l, -1) \, | c_l \in \mathcal{A}_j \}_{l=1}^{M} \bigcup \{(\boldsymbol{X}_l, 1) \, | c_l \in \mathcal{B}_j \}_{l=1}^{M}$ (Fig. 2). Thereby SVM is trained in the way that its output value is equal -1 if the label c_l of the object $\boldsymbol{X}_l$ belongs to $\mathcal{A}_j$, otherwise its output is configured as 1. In the listing 2 we present an algorithm of classifying the network attacks through a consistent dichotomy of the set $\mathcal{C}$.

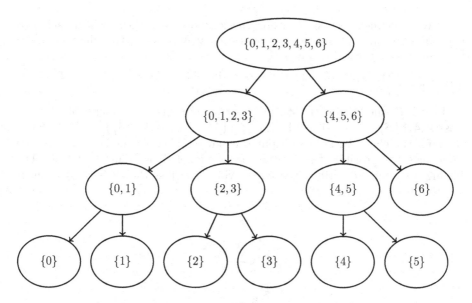

Fig. 2. Example of CBT

Listing 2. Classifying the network attacks using SVMs combined via CBT

---

    input   : Trained SVMs $Y_{\mathcal{AB}}$ represented as nodes of $CBT_{\mathcal{C}}$
               Input object $\boldsymbol{Z}$ which is to be classified
    output: Class label of the object $\boldsymbol{Z}$

```
 1 function F_CBT(CBT_D, Z)
 2 begin
 3     if CBT_D = D then
 4     |   return D
 5     else
 6     |   ⟨Y_AB, CBT_A, CBT_B⟩ := CBT_D
 7     |   if Y_AB(Z) = −1 then
 8     |   |   R := call recursively function F_CBT(CBT_A, Z)
 9     |   |   return R
10     |   else
11     |   |   R := call recursively function F_CBT(CBT_B, Z)
12     |   |   return R
13     |   end
14     end
15 end
16 R := call function F_CBT(CBT_C, Z)
```

DAG is defined recursively using the following formula in which each j-th node SVM $Y_{A_j B_j}$ is trained to recognize elements having the different labels from singleton class sets A_j and B_j:

$$DAG_{\mathcal{D}} = \begin{cases} \langle Y_{A_j B_j}, DAG_{\mathcal{D}\setminus A_j}, DAG_{\mathcal{D}\setminus B_j} \rangle, & \text{if } \#\mathcal{D} \geqslant 2, \text{ where } \#A_j = 1 \wedge \#B_j = 1 \\ \mathcal{D}, & \text{if } \#\mathcal{D} = 1. \end{cases}$$

In the scheme DAG each j-th SVM is trained using the elements of only two classes $A_j \bigcup B_j - \{(\boldsymbol{x}_l, -1)\,|\,\{c_l\} = A_j\}_{l=1}^{M} \bigcup \{(\boldsymbol{x}_l, 1)\,|\,\{c_l\} = B_j\}_{l=1}^{M}$. If the SVM votes for the class A_j, i.e. its output is equal -1, then the label B_j is removed from the set of possible classes, otherwise the label A_j is excluded (Fig. 3). The Listing 3 contains described procedure which specifies the element-by-element splitting from the set $\mathcal{C}$.

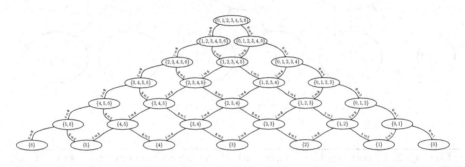

Fig. 3. Example of DAG

Listing 3. Classifying the network attacks using SVMs combined via DAG

input : Trained SVMs Y_{AB} represented as nodes of $DAG_{\mathcal{C}}$
　　　　　Input object $\boldsymbol{Z}$ which is to be classified
output: Class label of the object $\boldsymbol{Z}$

```
1  function F_DAG(DAG_D, Z)
2  begin
3      if DAG_D = D then
4          return D
5      else
6          ⟨Y_AB, DAG_D\A, DAG_D\B⟩ := DAG_D
7          if Y_AB(Z) = -1 then
8              R := call recursively function F_DAG(DAG_D\B, Z)
9              return R
10         else
11             R := call recursively function F_DAG(DAG_D\A, Z)
12             return R
13         end
14     end
15 end
16 R := call function F_DAG(DAG_C, Z)
```

Table 1. Comparison of graph-based schemes for combining the SVMs (the number of classes is $m + 1$, the cardinality of the training sample of each class is k)

Characteristic	Scheme	
	CBT	DAG
The number of SVMs to be trained	m	$\binom{m+1}{2} = \frac{(m+1)\cdot m}{2}$
The minimum number of SVMs when classifying the objects	1	m
The maximum number of SVMs when classifying the objects	m	m
The minimum cardinality of the training sample among all node SVMs	$2 \cdot k$	$2 \cdot k$
The maximum cardinality of the training sample among all node SVMs	$(m + 1) \cdot k$	$2 \cdot k$
The minimum number of different paths leading to the same terminal node among all class labels	1	$\min\limits_{i=0,\ldots,m} \binom{m}{i} = \binom{m}{0} = \binom{m}{m} = 1$
The maximum number of different paths leading to the same terminal node among all class labels	1	$\max\limits_{i=0,\ldots,m} \binom{m}{i} = \binom{m}{\lceil m/2 \rceil} = \binom{m}{\lfloor m/2 \rfloor}$
The average number of different paths leading to the same terminal node for each class label	1	$\frac{\sum\limits_{i=0}^{m} \binom{m}{i}}{m+1} = \frac{2^m}{m+1}$

The result of applying the Algorithms 2 and 3 is a set consisting of a single class label. In the Table 1 we give the main comparative parameters of the models considered. We suppose that the whole training data set includes $m + 1$ classes each of which contains the same number (k) of training instances.

We estimate the number of classifiers which are necessary for constructing a multiclass model for each of the proposed schemes. For CBT each internal node always has two child nodes, so if we consider the tree consisting of $m + 1$ leaves, then the quantity of nonterminal nodes is equal to m. Therefore for constructing the multiclass model based on CBT it is necessary to train m SVMs. For DAG each SVM is trained using unique unordered pairs of class labels C. Thereby the number of SVMs used in the scheme DAG is equal to $\binom{m+1}{2} = \frac{(m+1)\cdot m}{2}$.

While in the case of CBT the number of node SVMs depends linearly on the number of classes, the scheme DAG requires a significantly larger number of classifiers (quadratic dependence on the number of classes) to be trained and placed in its nodes.

In the process of object classification the scheme CBT uses a variable amount of node classifiers, varying from 1 to m (in the case of a balanced tree depicted in the Fig. 2 this value is equal to $\lfloor \log_2(m+1) \rfloor$ or $\lceil \log_2(m+1) \rceil$); whereas for the scheme DAG this quantity is always constant and equal to m.

All SVMs combined via DAG are trained using the sets of identical sizes. Unlike it the SVMs represented as nodes of CBT use the training sets of variable sizes.

All the objects recognized by CBT as elements of some fixed class pass through the same chain of nodes. Therefore the characteristic named as "the number of different paths leading to the same terminal node" in the Table 1 is equal 1 for any class in the case of CBT. However this characteristic is inconstant for DAG: 2 classes of objects are recognized by a single group of SVMs, for the others multiple paths are possible which connect the root node with the terminal node.

5 Experiments

In this section we describe the results of experiments aimed at calculating the performance indicators, time and system resources spent.

To estimate the models considered, we have used the open data set DARPA 1998 containing network records in pcap-files with corresponding class labels in csv-files. For extracting the network parameters the special software tool was developed which is based on an event-oriented mechanism for processing the packets. Using this tool we have extracted 106 parameters describing the network interaction between hosts. The most outdated attack types were excluded, thereby only seven classes were used in the experiments (normal; DoS: neptune, smurf; Probing: ipsweep, nmap, portsweep, satan) which take place in mobile Internet and networks. For correct interpreting the data transmitted in the packets, the algorithms of IP-defragmentation [17] inherent in the Linux OS were implemented.

We have used the well-known PCA as a preprocessing and compressing procedure for input 106-dimensional vectors.

Four performance indicators were selected for evaluating the multiclass model G constructed using CBT or DAG:

1. GPR—an indicator of generalization ability while detecting:

$$GPR = \frac{TP^*}{TP^*+FN^*} = \frac{\#\left\{ \boldsymbol{Z}_i \,\middle|\, \boldsymbol{Z}_i \in \mathcal{X}_C^{(TS)} \backslash \mathcal{X}_C^{(LS)} \wedge c_i \neq 0 \wedge 0 \notin G\left(\boldsymbol{Z}_i\right) \right\}_{i=1}^{M^*}}{\#\left\{ \boldsymbol{Z}_i \,\middle|\, \boldsymbol{Z}_i \in \mathcal{X}_C^{(TS)} \backslash \mathcal{X}_C^{(LS)} \wedge c_i \neq 0 \right\}_{i=1}^{M^*}},$$

where TP^* and FN^* represent the number of correctly recognized attacks and the number of errors with type II which were calculated using the unique elements of the testing data set $\mathcal{X}_C^{(TS)}$ strictly excluding any elements from the training data set $\mathcal{X}_C^{(LS)}$.

2. FPR—an indicator of false positive rates:

$$FPR = \frac{FP^*}{FP^*+TN^*} = \frac{\#\left\{\mathbf{Z}_i \;\middle|\; \mathbf{Z}_i \in \mathcal{X}_C^{(TS)} \backslash \mathcal{X}_C^{(LS)} \wedge c_i = 0 \wedge 0 \notin G\left(\mathbf{Z}_i\right)\right\}_{i=1}^{M^*}}{\#\left\{\mathbf{Z}_i \;\middle|\; \mathbf{Z}_i \in \mathcal{X}_C^{(TS)} \backslash \mathcal{X}_C^{(LS)} \wedge c_i = 0\right\}_{i=1}^{M^*}},$$

where FP^* and TN^* represent the number of errors with type I and the number of correctly recognized normal instances which were calculated using the unique elements of the testing data set $\mathcal{X}_C^{(TS)}$ strictly excluding any elements from the training data set $\mathcal{X}_C^{(LS)}$.

3. GCR—an indicator of generalization ability while classifying:

$$GCR = \frac{CC^*}{TP^*+FN^*+FP^*+TN^*} =$$
$$= \frac{\#\left\{\mathbf{Z}_i \;\middle|\; \mathbf{Z}_i \in \mathcal{X}_C^{(TS)} \backslash \mathcal{X}_C^{(LS)} \wedge \{c_i\} = G\left(\mathbf{Z}_i\right)\right\}_{i=1}^{M^*}}{\#\left\{\mathbf{Z}_i \;\middle|\; \mathbf{Z}_i \in \mathcal{X}_C^{(TS)} \backslash \mathcal{X}_C^{(LS)}\right\}_{i=1}^{M^*}},$$

where CC^* represent the number of elements from $\mathcal{X}_C^{(TS)} \backslash \mathcal{X}_C^{(LS)}$ which class label was predicted correctly.

4. ICR—an indicator of incorrect classification rates:

$$ICR = \frac{IC^*}{TP^*+FN^*+FP^*+TN^*} = \frac{\#\left\{\mathbf{Z}_i \;\middle|\; \mathbf{Z}_i \in \mathcal{X}_C^{(TS)} \backslash \mathcal{X}_C^{(LS)} \wedge c_i \notin G\left(\mathbf{Z}_i\right)\right\}_{i=1}^{M^*}}{\#\left\{\mathbf{Z}_i \;\middle|\; \mathbf{Z}_i \in \mathcal{X}_C^{(TS)} \backslash \mathcal{X}_C^{(LS)}\right\}_{i=1}^{M^*}},$$

where IC^* represent the number of elements from $\mathcal{X}_C^{(TS)} \backslash \mathcal{X}_C^{(LS)}$ which class label was predicted incorrectly.

The cardinality of subsamples corresponding each class is presented in the Table 2. This table contains the number of unique (non-duplicated) elements within each class.

Table 2. Cardinality of network attack classes

normal	neptune	smurf	ipsweep	nmap	portsweep	satan
40622	789	524	1264	1015	649	8870
53733						

Table 3. Indicators calculated using 3-fold cross-validation

Indicator (%)	Scheme					
	CBT			DAG		
	avg	min	max	avg	min	max
GPR	99.7590	99.7407	99.7788	99.7666	99.7635	99.7712
FPR	0.1088	0.0615	0.1477	0.1477	0.1477	0.1477
GCR	98.6586	98.3864	98.7978	98.71747	98.5893	98.8238
ICR	1.3414	1.2022	1.6136	1.2826	1.1762	1.4107
$GPR - FPR$	99.6502	99.6006	99.6791	99.6189	99.6158	99.6235
$GCR - ICR$	97.3171	96.7729	97.5955	97.4347	97.1787	97.6477

In the Table 3 we give the selected performance indicators for two graph-based schemes which are designed for combining the SVMs without applying the PCA.

For calculating these indicators the 3-fold cross-validation [18] was used. The testing data set $\mathcal{X}_C^{(TS)}$ containing 53733 elements was split into 3 parts in such a way that in each formed subset there are instances of all classes in approximately equal proportions. The training and testing samples are taken in a ratio of 2 : 1. Such a partitioning was performed ten times, and each time the content of each subset was generated randomly. Suppose that $\omega_i^{(j)}$ is one of the indicators which is calculated for the j-th testing sample ($j = 1, 2, 3$) on the i-th iteration ($i = 1, \ldots, 10$) then the following expressions $\frac{1}{30} \cdot \sum_{i=1}^{10} \sum_{j=1}^{3} \omega_i^{(j)}$, $\frac{1}{3} \cdot \min_{i=1,\ldots,10} \sum_{j=1}^{3} \omega_i^{(j)}$, $\frac{1}{3} \cdot \max_{i=1,\ldots,10} \sum_{j=1}^{3} \omega_i^{(j)}$ specify average, minimum and maximum values for the indicator $\omega_i^{(j)}$.

The Table 3 shows that the scheme DAG has slightly better indicators GPR, GCR and ICR compared to CBT. In the same time the false positive rate is less in the scheme CBT than DAG. However CBT possesses the greatest value of the indicator $GPR - FPR$. Due to the absence of conflict classification cases the value $GCR + ICR = 100\%$ anytime.

The Figs. 4, 5 and 6 show the dependence of indicators TP^*, FP^*, CC^*, IC^*, $TP^* - FP^*$ and $CC^* - IC^*$ on the number of principal components. The limits of change in indicators (when iterating over i and using the 3-fold cross-validation) are marked with a vertical line piercing each histogram column. From the Fig. 4 it can be judged that the earlier statement about the indicators GPR and FPR is preserved for different dimensions of analyzed vectors: in most cases the scheme DAG is superior to the scheme CBT in terms of GPR (TP^*), but the indicator FPR (FP^*) calculated for the scheme CBT is less in comparison with the scheme DAG. The indicator GCR (CC^*) is approximately the same for both schemes (Fig. 5). The scheme CBT is better able to detect anomalous network records (Fig. 6).

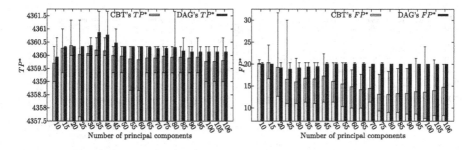

Fig. 4. Dependence of indicators TP^* and FP^* for CBT and DAG on the number of principal components

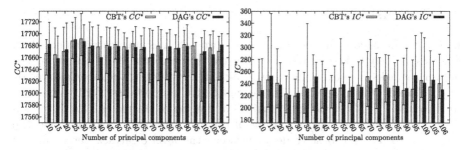

Fig. 5. Dependence of indicators CC^* and IC^* for CBT and DAG on the number of principal components

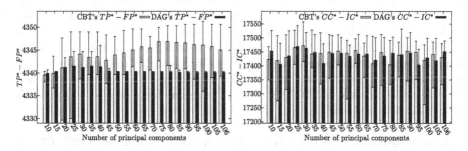

Fig. 6. Dependence of indicators $TP^* - FP^*$ and $CC^* - IC^*$ for CBT and DAG on the number of principal components

We have estimated the time and system resources spent on training of SVMs combined via CBT and DAG (Fig. 7). Despite the fact that the scheme DAG uses more SVMs than the scheme CBT, its training process requires less time and memory. This is due to the fact that each node classifier within DAG is trained on significantly smaller samples in terms of cardinality.

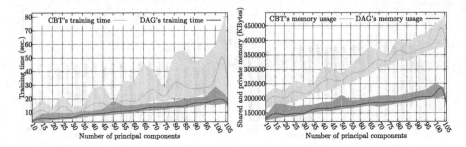

Fig. 7. Dependence of training time and memory usage for CBT and DAG on the number of principal components

6 Conclusion

In the paper a comparative analysis of two schemes was carried out. Both schemes, namely CBT and DAG, demonstrated a high quality of classifying the network attacks. The experiments were aimed at evaluating the models to recognize instances which were not seen during the training process. For this purpose we have used SVMs as binary classifiers and network traces DARPA 1998 as a data set for their testing. As a result of the experiments it was found that the scheme CBT has the best trade-off between the level of attack detection and false positives (indicator $GPP - FPR$), and the scheme DAG is characterized by less time and system resources spent on training of its node elements.

As directions for further research, the following should be noted. First, we plan to investigate applying other approaches for combining the SVMs (e.g., one-vs-all [19], one-vs-one [20], their combination [21], etc.). Second, we plan to increase the SVM-based attack detection system scalability, to this end it is proposed to use big data technologies such as Hadoop and Spark [22], while maintaining low resource consumption [23]. Third, we plan to generate the data set with modern network attacks which are characteristic of both the transport layer (e.g. for protocol MPTCP [24]), and the session layer (e.g. for the protocol SSL [25]) of the OSI model.

Acknowledgments. This research is being supported by the grant of RSF #18-11-00302 in SPIIRAS.

References

1. Branitskiy, A., Kotenko, I.: Network attack detection based on combination of neural, immune and neuro-fuzzy classifiers. In: IEEE 18th International Conference on Computational Science and Engineering (CSE), pp. 152–159 (2015)
2. Branitskiy, A., Kotenko, I.: Hybridization of computational intelligence methods for attack detection in computer networks. J. Comput. Sci. **23**, 145–156 (2017)
3. Lee, H., Song, J., Park, D.: Intrusion detection system based on multi-class SVM. In: Rough Sets, Fuzzy Sets, Data Mining, and Granular Computing, pp. 511–519 (2005)

4. Khan, L., Awad, M., Thuraisingham, B.: A new intrusion detection system using support vector machines and hierarchical clustering. VLDB J. Int. J. Very Large Data Bases **16**(4), 507–521 (2007)
5. Xu, X., Wang, X.: An adaptive network intrusion detection method based on PCA and support vector machines. In: International Conference on Advanced Data Mining and Applications, pp. 696–703 (2005)
6. Kim, D. S., Nguyen, H.-N., Park, J. S.: Genetic algorithm to improve SVM based network intrusion detection system. In: 19th International Conference on Advanced Information Networking and Applications, vol. 2, pp. 155–158 (2005)
7. Shon, T., Kim, Y., Lee, C., Moon, J.: A machine learning framework for network anomaly detection using SVM and GA. In: Information Assurance Workshop, IAW 2005, Proceedings from the Sixth Annual IEEE SMC, pp. 176–183 (2005)
8. Wang, J., Hong, X., Ren, R., Li, T.: A real-time intrusion detection system based on PSO-SVM. In: Proceedings of the International Workshop on Information Security and Application, pp. 319–321 (2009)
9. Li, L., Zhao, K.: A new intrusion detection system based on rough set theory and fuzzy support vector machine. In: 3rd International Workshop on Intelligent Systems and Applications (ISA), pp. 1–5 (2011)
10. Thaseen, I.S., Kumar, C.A.: Intrusion detection model using fusion of chi-square feature selection and multi class SVM. J. King Saud Univ. Comput. Inf. Sci. **29**(4), 462–472 (2017)
11. Abraham, A., Thomas, J.: Distributed intrusion detection systems: a computational intelligence approach. In: Applications of Information Systems to Homeland Security and Defense, pp. 107–137 (2006)
12. Peddabachigari, S., Abraham, A., Grosan, C., Thomas, J.: Modeling intrusion detection system using hybrid intelligent systems. J. Netw. Comput. Appl. **30**(1), 114–132 (2007)
13. Hsu, C.-W., Lin, C.-J.: A comparison of methods for multiclass support vector machines. IEEE Trans. Neural Netw. **13**(2), 415–425 (2002)
14. Drucker, H., Burges, C.J.C., Kaufman, L., Smola, A.J., Vapnik, V.: Support vector regression machines. In: Advances in Neural Information Processing Systems, pp. 155–161 (1997)
15. Müller, K.-R., Smola, A.J., Rätsch, G., Schölkopf, B., Kohlmorgen, J., Vapnik, V.: Predicting time series with support vector machines. In: International Conference on Artificial Neural Networks, pp. 999–1004 (1997)
16. Platt, J.: Sequential minimal optimization: a fast algorithm for training support vector machines (1998)
17. Stevens, W. R.: TCP/IP illustrated, volume 1: The protocols. Addison-Wesley Professional (1993)
18. Refaeilzadeh, P., Tang, L., Liu, H.: Cross-validation. Encyclopedia of Database Systems, pp. 532–538 (2009)
19. Rifkin, R., Klautau, A.: In defense of one-vs-all classification. J. Mach. Learn. Res. **5**, 101–141 (2004)
20. Galar, M., Fernández, A., Barrenechea, E., Bustince, H., Herrera, F.: An overview of ensemble methods for binary classifiers in multi-class problems: experimental study on one-vs-one and one-vs-all schemes. Pattern Recogn. **44**(8), 1761–1776 (2011)
21. García-Pedrajas, N., Ortiz-Boyer, D.: Improving multiclass pattern recognition by the combination of two strategies. IEEE Trans. Pattern Anal. Mach. Intell. **28**(6), 1001–1006 (2006)

22. Kotenko, I., Saenko, I., Kushnerevich, A.: Parallel big data processing system for security monitoring in Internet of Things networks. J. Wirel. Mobile Netw. Ubiquitous Comput. Dependable Appl. (JoWUA) **8**(4), 60–74 (2017)
23. Desnitsky, V., Levshun, D., Chechulin, A., Kotenko, I.: Design technique for secure embedded devices: application for creation of integrated cyber-physical security system. J. Wirel. Mobile Netw. Ubiquitous Comput. Dependable Appl. (JoWUA) **7**(2), 60–80 (2016)
24. Zeng, J., Ke, F., Zuo, Y., Liu, Q., Huang, M., Cao, Y.: Multi-attribute aware path selection approach for efficient MPTCP-based data delivery. J. Internet Serv. Inf. Secur. **7**(1), 28–39 (2017)
25. Kurokawa, T., Nojima, R., Moriai, S.: On the security of CBC mode in SSL3.0 and TLS1.0. J. Internet Serv. Inf. Secur. **6**(1), 2–19 (2016)

Generating Dynamic Box
by Using an Input String

Jia-Jia Liu, Yi-Li Huang, Fang-Yie Leu[✉],
Xing-You Pan, and Li-Ren Chen

Computer Science Department, TungHai University, Taichung, Taiwan
{s03353014v, yifung, leufy, g04350016,
s03353040}@thu.edu.tw

Abstract. Today, encrypting and decrypting data by looking up a table is quite popular and its processing speed is high. But currently, the table to be looked up is a static S-Box, the content of which is fixed and independent from its input string. In fact, its security can be enhanced by dynamically changing the table contents according to the input string. Basically, the table is unknown to hackers since they do not know the input string. On the other hand, encryption and decryption processes usually are accomplished by using control parameters, such as user's passwords or channel keys. Based on this, in this study, we propose an algorithm, namely Generating a Dynamic Box by using Input String (GDBIS for short), which produces a 16 x 16 dynamic box (D-Box for short) according to user's input string, the length of which should be longer than or equal to 8 bits, i.e., the length of one character. The GDBIS has three procedures with which to yield a D-Box. We also design a new key expansion algorithm, called Generation of D-Box and Round Keys (GDBRK for short), to substitute for the original key expansion algorithm of AES. According to our security analysis, the D-Box generated by GDBIS is irreversible with high degree of chaos and has excellent sensitivity on inputs. The Round Keys generated by the GDBRK have high degree of randomness and low relation among themselves. Our analysis also shows that the GDBIS and the GDBRK have excellent performance, able to meet the needs of practical applications.

Keywords: S-Box · GDBIS · D-Box · AES · GDBRK

1 Introduction

Currently, due to high performance of existing computers and communication technology, the security and efficiency problems of Advanced Encryption Standard (AES) are gradually clear. In 2010, Biryukov et al. [1] mentioned that the first 10 rounds of AES-256 have been solved. In addition, many researchers are trying to crack AES [2–5]. As a result, how to further improve security level of AES is an important issue today since it has been popularly employed in different applications. A typical application is encrypting sensitive information for our online-shopping transactions.

Many studies have investigated how to improve security of AES, such as those studying block cipher modes of operation [6] and those improving the complexity of the S-Box [7–9]. In AES, the SubBytes looks up a table to encrypt and decrypt data stream. The processing speed is high. Also, given different inputs (plaintext),

© Springer Nature Singapore Pte Ltd. 2019
I. You et al. (Eds.): MobiSec 2017, CCIS 971, pp. 17–29, 2019.
https://doi.org/10.1007/978-981-13-3732-1_2

the outputs of the encryption process are sensitively different. However, the contents of the lookup table in AES, i.e., S-Box, are fixed, thus greatly reducing its security level since the only nonlinear component of this block ciphering technique is the manipulation on S-Box. It is an important source that enhances AES's cryptographic strength. Our opinion is that if we can use Cipher Key to generate the corresponding dynamic box (D-Box) with which to substitute for the primary substitution box (S-Box), the security of AES will be significantly improved.

Generally, our D-Box is produced by invoking an algorithm, named Generating a 16×16 Dynamic Box by using an Input String (GDBIS for short) which consists of procedures that generate different keys for the production of D-Box based on a dynamic string input by user.

The advantages of GDBIS are that (1) its output sensitively varies on different input data; (2) the contents of D-Box are pseudo dynamically and randomly rearranged (we will describe this later) to significantly enhance its security; (3) the collision among different boxes produced by inputting different strings is low; (4) the GDBIS is a one-way function.

We also propose an algorithm, named Generation of D-Box and Round Keys (GDBRK for short) to substitute for the original Key-expansion algorithm of AES, which generates a D-Box and some necessary round keys sequentially for later encryption.

The rest of the paper is organized as follows. Section 2 reviews the related work of this study. Section 3 introduces architecture of the GDBIS. Security analysis is presented and discussed in Sect. 4. Performance is analyzed in Sect. 5. Section 6 concludes this paper and outlines our future studies.

2   Background

In this section, we briefly describe background techniques of this study and review the related literature.

2.1   The Dynamic S-Box

AES, announced by the U.S. National Institute of Standards and Technology (NIST) in 2001 [10], has become a federal government standard on May 26, 2002 after approved by the United States Secretary of Commerce. AES is widely used to secure data transmission in both software and hardware applications nowadays. It has 4 steps, including AddRoundKey, SubBytes, ShiftRows and MixColumns.

In AES, the S-box provides confusion capabilities to increase the computational complexity for breaking keys and the ciphertext by evenly diffusing employed keys into the produced ciphertext. As a result, it is hard for hackers to solve the ciphertext by using statistical techniques [11, 12]. However, the look-up table in AES is widely known. It is relatively easier to obtain the plaintext from the ciphertext if a fixed S-Box is adopted. In other words, the security of AES can be further improved.

In 2012, Hosseinkhani and Javadi [13] discussed how to generate a dynamic S-Box. They derive parameters from CipherKey, i.e., *CK*, and then accordingly swap rows and columns of the primary S-Box with a dynamic S-Box generation mechanism, named GenerateDynamicSbox () which receives *CK* as its input. Additionally, in 2003, Mahmoud *et al.* [14] proposed a method that derives a dynamic S-Box from a secret key. The process is that the secret key is invoked to generate the initial state of a pseudo random (PN) sequence generator. The output of this generator is inputted to a standard S-Box to dynamically permute its elements. Besides, many others studies also discuss how to improve the structure of the S-Box or generate a dynamic S-Box [15–17]. However, the methods that they frequently used are rearranging the primary one. But the data sensitivity and degree of data randomness of these methods can be further enhanced. Therefore, in this paper, a D-Box is generated according to the content of its input string to substitute for the S-Box in AES. The purpose is rising the security level of AES.

2.2   Three-Dimension Operation

In this paper, the GDBIS is developed by using several operations and algorithms to effectively reduce the relationship between two arbitrarily produced parameters, and significantly increase the complexity of the process producing these parameters. In 2015, Huang *et al.* [18] proposed an encryption method, called Secure Feedback Encryption Method (SeFEM for short), which utilizes three security mechanisms, including a sequential-logic style encryption method, a three-dimensional operation (3D operation, for short, including $\oplus$, $+_2$ and $\odot$) and a dynamic transition box. The content of a plaintext block is first rearranged by using a dynamic transition box and then manipulated by the three-dimensional operation with multiple keys so as to generate a complex ciphertext block. However, the exclusive-or operator, i.e., $\oplus$, and the equivalence operator, i.e., $\odot$, are mutually complemented. In other words, the relationship between the two operators is high.

In 2017, Huang *et al.* [19] proposed another scheme, named 3D Encryption with Shifting Mapping Substitution Mechanism (3DESME for short), which replaces the equivalence operator $\odot$ with an operator $\odot_R$, called the Rotate-Equivalence operator, to improve the security strength of the 3D operation. $\odot_R$ will be defined later. In this study, we use three fundamental operators and their reverse operators, including $\oplus/\oplus$, $+_2/-_2$ and $\odot_R/\odot_{IR}$, to generate Dynamic Keys where $\odot_{IR}$ is the reverse operator of $\odot_R$. With these Keys, the security level of the D-Box can be further improved.

3   The GDBIS and GDBRK

In this section, we will introduce the GDBIS and GDBRK algorithms.

3.1 The Parameters and Functions

The parameters and functions employed in this study are defined below.

(1) D-Box   A 16×16 dynamic box (D-Box) which is generated based on input strings. The 256 non-duplicated elements, ranging from 00 to FF, are randomly placed in the D-Box.

(2) *ISK*s   Initial Serial Keys, including ISK_1 and ISK_2, which are produced by a specific algorithm given an input string. The length of an initial serial key is 1024 bits.

(3) E-DASS   The Enhanced DASS which as a one-way function employs a dynamically accumulated shifting substitution mechanism to encrypt a plaintext into an irreversible ciphertext.

(4) *DK*s   Dynamic Keys, i.e., DK_1, DK_2 and DK_3, which are derived from ISK_1 and ISK_2 by employing the 3D operations [19] and E-DASS. The length of a dynamic key is 1024 bits.

(5) *FA*   Flag Array, which is used to identify the elements of the D-Box. With *FA*, we can guarantee that each element of the D-Box is unique without colliding with others. When the indexed content of Flag Array is "T"("F"), it means the index has (has not) been chosen.

(6) *IA*1   The 1st Insert Array, which is derived from DK_1 by removing the duplicated elements in DK_1 with the help of *FA*. The elements of *IA*1 are used to establish the D-Box.

(7) *IA*2   The 2nd Insert Array, which is derived from DK_2 and DK_3 by removing the duplicated elements in *IA*1, DK_2 and DK_3 with the help of *FA*. The elements of *IA*2 are used to establish the D-Box.

(8) *IAR*   Residual Insert Array, which consists of those unselected indexes of *FA*.

(9) *IA*3   The 3rd Insert Array, which is obtained by rearranging Residual Insert Array. The elements of *IA*3 are used to establish the D-Box.

(10) *RLi*   Real length of *IAi*, $1 \leq i \leq 3$.

(11) *RLR*   Real length of *IAR*.

3.2 Operators

Let p_i (c_i) be the plaintext (ciphertext) block and k is the encryption key. The encryption/decryption processes of these three fundamental operators are defined as follows.

$\oplus$ Exclusive-OR operator:

Encryption: $c_i = p_i \oplus k$;

Decryption: $p_i = c_i \oplus k$;

$+_2$ Encryption: $c_i = p_i +_2 k$, where the carry out of the most significant bit of the binary addition is dropped.

Decryption: $p_i = c_i -_2 k = \begin{cases} c_i - k, & if\ c_i \geq k \\ c_i + \bar{k} + 1, if\ c_i < k \end{cases}$, where $-_2$ is the inverse

operation of $+_2$.

$\odot_R$ Rotate-Equivalence operator:

Encryption: $c_i = p_i \odot_R k = p_{iR} \odot k$, where p_{iR} is the key obtained by continuously rotating plaintext p_i clockwise h bits where $h = |k|/4$, e.g., if $|k| = 128$, p_i will be rotated 32 bits.

Decryption: $p_i = c_i \odot_{IR} k =$ counter clockwise rotating $(c_i \odot k)$ $|k|/4$ bits.

3.3   The Enhanced DASS Algorithm

The DASS algorithm defined in [20] has a drawback since the shifting counter ct linearly changes and only ranges between 0 and 8 on each time of looking up S-Box so that it cannot effectively defense Brute-force Attacks. The following is its enhanced version, called Enhanced DASS (E-DASS for short), which as a one-way function employs a dynamically accumulated shifting substitution mechanism to encrypt a plaintext into an irreversible ciphertext. With the E-DASS, the mentioned problems on ct can be solved.

Algorithm 1: the E-DASS algorithm /* format is E-DASS(P, R-Box) */

Input: a plaintext P of n bits in length, and a 16 x16 random-box (R-Box for short) where n is a multiple of 8.

Output: ciphertext C.

1. Let $P = p_1 p_2 ... p_k$, and let $C = c_1 c_2 ... c_k$, where $k = n/8$;
   /* $|p_i| = |c_i| = 8$ bits, $1 \leq i \leq k$*/

2. $dsc = 256$; /*dsc: dynamic shifting count*/

3. For $i = 1$ to k {

4. $vp[i] = Int(p_i)$; /* $Int(p_i)$ retrieves the ACSII code of p_i*/

5. $dsc = dsc + (vp[i] +1)*i$;} /* yielding non-linear increment of dsc */

6. $vp[0] = vp[1] + vp[k]$;

7. For $i = 1$ to k {

8. $dsc = (dsc + (vp[i-1])*i)$ mod 65536;

9. $ch = str((vp[i] + dsc)$ mod 256); /* $str(X)$ returns ASCII code of X */

10. $c_i =$ the ciphertext which is the corresponding content in the R-Box after ch is looking up by using R-Box;}

3.4   Generating a 16 × 16 Dynamic Box from an Input String

The GDBIS consists of three procedures, namely (1) the one generating Initial Serial Keys, including ISK_1 and ISK_2; (2) the one producing Dynamic Keys, including DK_1, DK_2 and DK_3; (3) the one yielding D-Box by using an algorithm, named Dynamic Box Generator (DBG for short), which generates a 16 × 16 dynamic box from input strings. Let P represent the plaintext, and $|P| = l$ bits.

3.4.1   Generation of Initial Serial Key

If the length of the string P input by user is shorter than 1024 bits, the GDBIS employs the E-DASS_expansion () and Binaryadder_expansion () to lengthen it. The former expands P by invoking the E-DASS until $|P| \geqq 1024$, while the latter prolongs P by using the Binary-Adder ($+_2$) operation until $|P| \geqq 1024$. These two algorithms are described as follows.

> Algorithm 2: the E-DASS_expansion algorithm
> /* format is E-DASS_expansion (P) */
> Input: a string P with $|P| < 1024$ bits
> Output: a lengthened string P with $|P|$=1024
>   1. Do {
>   2. P'= E-DASS (P, S-Box);
>   3. $P = P\|P'$;}
>   4. while ($|P|$<1024)
>   5. P = E-DASS (P, S-Box);
>   6. return Right(P, 1024); /* return the 1024 right most bits of P */

> Algorithm 3: the Binaryadder_expansion algorithm
> /* format is Binaryadder_expansion (P) */
> Input: a string P with $|P| < 1024$ bits
> Output: a prolonged string P with $|P|$=1024
>   1. While ($|P|$<1024){
>   2. $P = (P\|P)+_2(P\|P)$; }
>   3. return Right(P,1024);

The generation process of IKSs is as follows.
    1. If $|P|$<1024, then
            {ISK_1= E-DASS_expansion (P);
            ISK_2= Binaryadder_expansion (P);}
    2. If $|P|$ =1024, then
            {ISK_1= E-DASS (P, S-Box);
            ISK_2=E-DASS (ISK_1, S-Box); }
    3. If $|P|$ >1024, then
            {(1) $P = p_1p_2p_3\ldots p_m$, where $|p_i|$=1024, $1 \leqq i \leqq m$, $m \geqq 2$;
            (2) if $|p_m|$<1024, then p_m=E-DASS_expansion(p_m);
            (3) ISK_1=$p_1 \oplus p_2 \oplus \ldots \oplus p_m$;
            (4) ISK_2=E-DASS (ISK_1, S-Box);}

3.4.2 Generation of Dynamic Keys
The process that generates Dynamic keys is as follows.

1. DK_1 = E-DASS ($ISK_1 \oplus ISK_2$, S-Box);
2. DK_2 = E-DASS ($DK_1 +_2 ISK_2$, S-Box);
3. DK_3 = E-DASS ($DK_1 \odot_R DK_2$, S-Box);

3.4.3 Dynamic Box Generator Algorithm
The DBG algorithm, which produces a D-Box, is as follows.

Algorithm 4: the DBG algorithm /* format is DGB(DK_1, DK_2, DK_3) */
Input: DK_1, DK_2, DK_3
Output: D-Box
{ Let $DK_1 = KA_0\|KA_1\|\dots\|KA_{127}$, where KA_j is 8 bits in length for all j, $0 \leq j \leq 127$;
Let $DK_2 = KB_0\|KB_1\|\dots\|KB_{127}$, where KB_j is 8 bits in length for all j, $0 \leq j \leq 127$;
Let $DK_3 = KC_0\|KC_1\|\dots\|KC_{127}$, where KC_j is 8 bits in length for all j, $0 \leq j \leq 127$;
For j = 0 to 127
    {$KA[j]$ = Int(KA_j); $KB[j]$ = Int(KB_j); $KC[j]$ = Int(KC_j); $IA1[j]$=0; }
For j = 0 to 255
    {D-Box[j]=0; $IA2[j]$=0; $IAR[j]$=0; $IA3[j]$=0;}
$RL1$=0; $RL2$=0; RLR=0;
For i = 0 to 127
  If ($FA[KA[i]]$ = "F")
        {$IA1[RL1]$ = $KA[i]$; $FA[KA[i]]$ = "T"; $RL1 = RL1+1$;}
For i = 0 to 127
  {If ($FA[KB[i]]$ = "F")
        {$IA2[RL2]$ = $KB[i]$; $FA[KB[i]]$ ="T"; $RL2 = RL2+1$;}
  If ($FA[KC[i]]$ = "F")
        {$IA2[RL2]$ = $KC[i]$; $FA[KC[i]]$ = "T"; $RL2=RL2+1$;}}
For i = 0 to 255
  If ($FA[i]$ = "F")
        {$IAR[RLR]$ = i; $RLR = RLR+1$;}
$HL = RLR/2$;
For i =0 to HL-1
    {$IA3[i]$ = $IAR[HL+i]$; $IA3[HL+i]$ = $IAR[i]$;}
If (RLR is odd)
    $IA3[RLR-1]$ = $IAR[RLR-1]$;
$t1$=0; $t2$=0; $t3$=0; j=0;
while ($j \leq 255$)
        If ($t1 < RL1$){
            {D-Box[j] = $IA1[t1]$; $j = j+1$; $t1 = t1+1$;}
        If ($t2 < RL2$)
            {D-Box[j] = $IA2[t1]$; $j = j+1$; $t2 = t2+1$;}
        If ($t3 < RLR$)
            {D-Box[j]=$IA3[t3]$; $j = j+1$; $t3 = t3+1$;}}}

3.5   Enhancing AES by Employing D-Box

To improve the security of AES, our idea is that an effective method should not lower AES's process performance. In this study, we rewrite its key expansion algorithm. Although performance of the original one is acceptable, its round keys are generated by invoking Exclusive-OR operator which is a reversible operation. From security viewpoint, it is relatively easy to be cracked. Therefore, the GDBRK employs the E-DASS and DBG Algorithms to substitute for the key expansion algorithm of AES. The GDBRK generates the D-Box and round keys sequentially. The D-Box is developed to replace the S-Box of AES so as to improve the security of its SubBytes step. The generated round keys are used to substitute for the original round keys of AES. It will also effectively improve the security level of AES. The GDBRK is described as follows:

> Algorithm 5: the GDBRK algorithm
> /* format is GDBRK(CK, n), where n is number of round keys */
> Input: Cipher Key (CK for short) and n
> Output: Round Keys and a D-Box
> {Part 1 /*Generation of D-Box */
> 1. ECK = E-DASS_expansion(CK); /*|CK|=128 bits, |ECK|=1024 bits*/
> 2. DK_0 = E-DASS($\overline{ECK}$, S-Box);
> CK_0 = Right(DK_0, 128);
> 3. DK_1 = E-DASS($ECK \oplus DK_0$, S-Box);
> CK_1 = Right(DK_1, 128);
> 4. DK_2 = E-DASS($DK_0 +_2 DK_1$, S-Box);
> CK_2 = Right(DK_2, 128);
> 5. DK_3 = E-DASS($DK_1 \odot_R DK_2$, S-Box);
> CK_3 = Right(DK_3, 128);
> 6. D-Box = DBG(DK_1, DK_2, DK_3); /* See Algorithm 4*/
> Part 2 /* Generation of Round Keys */
> 7. RK_i = E-DASS($CK_0 \oplus CK_i$, D-Box), $1 \leq i \leq 3$;
> 8. RK_{i+3} = E-DASS($CK_0 +_2 CK_i$, D-Box), $1 \leq i \leq 3$;
> 9. for i = 7 to n
>   {RK_i = E-DASS($RK_{i-6} \oplus RK_{i-3}$, D-Box);}}

4   Security Analysis

In the study, the randomness level of the generated dynamic keys, i.e., DK1 $\sim$ DK3 during the generation of D-Box, is one of our key concerns. In fact, they are derived from user's input string by invoking E-DASS_expansion (), Binaryadder_expansion () and E-DASS operation to sequentially produce them. The security of the E-DASS is discussed below. Due to rewriting the key expansion algorithms of AES, we will also analyze their security.

4.1   The Security of the E-DASS

In the E-DASS algorithm, the input string of n-bit long is first divided into k characters and the corresponding ciphertext of each input character is obtained by looking up a table, based on the value of the sum of its ASCII-code and the value of current dynamic shifting count (,i.e., dsc, see Step 5 of the E-DASS). Hence, the security of the E-DASS in the lookup and substitution process comes from the changing of dsc's value.

The original value of dsc is 256. But it is varied by the For loop between Step 3 and Step 5 of the E-DASS algorithm. In Step 5, each input character's ASCII and its corresponding index value are multiplied. The value of dsc is then increased by the multiplied product. Therefore, the same character appearing at different locations will result in different increment of dsc. Of course, the corresponding ciphertext will be different.

The For loop between Step 7 and Step 10 sequentially generates the ciphertext ci, which is the corresponding content in the R-Box after ch is looking up by using R-Box. The ASCII code of ch is $(vp[i] + dsc) \bmod 256$. In Step 8, the current value of dsc is the sum its previous value and the product of $vp[i-1]$ and i. The nonlinear and dynamic accumulative increment of dsc at each i enhances the randomness and non-linear characteristic of ci. Here, dynamic means the plaintext on each user input is different.

Based on the analysis above, we can conclude that:

A ciphertext character $cj, 1 \leq j \leq k$, is generated by the E-DASS which employs two dynamic parameters, $vp[j]$ and dsc. Therefore, even though the R-Box is widely known, it is still hard for hackers to break the plaintext character pj from an invalidly intercepted ciphertext character $cj, 1 \leq j \leq k$.

The ciphertext generated by the E-DASS has high input-data sensitivity because any tiny change on the plaintext will be magnified and reflected on the value of dsc by the For loop between Step 3 and Step 5.

Each $cj, 1 \leq j \leq k$, will be dynamically and nonlinearly influenced due to the sequentially accumulative change of dsc in Step 8.

In this paper, the GDBIS generates the dynamic keys, i.e., DK1, DK2 and DK3, by invoking the E-DASS algorithm many times given an input string, consequently generating a dynamic box. Basically, the GDBIS inherits the security of E-DASS, including high input-string sensitivity, and high level of randomness, so that it is hard to obtain the plaintext through the manipulation on the D-Box. Furthermore, the GDBIS does not limit the length of an input string, meaning that it is very flexible. In other words, the GDBIS is convenient to use and able to improve the security of the D-Box.

4.2   The Security of the GDBRK

In part 1 of the GDBRK algorithm, dynamic keys, i.e., DKis, $1 \leq i \leq 3$, are first sequentially generated according to the Expanded Cipher Key (ECK for short) which is expanded from CK by invoking the E-DASS algorithm and 3D operations, i.e., CK ECK → DK0 → DK1 → DK2 → DK3. In fact, all DK1, DK2 and DK3 are those with high level of randomness and secrecy. Given these keys as the input of the DBG algorithm, the generated D-Box inherits these keys' randomness and secrecy, thus significantly enhancing the security level of D-Box.

On the other hand, the round keys, namely RK1 to RKn, are sequentially derived from CK0 ~ CK3 with the operations of $\oplus$, +2 and the E-DASS algorithm (Step 7 ~ Step9). Here, the table that the E-DASS looks up is the D-Box (Step 7) generated by the GDBRK algorithm, rather than the S-Box known to the public. Since the D-Box is unknown to hackers, even though they may correctly guess the values of CK0 ~ CK3, they still cannot generate correct round keys. This will greatly enhance the security level of these round keys. Also, the E-DASS is an irreversible algorithm. Each round key is almost independent from others, meaning their relation is low and they have high level of security which is higher than that of the round keys generated in AES.

5   Performance Analysis

Performance is a key concern of an algorithm, especially in cryptography. Therefore, the efficiency of the E-DASS and GDBIS will be analyzed. The variable length of an input string is utilized to simulate the usage in real. The specifications of our simulation environment are shown in Table 1.

Table 1. The specifications of our simulation environment

CPU	AMD Phenom II X4 955 @ 3.20 GHz
RAM	12 GB
O.S.	Windows 10
Programming tools	C /Microsoft (R) C/C ++ Optimizing Compiler Version 19.00.24215.1

5.1   Performance of Fundamental Operators

The fundamental operators $\oplus$, $+_2$, $-_2$, $\odot_R$, and $\odot_{IR}$ are first tested, each for 12.5 million of times. Table 2 lists the average time consumed by an operator.

Table 2. The execution time of fundamental operators $\oplus$, $+_2$, $-_2$, $\odot_R$, and $\odot_{IR}$ employed in this study given keys of different lengths (a value is an average of 12.5 millions of execution times and the unit is ns).

Operator	Key size			
	128-bit	256-bit	512-bit	1024-bit
$\oplus$	10.77	20.59	38.37	76.09
$+_2$	11.08	23.94	68.22	155.35
$-_2$	11.12	23.30	67.21	146.05
$\odot_R$	22.98	42.73	84.22	169.29
$\odot_{IR}$	23.83	43.01	83.67	177.04

Operators, except XOR, were all implemented by software. However, the execution times are not very far away from those of XOR. In other words, if they all implemented with hardware, the times can be further shortened, but the improvement will not be significant.

5.2   Performance of the E-DASS and GDBIS

Basically, the E-DASS and GDBIS have good flexibility in use. Both are able to handle different lengths of inputs. But the process steps of the GDBIS differ. Also, the cost of the E-DASS increases when the input size is longer. Table 3 lists the experimental results.

Table 3. The execution times of the E-DASS given key sizes of 128, 256, 512 and 1024 bits (a value is an average of 12.5-million execution time and the unit is ns).

Input size			
128-bit	256-bit	512-bit	1024-bit
302.69	509.99	918.72	1744.11

Table 4 illustrates the execution time of the E-DASS, which linearly grows. But the increase is insignificant. Moreover, the cost of the GDBIS is appropriate for most usage since it is only used to initialize the system so as to provide a high-efficient environment for its following operations.

Table 4. The average execution times of the GDBIS given different input sizes (a value is an average of 2 million times of execution time and the unit is µs).

Input size (l)				
128-bit	$l < 1024$bits	$l = 1024$bits	1024bits $< l <$ 10 Kb	10 Kb $< l <$ 100 Kb
16.6192	17.98	15.73	15.67	18.75

5.3   Performance of the GDBRK

To improve AES, the GDBRK can be a part of it. The reliability will be boosted without losing its performance. Besides, D-Box could increase the confusability of SubBytes, and the round keys generated by the GDBRK would enhance the robustness of AES. Consequently, the number of rounds in the AES can be reduced, making AES more efficient (Table 5).

Table 5. The average time consumed for generating the round keys and D-Box for AES (unit: μs, average of 200-thousand times of execution)

AES-128 (128-bit, 10 round keys)	AES-192 (192-bit, 12 round keys)	AES-256 (256-bit, 14 round keys)
20.7921	24.1367	24.4706

6 Conclusions and Future Studies

In this study, a 16×16 dynamic box is produced by using an input string (please refer to the GDBIS in Sect. 3.4) without limiting the length of its input string. In other words, the GDBIS has high flexibility, and the D-Box has high level of randomness. Also, the GDBIS has high input-data sensitivity and an irreversible characteristic because it inherits the characteristics of the E-DASS. The other algorithm developed in this study, i.e., the GDBRK, uses Cipher Key to generate D-Box as its lookup table. After the 3D operation and the invocation of the E-DASS, the Round Keys will be sequentially produced. As a result, the Round Keys generated by the GDBRK have low relation among themselves, thus greatly enhancing the security level of the proposed system. If the Cipher Key is unknown, the D-Box follows. In this circumstance, using the GDBRK to replace the original Key Expansion algorithm of AES has significantly improved the security of the Round Keys, and dramatically increased the difficulty of cracking AES.

In the future, due to the 3D operations, the E-DASS and GDBIS are very efficient and secure. We can apply them to many fields, such as generating a faster and more secure Hash-based Message Authentication Code (HMAC), or developing a new data encryption method to substitute for AES. New research topics can be found in [21–24] These constitute our future studies.

References

1. Biryukov, A., Dunkelman, O., Keller, N., Khovratovich, D., Shamir, A.: Key recovery attacks of practical complexity on AES-256 variants with up to 10 rounds. In: Gilbert, H. (ed.) EUROCRYPT 2010. LNCS, vol. 6110, pp. 299–319. Springer, Heidelberg (2010). https://doi.org/10.1007/978-3-642-13190-5_15
2. Li, R., Jin, C.: Meet-in-the-middle Attacks on 10-round AES-256. Des. Codes Crypt. **80**(3), 459–471 (2016)
3. Bogdanov, A., Khovratovich, D., Rechberger, C.: Biclique cryptanalysis of the full AES. In: Lee, D.H., Wang, X. (eds.) ASIACRYPT 2011. LNCS, vol. 7073, pp. 344–371. Springer, Heidelberg (2011). https://doi.org/10.1007/978-3-642-25385-0_19
4. Biryukov, A., Khovratovich, D.: Related-key cryptanalysis of the full AES-192 and AES-256. In: Matsui, M. (ed.) ASIACRYPT 2009. LNCS, vol. 5912, pp. 1–18. Springer, Heidelberg (2009). https://doi.org/10.1007/978-3-642-10366-7_1
5. Kim, J., Hong, S., Preneel, B.: Related-key rectangle attacks on reduced AES-192 and AES-256. In: Biryukov, A. (ed.) FSE 2007. LNCS, vol. 4593, pp. 225–241. Springer, Heidelberg (2007). https://doi.org/10.1007/978-3-540-74619-5_15

6. Rogaway, P., Bellare, M., Black, J., Krovetz, T.: OCB: A Block-cipher Mode of Operation for Efficient Authenticated Encryption CCS-8, pp. 196–205 (2001)
7. Manjula, G., Mohan, H.S.: Constructing Key Dependent Dynamic S-Box for AES Block Cipher System iCATccT, pp. 613–617 (2017)
8. Alabaichi, A., Salih, A.I.: Enhance security of advance encryption standard algorithm based on key-dependent s-box. In: ICDIPC, pp. 44–53 (2015)
9. Arrag, S., Hamdoun, A., Tragha, A., Khamlich Salah, E.: Implementation of stronger AES by using dynamic S-box dependent of masterkey. J. Theoret. Appl. Inf. Technol. **53**(2), 196–204 (2013)
10. Announcing the Advanced Encryption Standard (AES), Federal Information Processing Standards Publication 197, United States National Institute of Standards and Technology (NIST), 26 November 2001
11. Hussain, I., Shah, T., Gondal, M.A., Khan, W.A., Mahmood, H.: A group theoretic approach to construct cryptographically strong substitution boxes. Neural Comput. Appl. **23**(1), 97–104 (2013)
12. Shah, T., Hussain, I., Gondal, M.A., Mahmood, H.: Statistical analysis of S-box in image encryption applications based on majority logic criterion. Int. J. Phys. Sci. **6**(16), 4110–4127 (2011)
13. Hosseinkhani, R., Javadi, H.H.S.: Using cipher key to generate dynamic S-box in AES cipher system. Int. J. Comput. Sci. Secur. **6**(1), 19–28 (2012)
14. Mahmoud, E.M., El Hafez, A.A., Elgarf, T.A., Abdelhalim, Z.: Dynamic AES-128 with key-dependent S-box. Int. J. Eng. Res. Appl. **3**(1), 1662–1670 (2013)
15. Kaul, V., Bharadi, V.A., Choudhari, P., Shah, D., Narayankhedkar, S.K.: Security enhancement for data transmission in 3G/4G networks. In: ICCUBEA, pp. 95–102 (2015)
16. Nejad, F.H., Sabah, S., Jam, A.J.: Analysis of avalanche effect on advance encryption standard by using dynamic S-box depends on rounds keys. In: ICCST, no. 7045184 (2014)
17. Wang, X., Wang, Q.: A novel image encryption algorithm based on dynamic S-boxes constructed by chaos. Nonlinear Dyn. **75**(3), 567–576 (2014)
18. Huang, Y.L., Dai, C.R., Leu, F.Y., You, I.: A secure data encryption method employing a sequential-logic style mechanism for a cloud system. Int. J. Web Grid Serv. **11**(1), 102–124 (2015)
19. Huang, Y.L., Leu, F.Y., You, I., Su, R.Y., Su, P.H., Chen, H.C.: A 3D encryption with shifting mapping substitution mechanism. In: The 5th IEEE CCNC International Workshop on Security and Cognitive Informatics for Homeland Defense (SeCIHD 2017), Las Vegas, USA, (2017)
20. Huang, Y.L., Leu, F.Y., Su, P.H., Sung, T.H., Liu, S.C.: A secure and high performance wireless sensor network based on symmetric key matrix. In: Tenth International Conference on Innovative Mobile and Internet Services in Ubiquitous Computing (IMIS-2016), Fukuoka Institute of Technology (FIT), Fukuoka, Japan (2016)
21. Hartl, A., Annessi, R., Zseby, T.: Subliminal channels in high-speed signatures. J. Wirel. Mobile Netw. Ubiquitous Comput. Dependable Appl. **9**(1), 30–53 (2018)
22. Harilal, A., et al.: The wolf of SUTD (TWOS): a dataset of malicious insider threat behavior based on a gamified competition. J. Wirel. Mobile Netw. Ubiquitous Comput. Dependable Appl. **9**(1), 54–85 (2018)
23. Vidhya, R., Brindha, M.: A novel dynamic key based chaotic image encryption. J. Internet Serv. Inf. Secur. **8**(1), 46–55 (2018)
24. Li, G., Zhou, H., Li, G., Feng, B.: Application-aware and dynamic security function chaining for mobile networks. J. Internet Serv. Inf. Secur. **7**(4), 21–34 (2017)

SAAS: A Secure Anonymous Authentication Scheme for PMIPv6

Tianhan Gao$^{(\boxtimes)}$, Xinyang Deng, and Fanghua Geng

Northeastern University, Shenyang, Liaoning, China
gaoth@mail.neu.edu.cn, xinyang1121@sina.com, gfh4056@163.com

Abstract. Proxy MIPv6 (PMIPv6) provides network-based mobility management without the participation of mobile node. Security and privacy issues are the main obstacles during mobile's access authentication in PMIPv6 network. A secure anonymous authentication scheme (SAAS) based on proxy group signature is proposed in this paper to achieve mutual authentication between mobile node and mobility access gateway. Anonymity is guaranteed through the identity-based proxy group signature. The formal security proof through SVO logic and the performance analysis demonstrate that the proposed scheme is both robust and efficient.

Keywords: PMIPv6 · Identity-based proxy group signature
Anonymous authentication · Mutual authentication

1 Introduction

With the rapid development of mobile network technology, wireless access needs become urgent. MIPv6 [1], suggested by IETF, provides mobility support for mobile node (MN), and is used in a variety of network scenarios, like VANETs [2, 3], WSN [4,5] etc. However, MIPv6 still faces with some problems, such as high handover latency, high package loss rate, and large signaling overheads [6]. Hence, to overcome the disadvantages of MIPv6, PMIPv6 [7], a network-based localized mobility management scheme, is proposed which holds the following features:

(1) Mobility management can be achieved by auxiliary network entity without the participation of MN [8];
(2) The complexity of MN's protocol stack is reduced to improve the handover performance of MN;
(3) Handover is achieved without changing IP address.

As shown in Fig. 1, PMIPv6 introduces two entities: LMA (local mobility anchor) and MAG (mobility access gateway). LMA is the topological anchor for the MN's home network prefix and is responsible to manage MN's reachability status. MAG is responsible for detecting MN's mobility status and performing mobility management on behalf of MN. However, security and privacy

© Springer Nature Singapore Pte Ltd. 2019
I. You et al. (Eds.): MobiSec 2017, CCIS 971, pp. 30–50, 2019.
https://doi.org/10.1007/978-981-13-3732-1_3

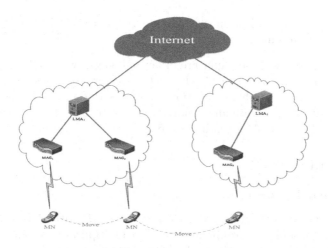

Fig. 1. PMIPv6 network architecture

issues become the main obstacles for PMIPv6's wide deployment, such as mutual authentication, privacy preserving, as well as key agreement. Thus, many access authentication schemes for PMIPv6 are proposed recent years [9–13].

In [9], LMA and MN shares a time-synchronized key to authenticate each other remotely, which causes low authentication efficiency and much communication overhead. Chuang and Lee propose SF-PMIPv6 [10], where local authentication, fast handover, and buffering scheme are adopted to reduce authentication delay, signaling overhead, and package loss. However, all entities depend on one key for authentication process, SPF (Single Point of Failure) may occur. SPAM [11] presents a secure password authentication scheme, that implements seamless handover authentication for PMIPv6. While with the hops between MAG and AAA increased, authentication overhead increases sharply. Furthermore, the scheme is vulnerable to impersonation and password guessing attacks. [12] combines PMIPv6 and SIP to gain high authentication efficiency. However, the inside attack is existed. The above authentication schemes are accomplished using symmetric cryptosystem. In 2014, Kim proposed a PMIPv6 authentication scheme [13] based on public key system where fast handover is adopted to decrease the handover latency and package loss. While public key encryption has high computation cost. In summary, most of the above schemes don't take MN's privacy into account during authentication. A secure anonymous PMIPv6 authentication scheme based on proxy group signature is then proposed in this paper which achieves secure anonymous mutual authentication between MN and MAG with the help of fast handover mechanism. The main contributions of this paper are as below:

(1) Secure Mutual authentication is achieved between MN and MAG.
(2) Handover authentication efficiency is guaranteed in terms of fast handover mechanism.

(3) Anonymous authentication is achieved based on the efficient ID-based proxy group signature mechanism.

The rest sections of the paper are organized as follows. Section 2 introduces the related technology. Section 3 elaborates the proposed secure anonymous mutual authentication scheme. Section 4 presents the formal security proof of the main protocols. Performance analysis is shown in Sect. 5. Conclusion and future research are finally given in Sect. 6.

2 Preliminaries

2.1 Bilinear Pairings

Let G_1 and G_2 be two cycle groups generated by P with the same order q, where G_1 is an additive groups and G_2 is a multiplicative group. A bilinear pairing $e : G_1 \times G_1 \to G_2$ satisfies the following properties:

(1) Bilinear: For all $P, Q \in G_1$ and $a, b \in Z_q^*$, we have $e(aP, bQ) = e(P, Q)^{ab}$.
(2) Non-degenerate: There exists $P, Q \in G_1$ such that $e(P, Q) \neq 1$.
(3) Computable: There is an efficient algorithm to compute $e(P, Q)$ for any $P, Q \in G_1$.

2.2 Identity-Based Proxy Group Signature

In proxy signature, the original signer delegates the signing right to proxy signer, who can sign message instead of the original signer [14]. In order to protect proxy signer's privacy, [15] first proposed the concept of proxy group signature. The proxy group signature scheme contains four entities:

(1) Original signer: Issuing proxy authorization to proxy manager.
(2) Proxy manager: Delegate signing right to the group manager.
(3) Proxy signer: Signing message instead of original signer.
(4) Group manager: Issuing signing key to proxy signer.

In this paper, a new proxy group signature scheme that integrates [15] and [16] is proposed where the proxy manager is removed to reduce the computation cost and signaling overhead. The details of the scheme are as below.

(1) Initialization: PKG chooses a cycle additive group G_1, a multiplicative group G_2 generated by P, whose order is prime q respectively, a bilinear pairing $e : G_1 \times G_1 \to G_2$, and three hash functions $H : \{0,1\} \to G_1, H_1 : \{0,1\} \times G_1 \to G_2, H_2 : \{0,1\} \to Z_q^*$. Original signer selects private key $s \in Z_q^*$, and the public key is $P_{pub} = sP$. Group manager's private key is $a \in Z_q^*$, group public key is $P_g = aP$. System public parameters are $\{G_1, G_2, q, P, P_{pub}, H, H_1, H_2, e\}$. Group manager issues private key to proxy signer: $sk_i = aPK_u$, where $PK_u = H(ID_u)$ is proxy signer's public key. Proxy signer computes a random number $b \in Z_q^*$ satisfying $bH_2(ID_u) \equiv 1 mod\varphi(n)$, where $\varphi(n)$ is the euler function, n is the product of two large prime numbers. Proxy signer's signing key is (sk_i, b).

(2) Delegation: Original signer selects warrant w, computes $S_w = sH(w)$, and delegates w and S_w to group manager. Group manager ensures whether the warrant is legal through checking the equation $e(P, S_w) =?e(P_{pub}, H(w))$.

(3) Signing: Proxy signer selects a random number $x \in Z_q^*$, computes $A = xP; B = x^{-1}sk_i + H_1(m, S_w)b; C = H_2(ID_u)PK_u; D = H_2(ID_u)A$, the signature on message m is $\{A, B, C, D, w, S_w\}$.

(4) Verification: Verifier uses original signer's public key to verify w first. If legal, verifier uses group public key to compute $\alpha = e(P_g, C); \beta = e(D, B); \sigma = e(A, H_1(r_5P, S_{w1}))$. Through checking $\beta =?\alpha\sigma$, verifier checks whether the signature is legal or not.

3   The Proposed Scheme

3.1   Network Architecture and Trust Model

The network architecture of the proposed scheme consists of four layers as described in Fig. 2. The first layer is TR, which acts as the original signer to issue private key to other entities. The second layer is LMA, the group manager, which is responsible for issuing proxy signing key to legal group member: MAG and MN. The last two layers are MAG and MN respectively. In terms of the network architecture, the trust model is also presented. TR is the root trust for all the entities in the architecture. LMA and MAGs under the same group trust each other. Although the entities in different group has no trust relationship

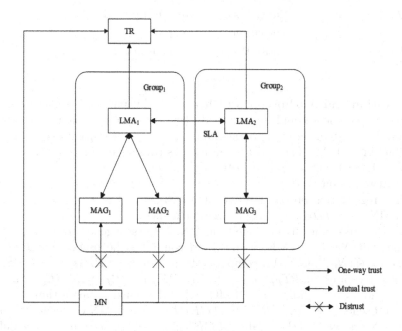

Fig. 2. Trust model

between each other, inter-LMA is able to establish a secure channel through SLA(service-level agreement). Both MN and the accessed MAG distrusts each other. The proposed authentication scheme will establish such trust relationship.

3.2 Secure Anonymous Authentication Scheme

The access authentication scheme consists of four phrases: registration and authorization, initial authentication protocol, intra-group handover authentication protocol, inter-group handover authentication protocol. In order to facilitate the following description, Table 1 shows the relevant identifications and meanings.

Table 1. Relevant identifications and meanings

Identification	Meaning
ID_A	The identity of entity A
$PK_A PR_A$	The public/private key of entity A
PSE	MN's pseudonym
K_{A-B}	The shared key between entity A and B
$ENCR\_ALG\_PK_A\{M\}$	Encrypt message M using PK_A through ALG algorithm
$SIGN\_ALG\_PR_A\{M\}$	Sign message M using PR_A through ALG algorithm
$E_{K_{A-B}}\{M\}$	Encrypt message M using K_{A-B}
w	The warrant generated by original signer TR
$CERT_{A-B}$	Entity B's certificate issued by entity A
T_i	The current timestamp
$auth_{A-B}$	Entity B's authorization issued by entity A

Registration and Authorization Phrase. In this phrase, TR generates system public parameters and issues private key and signing right to the related entities. The system public parameters are $\{G_1, G_2, q, P, P_{pub}, H, H_1, H_2, e\}$ as described in Sect. 2.2. The registration process consists of three steps: MN registration, LMA registration and MAG registration.

(1) Registration of MN

MN's registration process is shown as Fig. 3.

①: MN sends ID_{MN} to TR via secure channel.

②: After receiving the message from MN, TR firstly generates multiple random number $N_1, N_2 \cdots\cdots N_m \in Z_q^*$, and computes the pseudonym $PSE_i = H_2(ID_{MN}) \bigoplus N_i$. Finally, TR computes the private keys: $PR_{MN} = sH(PSE_i)$, and the certificates $CERT_{TR-MN} = SIGN\_BLMQ\_PR_{TR}\{t_i, PSE_i\}$, where t_i is the pseudonym's validity and BLMQ [17] is the signature algorithm.

③: TR sends PSE_i, t_i, PR_{MN}, and $CERT_{TR-MN}$ to MN via secure channel.

④: MN first verifies the legality of $CERT_{TR-MN}$, then computes the public key $PK_{MN} = H(PSE_i)$ and stores $PSE_i, CERT_{TR-MN}, PR_{MN}$ locally.

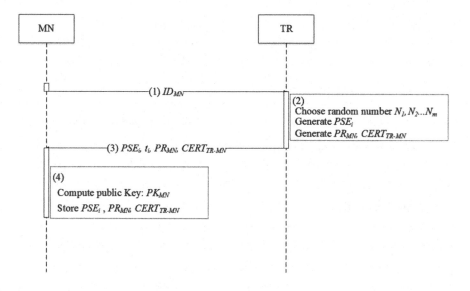

Fig. 3. MN's registration process

(2) Registration of LMA

①: TR generates warrant w, and $S_w = sH(w)$.

②: TR sends w and S_w to LMA.

③: After receiving the message from TR, LMA verifies whether $e(P, S_w) = ?e(P_{pub}, H(w))$ holds. If yes, LMA accepts S_w. Otherwise, LMA discards it.

(3) Registration of MAG

MAG's registration process is shown as Fig. 4.

①: MAG sends ID_{MAG} and PK_{MAG} to LMA.

②: LMA derives $PR_{MAG} = aPK_{MAG}$ and issues authorization: $auth_{LMA-MAG} = S_w + aH(ID_{MAG})$ to MAG, where $a \in Z_q^*$.

③: LMA sends PR_{MAG} and $auth_{LMA-MAG}$ to MAG through the secure channel.

④: MAG stores $auth_{LMA-MAG}$ and PR_{MAG} locally.

Initial Authentication Protocol. While MN first accessing the PMIPv6 network, the initial authentication protocol will be executed between MN and the accessed MAG(MAG$_1$) as shown in Fig. 5.

①: MN generates $r_1 \in Z_q^*$ randomly, computes r_1P as the key agreement parameter. Then MN signs message $\{r_1P, PSE_i, T_1, CERT_{TR-MN}\}$ to get $Sign_{MN} = SIGN\_BLMQ\_PR_{MN}\{r_1P, PSE_i, T_1, CERT_{TR-MN}\}$.

②: MN sends $Sign_{MN}$, $CERT_{TR-MN}$, r_1P, PSE_i, and T_1 to MAG$_1$.

③: When getting the message from MN, MAG$_1$ first checks the freshness of T_1, if T_1 is fresh, then MAG$_1$ verifies $CERT_{TR-MN}$ and $Sign_{MN}$ respectively. If both are confirmed to be legal, MAG$_1$ regards MN as a legal user. Otherwise MAG$_1$ rejects MN's access.

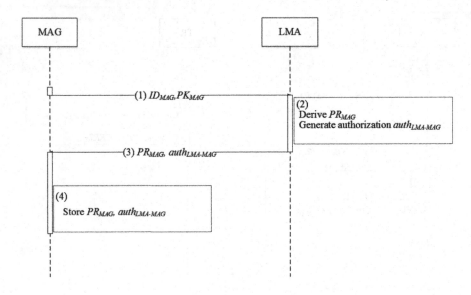

Fig. 4. MAG's registration process

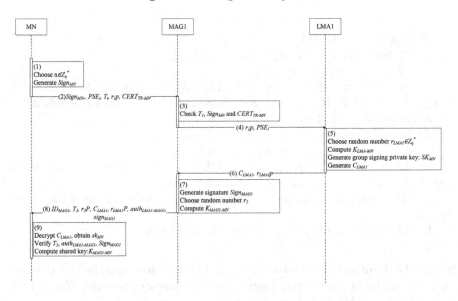

Fig. 5. MN's initial access authentication protocol

④: MAG_1 transfers PSE_i and r_1P to LMA_1.

⑤: LMA_1 generates $r_{LMA_1} \in Z_q^*$, and computes the shared key: $K_{LMA_1-MN} = r_{LMA_1}r_1P$. Then LMA_1 generates the group signing key: $sk_{MN} = aH(PSE_i)$ and encrypts $\{sk_{MN}, S_{w_1}, w_1, P_{g_1}\}$ to get $C_{LMA_1} = E_{K_{LMA_1-MN}}\{sk_{MN}, S_{w_1}, w_1, P_{g_1}\}$.

⑥: LMA_1 transfers C_{LMA_1} and $r_{LMA_1}P$ to MAG_1.

⑦: MAG_1 chooses $r_2 \in Z_q^*$, and signs $\{ID_{MAG_1}, auth_{LMA_1-MAG_1}, r_2P, T_2\}$ to get $Sign_{MAG_1} = SIGN\_BLMQ\_PR_{MAG_1}\{ID_{MAG_1}, auth_{LMA_1-MAG_1}, r_2P, T_2\}$. Then MAG_1 computes shared key: $K_{MAG_1-MN} = r_2r_1P$.

⑧: MAG_1 sends $Sign_{MAG_1}, auth_{LMA_1-MAG_1}, C_{LMA_1}, r_{LMA_1}P, ID_{MAG_1}, r_2P, T_2$ to MN.

⑨: After receiving the message from MAG_1, MN first computes: $K_{LMA_1-MN} = r_1r_{LMA_1}P$, decrypts C_{LMA_1}, and obtains sk_{MN}. MN computes $b_{MN} \in Z_q^*$ satisfying $b_{MN}H_2(ID_{MN}) \equiv 1mod\varphi(n)$. Then MN verifies $T_2, auth_{LMA_1-MAG_1}$, and $Sign_{MAG_1}$ respectively. If they are legal, MN takes MAG_1 as a reliable MAG. Otherwise, MN refuses to access into MAG_1. Finally, MN computes and stores $K_{MN-MAG_1} = r_1r_2P$.

Intra-group Handover Authentication Protocol. Intra-group handover authentication protocol takes into action when MN handovers among different MAGs in the same group. When MN is about to handover, the old MAG (i.e. MAG_1) is able to predict the new access MAG (MAG_2) with fast handover mechanism [18]. MAG_1 then sends the shared key between MAG_1 and MN to MAG_2 through the secure channel, where K_{MAG_1-MN} is a credential for the mutual authentication. Take the scenario in Fig. 1 for example, the steps of intra-group handover authentication protocol are shown in Fig. 6.

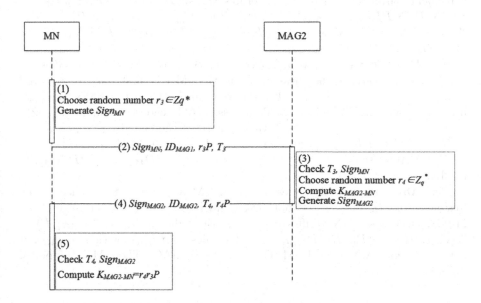

Fig. 6. Intra-group handover authentication protocol

①: MN generates random number $r_3 \in Z_q^*$. Using K_{MAG_1-MN}, MN computes the signature $Sign_{MN} = SIGN\_HMAC\_K_{MAG_1-MN}\{ID_{MAG_1}, r_3P, T_3\}$.

②: MN transfers $Sign_{MN}, ID_{MAG_1}, r_3P, T_3$ to MAG_2.

③: Once receiving the message, MAG_2 first checks the freshness of T_3. If T_3 is not fresh, MAG_2 rejects the access request from MN. Otherwise, MN continues to verify $Sign_{MN}$ with K_{MAG_1-MN}. If the $Sign_{MN}$ is legal, MAG_2 regards MN as a legal user. Otherwise MAG_2 rejects MN's access. Finally, MAG_2 chooses random $r_4 \in Z_q^*$, computes: $K_{MAG_2-MN} = r_4r_3P$ and $Sign_{MAG_2} = SIGN\_HMAC\_K_{MAG_1-MN}\{ID_{MAG_2}, r_4P, T_4\}$.

④: MAG_1 sends $Sign_{MAG_2}, ID_{MAG_2}, r_4P, T_4$ to MN.

⑤: MN first checks whether T_4 is fresh. If T_4 is not fresh, MN discards the message from MAG_2. Otherwise, MN verifies $Sign_{MAG_2}$ with K_{MAG_1-MN}. If $Sign_{MAG_2}$ is legal, MN regards MAG_2 as a legal MAG. Finally MN computes: $K_{MAG_2-MN} = r_3r_4P$.

Inter-group Handover Authentication Protocol. Inter-group handover authentication happens while MN roaming across different MAGs in different groups. The details of inter-group handover authentication protocol are shown in Fig. 7.

①: MN chooses random number $x, r_5 \in Z_q^*$, and computes r_5P as the key agreement parameter, then MN generates the signature on r_5P: $Sign_{MN} = SIGN\_PGS\_PR_{LMA_1-MN}\{A, B, C, D, r_5P, w_1, S_{w_1}, ID_{LMA_1}, r_5P\}$, where $A = xP; B = x^{-1}sk_{MN} + H_1(r_5P, S_{w_1})b_{MN}; C = H_2(PSE_i)PK_{MN}; D = H_2(PSE_i)A$.

②: MN sends $Sign_{MN}, A, B, C, D, r_5P, w_1, S_{w_1}, ID_{LMA_1}, r_5P$ to MAG_3.

③: After receiving the message from MN, MAG_3 first verifies S_{w_1} and $Sign_{MN}$ with P_{pub} and PK_{MN}. If both are legal, MAG_3 regards MN as a legal user. Otherwise MAG_3 rejects MN's access. MAG_3 chooses random $r_6 \in Z_q^*$, computes: $K_{MAG_3-MN} = r_6r_5P$, then generates the signature $Sign_{MAG_3} = SIGN\_BLM\text{-}Q\_PR_{MAG_3}\{auth_{LMA_2-MAG_3}, ID_{MAG_3}, w_2, ID_{LMA_2}, T_5\}$.

④: MAG_3 sends $Sign_{MAG_3}, auth_{LMA_2-MAG_3}, ID_{MAG_3}, w_2, ID_{LMA_2}, T_5$ to MN.

⑤: After receive the message from MAG_3, MN first checks the freshness of T_5. If T_5 is not fresh, MN discards the message from MAG_3. Otherwise, MN verifies $Sign_{MAG_3}$ through $e(auth_{LMA_2-MAG_3}, P) = ?e(P_{pub}, H(w_2))e(P_{g_2}, H(ID_{MAG_3}))$, and verifies $Sign_{MAG_3}$ with PK_{MAG_3}. If both are legal, MN regards MAG_3 as a legal MAG. Then MN computes: $K_{MAG_3-MN} = r_5r_6P$.

Table 2. Symbols of computation cost

Formula	Explanation
$F(X_1...X_n)$	X donates message, F is a function with variable
$SharedKey(K, P, Q)$	K is the sharedkey between P and Q
T_{EXP}	Exponentiation's computation cost
T_{RSA}	RSA's computation cost
T_{HMAC}	HAMC's computation cost

4 Security Proof

We adopt SVO logical [19] to analyze the core protocols in our scheme. Compared with other logical analysis method, the advantages of SVO logical are as follows:

(1) SVO establishes clear semantic and ensures the logical inference reliable.
(2) SVO has a detailed model, that eliminates fuzzy understanding issues.
(3) SVO owns concise logic, like BAN logic [20], which is easy to extend with logical semantics.

4.1 SVO Logic Rules and Axioms

The initial rules and some axioms used in this paper are presented below. Some meanings of the formula are listed in Table 2.

Two initial rules:
(1) MP(Modus Ponens):$\varphi \wedge \varphi \subset \psi \rightarrow \psi$
(2) Nec(Necessitation):$\vdash \varphi \rightarrow P$ believes φ

Twenty axioms:
(1) Believing
Ax1: P believes $\varphi \wedge P$ believes$(\varphi \subset \psi) \subset P$ believes ψ
Ax2: P believes $\varphi \subset P$ believes $Pbelieves\varphi$
(2) Source Association
Ax3: $SharedKey(K, P, Q) \wedge R$ received $\{X^Q\}_K \wedge Q$ said $X \wedge Q$ sees K
Ax4: $PK_\sigma(Q, K) \wedge R$ received $X \wedge SV(X, K, Y) \subset Q$ said Y
(3) Key agreement
Ax5: $PK_\delta(P, K_P) \wedge PK_\delta(Q, K_Q) \subset SharedKey(F_0(K_P, K_P), P, Q)$
Ax6: $\varphi \equiv \varphi[F_0(K, K')/F0(K', K)]$
(4) Receiving
Ax7: P received $\{X_1, X_2...X_n\} \subset P$ received X_i
Ax8: P received $\{X\}_K \subset P$ received X
(5) Seeing
Ax10: P received $X \subset P$ sees X
Ax11: P sees $\{X_1, X_2...X_n\} \subset P$ sees X_i
Ax12: P sees $X_1 \wedge ... \wedge P$ sees $X_n \subset P$ sees $F(X_1, X_2...X_n)$
(6) Comprehending
Ax13: P believes $(P$ sees $F(X)) \subset P$ believes $(P$ sees $X)$

(7) Saying

Ax14: P said $\{X_1, X_2...X_n\} \subset P$ said $X_i \wedge P$ sees X_i

Ax15: P says $\{X_1, X_2...X_n\} \subset P$ says $X_i \wedge P$ said $(X_1, X_2...X_n)$

(8) Jurisdiction

Ax16: P controls $\varphi \wedge P$ says $\varphi \subset \varphi$

(9) Freshness

Ax17: fresh$(X_i) \subset$ fresh$(X_1...X_n)$

Ax18: fresh$(X_1...X_n) \subset$ fresh$(F(X_1...X_n))$

(10) Nonce-Verification

Ax19: fresh$(X) \wedge P$ said $X \subset P$ says X

(11) Symmetric goodness of shared keys

Ax20: $SharedKey(K, P, Q) \equiv SharedKey(K, Q, P)$

4.2   Formal Security Proof

The formal security proof of the authentication protocols in the proposed scheme will be given in this section.

Security Proof of Initial Authentication Protocol. From the perspective of MN, we give the following security proof. The SVO proof of MAG can also be proved similarly.

Assumptions

P1 : MN believes $PK_\sigma(TR, PK_{TR})$;

MAG$_1$ believes $PK_\sigma(TR, PK_{TR})$;

LMA$_1$ believes $PK_\sigma(TR, PK_{TR})$;

P2 : MN believes $SV(Sign_{MAG_1}, ID_{MAG_1}, (ID_{MAG_1}, r_2P, T_2, auth_{LMA_1-MAG_1}))$;

MN believes $SV(auth_{LMA_1-MAG_1}, PK_{TR}, (w_1, ID_{MAG_1}))$;

MAG$_1$ believes $SV(CERT_{TR-MN}, PK_{TR}, (t_i, PSE_i))$;

MAG$_1$ believes $SV(Sign_{MN}, PK_{MN}, (ID_{MN}, T_1, r_1P, CERT_{TR-MN}))$;

P3 : MAG$_1$ believes (TR said $PSE_i \subset$ TR said $PK_\sigma(PSE_i, PK_{MN})$);

MN believes TR says (S_{w_1}, w_1);

P4 : MN believes $PK_\delta(MN, r_1P)$;

MAG$_1$ believes $PK_\delta(ID_{MAG_1}, r_2P)$;

LMA$_1$ believes $PK_\delta(ID_{LMA_1}, r_{LMA_1}P)$;

P5 : MN believes fresh(r_1);

MAG$_1$ believes fresh(r_2);

P6 : MN believes MN sees r_1P;

MAG$_1$ believes MAG$_1$ sees r_2P;

LMA$_1$ believes LMA$_1$ sees $r_{LMA_1}P$;

P7 : MN received $(ID_{MAG_1}, T_2, r_2P, r_{LMA_1}P, \{sk_{MN}, S_{w_1}, w_1, P_{g_1}\}K_{LMA_1-MN},$ $[ID_{MAG_1}, r_2P, T_2, auth_{LMA_1-MAG_1}]PR_{MAG_1})$;

MAG$_1$ received $(PSE_i, T_1, r_1P, CERT_{TR-MN}, [PSE_i, T_1, r_1P, CERT_{TR-MN}]$ $PR_{MN})$;

P8 : MN believes MN received $(ID_{MAG_1}, T_2, r_2P, r_{LMA_1}P, \{sk_{MN}, S_{w_1}, w_1, P_{g_1}\}$
$K_{LMA_1-MN}, [ID_{MAG_1}, r_2P, T_2, auth_{LMA_1-MAG_1}]PR_{MAG_1})$;

MAG$_1$ believes MAG$_1$ received $(PSE_i, T_1, r_1P, CERT_{TR-MN}, [PSE_i,$
$T_1, r_1P, CERT_{TR-MN}]PR_{MN})$;

P9 : MN believes -(MN said r_2P); MN believes -(MN said $r_{LMA_1}P$);

MAG$_1$ believes -(MAG$_1$ said r_1P); LMA$_1$ believes -(LMA$_1$ said $r_{LMA_1}P$);

P10 : MN believes fresh(T_2); MAG$_1$ believes fresh(T_1);

Goals

G1(Far-End Operative): MN believes MAG$_1$ says$\{ID_{MAG_1}, r_2P, T_2,$
$auth_{LMA_1-MAG_1}\}$;

G2(Secure Key Establishment): MN believes $SharedKey(K_{MN-MAG_1}-,$
MN, MAG$_1$);

G3(Key Confirmation): MN believes $SharedKey(K_{MN-MAG_1}+,$ MN,
MAG$_1$);

G4(Key Freshness): MN believes $fresh(K_{MN-MAG_1})$;

Security proof

From $P8, Ax1, Ax7$ and Nec, get:

MN believes MN received $(C_{LMA_1}, r_{LMA_1}P)$;   (1)

From $(1), P4, Ax1, Ax5$ and Nec, get:

MN believes $SharedKey(K_{MN-LMA_1},$ MN, LMA$_1$), K_{MN-LMA_1}
$= F_0(r_1, r_{LMA_1}P)$;   (2)

From $P6, P8, Ax1, Ax9, Ax11, Ax12$ and Nec, get:

MN believes MN sees K_{MN-LMA_1};   (3)

From $(1), (3), Ax1, Ax8$ and Nec, get:

MN believes MN received$\{PR_{MN}, S_{w_1}, w_1, P_{g_1}\}$;   (4)

From $P1, P2, P3, P8, Ax1, Ax7$, get:

MN believes $(PK_\sigma(ID_{MAG_1}, PK_{MAG_1}))$;   (5)

From $(5), P2, P8, Ax1, Ax4, Ax7$ and Nec, get:

MN believes MAG$_1$ said $(ID_{MAG_1}, r_2P, T_2, auth_{LMA_1-MAG_1})$;   (6)

From $(6), P10, Ax1, Ax17$ and Nec, get:

MN believes fresh $(ID_{MAG_1}, r_2P, T_2, auth_{LMA_1-MAG_1})$;   (7)

From $(6), (7), P10$ and $Ax19$, get:

MN believes MAG$_1$ says $\{ID_{MAG_1}, r_2P, T_2, auth_{LMA_1-MAG_1}\}$;   (8)

($G1$ is proved)

From $(8), P4, Ax1, Ax5$ and Nec, get:

MN believes $SharedKey(K_{MN-MAG_1},$ MN, MAG$_1$),K_{MN-MAG_1}
$= F_0(r_1, r_2)$;   (9)

($G2$ is proved)

From $(9), P6, Ax1$ and the definition of $SharedKey(K_{MN-MAG_1}-,$ MN,
MAG$_1$)

MN believes $SharedKey(K_{MN-MAG_1}-,$ MN, MAG$_1$);   (10)

From $(7), P5$ and $Ax18$, get:

MN believes $fresh(K_{MN-MAG_1})$;   (11)

($G4$ is proved)

From $(11), P8, P9, Ax1$ and definition of $confirm_P(X)$

MN believes $confirm_{MN}(K_{MN-MAG_1})$; (12)

From (10), (12), $Ax1$ and definition of $SharedKey(K+, A, B)$:

MN believes $SharedKey(K_{MN-MAG_1}+, MN, MAG_1)$; (13)

($G3$ is proved)

Security Proof of Intra-group Handover Authentication Protocol. From the perspective of MN, we give the following security proof. The SVO proof of MAG can also be proved similar with MN, so we don't give the prove detail from the perspective of MAG.

Assumptions

P1 : MN believes MN sees $SharedKey(K_{MN-MAG_1}, MN, MAG_1)$;

$\quad$ MAG_2 believes MAG_2 sees $SharedKey(K_{MN-MAG_1}, MN, MAG_1)$;

P2 : MN believes $SV(Sign_{MAG_2}, K_{MN-MAG_1}, (ID_{MAG_1}, T_4, r_4P))$;

$\quad$ MAG_2 believes $SV(Sign_{MN}, K_{MN-MAG_1}, (ID_{MAG_2}, T_3, r_3P))$;

P3 : MN believes $fresh(r_3)$;

$\quad$ MAG_2 believes $fresh(r_4)$;

P4 : MN believes $PK_\delta(PSE_i, r_3P)$;

$\quad$ MAG_2 believes $PK_\delta(ID_{MAG_2}, r_4P)$;

P5 : MN believes MN sees r_3P;

$\quad$ MAG_2 believes MAG_2 sees r_4P;

P6 : MN believes MN sees K_{MAG_2-MN};

$\quad$ MAG_2 believes MAG_2 sees K_{MAG_2-MN};

P7 : MN received $ID_{MAG_2}, T_4, r_4P, [ID_{MAG_2}, T_4, r_4P]K_{MAG_1-MN}$;

$\quad$ MAG_2 received $ID_{MAG_1}, T_3, r_3P, [ID_{MAG_1}, T_3, r_3P]K_{MAG_1-MN}$;

P8 : MN believes MN received $(ID_{MAG_2}, T_4, r_4P, [ID_{MAG_2}, T_4, r_4P]$ $K_{MAG_1-MN})$;

$\quad$ MAG_2 believes MAG_2 received $(ID_{MAG_1}, T_3, r_3P, [ID_{MAG_1}, T_3, r_3P]$ $K_{MAG_1-MN})$;

P9 : MN believes ?(MN said r_4P);

$\quad$ MAG_2 believes ?(MAG_2 said r_3P);

P10 : MN believes $fresh(T_4)$;

$\quad$ MAG_2 believes $fresh(T_3)$;

Goals

G1(Far-End Operative): MN believes MAG_2 says $\{ID_{MAG_2}, r_4P, T_4\}$;

G2(Secure Key Establishment): MN believes $SharedKey(K_{MN-MAG_2}-, MN, MAG_2)$;

G3(Key Confirmation): MN believes $SharedKey(K_{MN-MAG_2}+, MN, MAG_2)$;

G4(Key Freshness): MN believes $fresh(K_{MN-MAG_2})$;

Security proof

From $P8, Ax1, Ax7$ and Nec, get:

MN believes MN received (ID_{MAG_2}, r_4P, T_4); (1)

From (1), $P1, P2, Ax1, Ax4$ and Nec, get:

MN believes MAG_2 said $\{ID_{MAG_2}, r_4P, T_4\}$; (2)

From (2), $P3, P10, Ax1, Ax19$ and Nec, get:

MN believes MAG_2 says $\{ID_{MAG_2}, r_4P, T_4\}$;   (3)
($G1$ is proved)
From $(1), P1, P4$ and $Ax1$, get:
MN believes $PK_\delta(ID_{MAG_2}, r_4P)$;   (4)
From $(4), P4, Ax1, Ax5$ and Nec, get:
MN believes $SharedKey(K_{MN-MAG_2}, MN, MAG_2)$;   (5)
From $(5), P5, Ax1$ and definition of $SharedKey(K, A, B)$:
MN believes $SharedKey(K_{MN-MAG_2}-, MN, MAG_2)$;   (6)
($G2$ is proved)
From $(6), P4$ and $Ax18$, get:
MN believes $fresh(K_{MN-MAG_2})$;   (7)
($G4$ is proved)
From $(7), P8, P9, Ax1$ and definition of $confirm_P(X)$:
MN believes $confirm_{MN}(K_{MN-MAG_2})$;   (8)
From $(6), (8), Ax1$ and definition of $SharedKey(K+, A, B)$:
MN believes $SharedKey(K_{MN-MAG_2}+, MN, MAG_2)$;   (9)
($G3$ is proved)

Security Proof of Inter-group Handover Authentication Protocol.
Assumptions:
P1: MN believes $PK_\sigma(TR, PK_{TR})$;
  MAG_3 believes $PK_\sigma(TR, PK_{TR})$;
P2: MN believes $SV(Sign_{MAG_3}, PK_{MAG_3}, (ID_{MAG_3}, T_5, auth_{LMA_2-MAG_3},$
$ID_{LMA_2}, r_6P))$;
  MN believes $SV(auth_{LMA_2-MAG_3}, PK_{TR}, (w_2, ID_{MAG_3}))$;
  MN believes $SV(S_{w_1}, PK_{TR}, (w_1))$;
  MAG_3 believes $SV(S_{w_2}, PK_{TR}, (w_2))$;
  MAG_3 believes $SV(Sign_{MN}, P_{g_1}, (A, ID_{LMA_1}, B, C, D, r_5P, w_1, S_{w_1}))$;
P3: MN believes $PK_\sigma(ID_{LMA_2}, P_{g_2})$;
  MAG_3 believes $PK_\sigma(ID_{LMA_1}, P_{g_1})$;
P4: MN believes $PK_\delta(ID_{MN}, r_5P)$;
  MAG_3 believes $PK_\delta(ID_{MAG_3}, r_6P)$;
P5: MN believes fresh(r_5);
  MAG_3 believes fresh(r_6);
  MAG_3 believes fresh(r_5P);
P6 : MN believes MN sees r_5P;
  MAG_3 believes MAG_3 sees r_6P;
  MN believes MN sees K_{MAG_3-MN};
  MAG_3 believes MAG_3 sees K_{MAG_3-MN};
P7 : MN received ID_{MAG_3}, T_5, ID_{LMA_2}, $auth_{LMA_2-MAG_3}$, r_6P, w_2,
$[w_2, ID_{MAG_3}]PK_{TR}$, $[ID_{MAG_3}$, T_5, ID_{LMA_2}, $auth_{LMA_2-MAG_3}$, r_6P,
$w_2]PK_{MAG_3}$;
  MAG_3 received A, B, C, ID_{LMA_1}, D, r_5P, w_1, S_{w_1}, $[w_1]PK_{TR}, [A, B,$
$C, ID_{LMA_1}, D, r_5P, w_1, S_{w_1}]sk_{MN}$;
P8 : MN believes MN received $(ID_{MAG_3}, T_5, ID_{LMA_2}, auth_{LMA_2-MAG_3},$

r_6P, w_2, $[w_2, ID_{MAG_3}]PK_{TR}$, $[ID_{MAG_3}, T_5, ID_{LMA_2}, auth_{LMA_2-MAG_3}, r_6P, w_2]PK_{MAG_3})$;

MAG$_3$ believes MAG$_1$ received $(A, B, C, ID_{LMA_1}, D, r_5P, w_1, S_{w_1}, [w_1]PK_{TR}, [A, B, C, ID_{LMA_1}, D, r_5P, w_1, S_{w_1}]sk_{MN})$;

P9 : MN believes ?(MN said r_6P);

MAG$_3$ believes ?(MAG$_3$ said r_5P);

P10 : MN believes fresh(T_5);

Goals

From the perspective of MN, goals are as follows:

G1(Far-End Operative): MN believes MAG$_3$ says $\{ID_{MAG_3}, T_5, auth_{LMA_2-MAG_3}, r_6P, ID_{LMA_2}, w_2\}$;

G2(Secure Key Establishment): MN believes $SharedKey(K_{MN-MAG_3}-, MN, MAG_3)$;

G3(Key Confirmation): MN believes $SharedKey(K_{MN-MAG_3}+, MN, MAG_3)$;

G4(Key Freshness): MN believes fresh K_{MN-MAG_3};

Prove process is as follows:

From $P8, Ax1, Ax7$ and Nec, get:

MN believes MN received $(ID_{MAG_3}, ID_{LMA_2}, T_5, auth_{LMA_2-MAG_3}, r_6P, w_2)$; (1)

From $(1), P1, P2, P3, Ax1, Ax4, Ax7$ and Nec, get:

MN believes LMA$_2$ said $\{auth_{LMA_2-MAG_3}\}$; (2)

MN believes $(TRsaid\{S_{w_2}, w_2\} \subset PK_\sigma(ID_{LMA_1}, P_{g_1}))$; (3)

MN believes MAG$_3$ said $\{Sign_{MA_3}, ID_{MAG_3}, ID_{LMA_2}, T_5, auth_{LMA_2-MAG_3}, r_6P, w_2\}$; (4)

From $(4), P5, Ax1, Ax19$ and Nec, get:

MN believes $fresh\{Sign_{MAG_3}, ID_{MAG_3}, ID_{LMA_2}, T_5, auth_{LMA_2-MAG_3}, r_6P, w_2\}$; (5)

MN believes MAG$_3$ says $\{Sign_{MAG_3}, ID_{MAG_3}, T_5, ID_{LMA_2}, auth_{LMA_2-MAG_3}, r_6P, w_2\}$; (6)

($G1$ is proved)

From $P4, P8, Ax1, Ax5$ and Nec, get:

MN believes $SharedKey(K_{MN-MAG_3}, MN, MAG_3)$; (7)

From $(7), P6, Ax1$ and definition of $SharedKey(K, A, B)$, get:

MN believes $SharedKey(K_{MN-MAG_3}-, MN, MAG_3)$; (8)

($G2$ is proved)

From $(8), P5$ and $Ax18$, get:

MN believes $fresh(K_{MN-MAG_3})$; (9)

($G4$ is proved)

From $P8, P9, Ax1$ and definition of $confirm_P(X)$:

MN believes $confirm_{MN}(K_{MN-MAG_3})$; (10)

From $(8), (10), Ax1$ and definition of $SharedKey(K+, A, B)$:

($G3$ is proved)

MN believes $SharedKey(K_{MN-MAG_3}+, MN, MAG_3)$; (11)

Goals

From the perspective of MAG_3, goals are as follows:

G1(Far-End Operative): MAG_3 believes MN says $\{A, ID_{LMA_1}, B, C, D, r_5P, w_1, S_{w_1}\}$;

G2(Secure Key Establishment): MAG_3 believes $SharedKey(K_{MN-MAG_3}-, MN, MAG_3)$;

G3(Key Confirmation): MAG_3 believes $SharedKey(K_{MN-MAG_3}+, MN, MAG_3)$;

G4(Key Freshness): MAG_3 believes fresh K_{MN-MAG_3};

Prove process is as follows:

From $P8, Ax1, Ax7$ and Nec, get:

MAG_3 believes MAG_3 received $(A, B, C, D, ID_{LMA_1}, r_5P, w_1, S_{w_1})$;   (1)

From $P3, Ax1, Ax7$ and Nec, get:

MAG_3 believes MN said $(A, B, ID_{LMA_1}, C, D, r_5P, w_1, S_{w_1})$;   (2)

From (2), $P5, Ax1, Ax19$ and Nec, get:

MAG_3 believes $fresh\{A, B, C, D, ID_{LMA_1}, r_5P, w_1, S_{w_1}\}$;   (3)

MAG_3 believes MN says $\{A, B, C, D, ID_{LMA_1}, r_5P, w_1, S_{w_1}\}$;   (4)

($G1$ is proved)

From $P4, P8, Ax1, Ax5$ and Nec, get:

MAG_3 believes $SharedKey(K_{MN-MAG_3}, MN, MAG_3)$;   (5)

From (5), $P6, Ax1$ and definition of $SharedKey(K, A, B)$:

MAG_3 believes $SharedKey(K_{MN-MAG_3}-, MN, MAG_3)$;   (6)

($G2$ is proved)

From (6), $P5$ and Ax18, get:

MAG_3 believes $fresh(K_{MN-MAG_3})$;   (7)

($G4$ is proved)

From (7), $P8, P9, Ax1$ and definition of $confirm_P(X)$:

MAG_3 believes $confirm_{MN}(K_{MN-MAG_3})$;   (8)

From (6), (8), $Ax1$ and definition of $SharedKey(K+, A, B)$:

MN believes $SharedKey(K_{MN-MAG_3}+, MN, MAG_3)$;   (9)

($G3$ is proved)

5   Performance Analysis

We will give a performance analysis among HOTA [21], CSS [22], 2-HIBS [23], and our proposed scheme (SAAS) in terms of authentication delay during different authentication phrase.

Authentication delay(T_a) contains transfer delay(T_t), computational delay(T_c), and process delay(T_p). Transfer delay consists of wireless link transfer delay L_w, local domain transfer delay L_l and foreign domain transfer delay L_f. We have $L_f = hL_l + (h-1)T_p$, where h is the hop account between two communication entities. In general, $L_f > L_w > L_l$. T_p is the processing delay at intermediate routers. Table 3 gives some symbols of computation cost of different operations.

Table 3. Symbols of computation cost

Symbols	Meanings
T_{BP}	Bilinear pairing's computation cost
T_{MP}	Dot multiplication's computation cost
T_{EXP}	Exponentiation's computation cost
T_{RSA}	RSA's computation cost
T_{HMAC}	HAMC's computation cost

(1) Initial authentication delay.

In initial authentication phrase, HOTA doesn't support local authentication and has inter-domain transfer delay. HOTA mainly uses symmetric encryption and HMAC/SHA1 operations. The computation delay is negligible compared with bilinear pairing. The initial authentication delay of HOTA is:

$$Ta - initial - HOTA = 2L_w + (2 + 2h)L_l + (2h + 5)T_P \qquad (1)$$

CSS scheme achieves mutual authentication through a series of signing and verifying operations. The initial authentication delay of CSS is:

$$Ta - initial - CSS = 4L_w + (2 + 4h)L_l + (4h + 9)T_P + 4T_{BP} + 4T_{PM} + 4T_{EXP} \qquad (2)$$

2-HIBS is a local authentication scheme depending on identity-based cryptography. As for transfer delay, it doesn't exist the inter-domain transfer delay, The scheme mainly utilizes bilinear pairing and exponentiation. The initial authentication delay of 2-HIBS is:

$$Ta - initial - 2 - HIBS = 2L_w + 2L_l + 5T_P + 4T_{BP} + 2T_{EXP} \qquad (3)$$

In SAAS, the transfer delay only contains wireless transfer delay and local domain transfer delay. As for computation delay, SAAS mainly uses bilinear pairing and dot multiplication operations. The initial authentication delay of SAAS is:

$$Ta - initial - SAAS = 2L_w + 5T_P + T_{BP} + 2T_{EXP} \qquad (4)$$

From [24,25], we know that $T_{BP} = 2 \sim 3T_{RSA}, T_{EXP} = T_{PM} = 0.5 \sim 1T_{RSA}$. In this paper, we set $T_{BP} = 2T_{RSA}, T_{EXP} = T_{PM} = 0.5T_{RSA}$. [26] points out that $L_w = 4\,\mathrm{ms}, L_l = 2\,\mathrm{ms}, T_P = 0.5\,\mathrm{ms}$. According to the above result (1)–(4), we present the comparison of initial authentication delay of the related schemes as Fig. 7. From Fig. 7, we can see that CSS owns the highest authentication delay compared with other schemes. When h is small, HOTA owns the lowest authentication delay. But with the increasing of h, the authentication delay of HOTA is higher than SAAS and 2-HIBS. To sum up, SAAS has better performance in initial authentication delay.

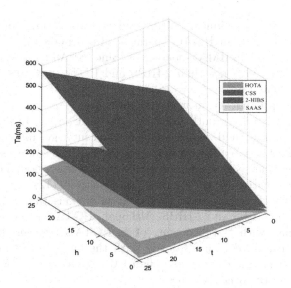

Fig. 7. Initial authentication delay

(2) Intra-group authentication delay

In intra-group handover authentication phrase, HOTA achieves handover authentication through the $TICKET$ obtained from the initial access phrase without inter-domain data exchange. HOTA depends on HMAC for computation. The intra-group handover authentication delay of HOTA is:

$$Ta - intra - HOTA = 2L_w + 2L_l + 4T_P + 2T_{HMAC} \tag{5}$$

CSS doesn't give the specific handover approach, we assume that the authentication delay is the same with the initial access phrase. So, the intra-group handover authentication delay of CSS is:

$$Ta - intra - CSS = 4L_w + (2 + 4h)L_l + (4h + 9)T_P + 4T_{BP} + 4T_{PM} + 4T_{EXP} \tag{6}$$

2-HIBS achieves the intra-group handover through shared key between MN and MAG without the participation of LMA, which reduces the transfer delay. 2-HIBS also utilizes HMAC for authentication computation. The intra-group handover authentication delay of 2-HIBS is:

$$Ta - intra - 2HIBS = 2L_w + 2L_l + 5T_P + 2T_{HMAC} \tag{7}$$

SAAS employs the same authentication method to achieve handover authentication as 2-HIBS. SAAS's transfer delay occurs between MN and MAG. While in 2-HIBS, intra-group handover authentication needs the participation of LMA, which cause extra transfer delay between LMA and MAG. The intra-group handover authentication delay of SAAS is:

$$Ta - intra - SAAS = 2L_w + 3T_P + 2T_{HMAC} \tag{8}$$

Obviously, CSS uses bilinear pairing and exponentiation from formula (6), which is much larger than HMAC operation. In formula (5), (7), (8), all the three schemes depend on HMAC operations. Since SAAS has less transfer delay, so it has better performance than 2-HIBS and HOTA in terms of intra-group authentication delay.

(3) Inter-group handover authentication delay

In inter-group handover authentication, HOTA, CSS, 2-HIBS don't give specific authentication method, we assume that their inter-group handover delay is the same as initial access authentication phrase. SAAS introduces local authentication with bilinear pairing and dot multiplication operation. The inter-group handover authentication delay of each scheme is as (9)–(12).

Figure 8 gives the comparison results. It is obvious that SAAS has lower authentication than CSS and 2-HIBS. Although, HOTA has low authentication at the beginning, with the increasing of h, HOTA's transfer delay increases quickly. SAAS has fixed transfer delay. With the increase of t and h, SAAS's authentication delay increases slower than HOTA. Generally, SAAS has better performance than the other schemes.

$$Ta - inter - HOTA = 2L_w + (2 + 2h)L_l + (2h + 5)T_P \tag{9}$$

$$Ta - inter - CSS = 4L_w + (2 + 4h)L_l + (4h + 9)T_P \\ + 4T_{BP} + 4T_{PM} + 4T_{EXP} \tag{10}$$

$$Ta - inter - 2HIBS = 2L_w + 2L_l + 5T_P + 4T_{BP} + 2T_{PM} \tag{11}$$

$$Ta - inter - SAAS = 2L_w + 3T_P + 3T_{BP} + T_{PM} \tag{12}$$

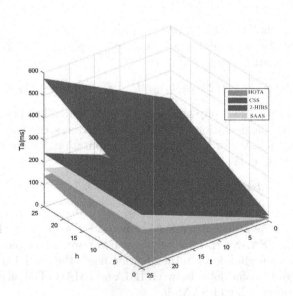

Fig. 8. Inter-group handover authentication delay

6 Conclusion

Aiming at the privacy issues during access authentication in PMIPv6 network, a secure anonymous authentication scheme is proposed in this paper. Based on the hierarchical network architecture and trust model, mutual authentication is achieved between MN and MAG for both intra-group and inter-group scenario. MN's privacy is preserved with the help of proxy group signature mechanism.

We further give the formal security proof and performance analysis of our proposed scheme to show its robustness and efficiency. In future research, we will focus on the location privacy of MN in PMIPv6 network.

References

1. Johnson, D., Perkins, C., Arkko, J.: Mobility support in IPv6. Technical report (2004)
2. Bhargava, B., Johnson, A.M., Munyengabe, G.I., Angin, P.: A systematic approach for attack analysis and mitigation in V2V networks. J. Wirel. Mob. Netw. Ubiquitous Comput. Dependable Appl. 7(1), 79–96 (2016)
3. Sanchez-Iborra, R., et al.: Integrating LP-WAN communications within the vehicular ecosystem. J. Internet Serv. Inf. Secur. 7(4), 45–56 (2017)
4. Taqieddin, E., Awad, F., Ahmad, H.: Location-aware and mobility-based performance optimization for wireless sensor networks. J. Wirel. Mob. Netw. Ubiquitous Comput. Dependable Appl. 8(4), 37–59 (2017)
5. Weng, C.-E., Sharma, V., Chen, H.-C., Mao, C.-H.: PEER: proximity-based energy-efficient routing algorithm for wireless sensor networks. J. Internet Serv. Inf. Secur. 6(1), 47–56 (2016)
6. Wu, T.-Y., Chen, W., Lee, W.-T., Liu, F.-H., Huang, Y.-P.: SeMIPv6: secure and efficient roaming mechanism based on IEEE 802.11 r and MIH. J. Internet Technol. 11(7), 909–916 (2010)
7. Gundavelli, S., Leung, K., Devarapalli, V., Chowdhury, K., Patil, B.: Proxy mobile IPv6. Technical report (2008)
8. Kang, D., Jung, J., Lee, D., et al.: Security analysis and enhanced user authentication in proxy mobile IPv6 networks. Plos One 12(7), e0181031 (2017)
9. Song, J., Han, S.: One-time key authentication protocol for PMIPv6. In: Third International Conference on Convergence and Hybrid Information Technology, ICCIT 2008, vol. 2, pp. 1150–1153. IEEE (2008)
10. Chuang, M.-C., Lee, J.-F.: SF-PMIPv6: a secure fast handover mechanism for proxy mobile IPv6 networks. J. Syst. Softw. 86(2), 437–448 (2013)
11. Chuang, M.-C., Lee, J.-F., Chen, M.-C.: SPAM: a secure password authentication mechanism for seamless handover in proxy mobile IPv6 networks. IEEE Syst. J. 7(1), 102–113 (2013)
12. Zubair, M., Kong, X., Mahfooz, S.: CLAM: cross-layer localized authentication mechanism based on proxy MIPv6 and SIP in next generation networks. J. Commun. 9(2), 144–156 (2014)
13. Kim, J.H., Song, J.S.: A public key based PMIPv6 authentication scheme. In: 2014 IEEE/ACIS 13th International Conference on Computer and Information Science (ICIS), pp. 5–10. IEEE (2014)
14. Agarwal, N., Rana, A., Pandey, J.P.: Proxy signatures for secured data sharing. In: Cloud System and Big Data Engineering, pp. 255–258. IEEE (2016)

15. Wu, K., Zou, J., Wei, X.-H., Liu, F.-Y.: Proxy group signature: a new anonymous proxy signature scheme. In: Machine Learning, vol. 3, pp. 1369–1373. IEEE (2008)
16. Han, S., Wang, J., Liu, W.: An efficient identity-based group signature scheme over elliptic curves. In: Freire, M.M., Chemouil, P., Lorenz, P., Gravey, A. (eds.) ECUMN 2004. LNCS, vol. 3262, pp. 417–429. Springer, Heidelberg (2004). https://doi.org/10.1007/978-3-540-30197-4_42
17. Barreto, P.S.L.M., Libert, B., McCullagh, N., Quisquater, J.-J.: Efficient and provably-secure identity-based signatures and signcryption from bilinear maps. In: Roy, B. (ed.) ASIACRYPT 2005. LNCS, vol. 3788, pp. 515–532. Springer, Heidelberg (2005). https://doi.org/10.1007/11593447_28
18. Yokota, H.: Fast handovers for proxy mobile IPv6. Heise Zeitschriften Verlag (2010)
19. Syverson, P.F., Oorschot, P.C.V.: On unifying some cryptographic protocol logics. In: Proceedings of the 1994 IEEE Computer Society Symposium on Research in Security and Privacy, pp. 14–28 (1994)
20. Burrows, M., Abadi, M., Needham, R.: A logic of authentication. Proc. R. Soc. Math. Phys. Eng. Sci. **426**(1871), 1–13 (1989)
21. Lee, J.H., Bonnin, J.M.: HOTA: handover optimized ticket-based authentication in network-based mobility management. Inf. Sci. **230**(4), 64–77 (2013)
22. Zhang, L., Mo, T., Zhao, L.: Authentication scheme based on certificateless signcryption in proxy mobile IPv 6 network. Jisuanji Yingyong Yanjiu **29**(2), 640–643 (2012)
23. Gao, T., Tan, L., Qiao, P., Yim, K.: An access authentication scheme based on hierarchical IBS for proxy mobile IPv6 network. Intell. Autom. Soft Comput. **22**(3), 389–396 (2016)
24. Konstantinou, E.: Efficient cluster-based group key agreement protocols for wireless ad hoc networks. J. Netw. Comput. Appl. **34**(1), 384–393 (2011)
25. Xiong, X., Wong, D.S., Deng, X.: TinyPairing: a fast and lightweight pairing-based cryptographic library for wireless sensor networks. In: 2010 IEEE Wireless Communications and Networking Conference (WCNC), pp. 1–6. IEEE (2010)
26. Tian, Y., Zhang, Y., Zhang, H., Li, Z.: Identity-based hierarchical access authentication in mobile IPv6 networks. In: IEEE International Conference on Communications, ICC 2006, vol. 5, pp. 1953–1958. IEEE (2006)

FAIR-Based Cyber Influence Damage Assessment for Exploit in Mobile Device

Mookyu Park[1], Jaehyeok Han[1], Junwoo Seo[1], Haengrok Oh[2],
and Kyungho Lee[1(✉)]

[1] School of Information Security, Korea University, Seoul, Republic of Korea
{ctupmk,one01h,junuseo,kevinlee}@korea.ac.kr
[2] Agency for Defense Development (ADD), Seoul, Republic of Korea

Abstract. Recently, as the utilization rate for mobile devices has increased, cyber attacks targeting them have been increasing. Cyber attacks such as ransomware in general network space have started to spread to mobile devices. In addition, malware that exploits mobile vulnerabilities is also increasing rapidly. Threats to these mobile devices could cause negative damage to human life. Thus, the cyber attack that causes secondary damage to the real world is called a *Cyber Influence Attack*. This paper presents an influence attack scenario in which the exploit of the Android OS acquires the permission of the mobile device for propagating false information. Based on this scenario, we analyze the damage assessment of mobile device exploit that can cause real social damage as well as damage to cyberspace assets through FAIR (Factor Analysis of Information Risk) model.

Keywords: Exploit · Cyber influence attack
Damage assessment · FAIR (Factor Analysis of Information Risk)

1 Introduction

Recent cyber attacks are damaging not only cyberspace assets but also real world assets. If past cyber attacks (hacking, DDoS, APT etc) were limited to cyberspace, current cyber attacks are expanding the damage to the real world by using communication services such as social network, messenger, etc. As a result of these changes, the frequency of cyber attacks on mobile devices, which have become a necessity in life, is also increasing. A typical example is the case where the spy application was installed on the smartphone of domestic defense, diplomacy and security personnel in South Korea in 2016 to take information. 35% of attackers use this attack method targeting mobile devices.

The ability to monitor, reconnaissance, and collect information through vulnerabilities of these mobile devices (Android, IOS etc.) is recognized as an important factor in the development of cyber weapons. This can be confirmed in the Italian Hacking email that leaked to WikiLeaks in 2014. According to the leaked

© Springer Nature Singapore Pte Ltd. 2019
I. You et al. (Eds.): MobiSec 2017, CCIS 971, pp. 51–64, 2019.
https://doi.org/10.1007/978-981-13-3732-1_4

information, national authorities requested the production of exploit kit for monitoring or inspection purposes [9]. In addition, the US CIA and the UK GCHQ leaked information that they developed a Weeping Angel for monitoring through IoT devices [22]. According to RSA's Current State of Cybercrime report published in 2016, the threat to mobile devices in 2013 and 2015 has increased by about 173% [24].

Since the mobile device is closely related to human life, the cyber attack against it has a greater impact on the secondary damage than the general device. This research assumes cyber influence attack scenarios by selecting exploits, which related to simishing (combination of SMS message and phishing) attack, that could damage the real world among vulnerabilities of Android OS. This paper proposes a damage assessment scheme using FAIR (Factor Analysis of Information Risk) based on hypothetical scenarios.

2   Related Works

As mobile devices begin to become a necessity for human life, the frequency of attacks against them is also increasing. In addition, the vulnerability of mobile devices is also diversifying the attack methods such as information leakage and illegal surveillance. This section describes the research on exploits of mobile devices and related research on cyber BDA (Battle Damage Assessment).

2.1   Exploits of Mobile Platforms

Most of the attacks of mobile device OS are made through the malicious application. Especially, the Google Marketplace is much higher than Apple App Store. At the 2009 Black Hat Conference, Lookout Mobile Security detected malicious apps that had access to personal data in the application market. As a result, the number of malicious applications using Android's vulnerabilities (64%) was about 2.2 times higher than the number of applications of iOS (28%).

Shezan et al. conducted research on detecting vulnerabilities in the Android apps. The study extracted eight common vulnerabilities for Android apps. As a result of this study, "Webview Vulnerability", "Storage Access Vulnerability", "Advertisement Vulnerability" and "Database Vulnerability" were detected as characteristics of malicious apps. Among them, "Webview vulnerability" was identified as a threat to users with about 68.4% of all vulnerabilities [26]. Orazio conducted research on vulnerability detection of iOS devices and iOS apps. This study presents an approach to applying attack models to DRM (Digital Right Management) apps, detecting vulnerable iOS devices, and analyzing non-DRMs for potentially exploitable vulnerabilities. As a result, this study identified vulnerabilities using popular apps from the Google Marketplace and could exploit them to design vulnerabilities that compromise the confidentiality, integrity, and availability of data stored on the device [4]. Recently, attacks on mobile banking apps targeting financial damage have also occurred. Saenko studied the analytical modeling approach of mobile banking attacks based on stochastic network transformation techniques. In particular, the proposed approach was used for modeling the most dangerous ZITMO attacks during mobile banking attacks and developed a reliable analysis model [25].

Research on cyber weapons using vulnerabilities of a mobile devices operating system has also been going on Herr proposed a framework for classifying and evaluating cyber weapons based on various malicious codes that make up cyber weapons. The study defined cyber weapons as a combination of three software components: propagation methods, types of exploits, and payloads designed to create physical or logical effects [10]. Joshi et al. extracted vulnerabilities in Android OS from OSVDB (Open Source Vulnerability Database) and NVD (National Vulnerability Database). This study also proposed a metadata model for vulnerability assessment. This study found that an attacker was able to get users to download and install malicious applications with ease [17].

These studies are important because the target is changed from the local device to the mobile device. In addition, vendors such as Zerodium are also highly pricing of iOS and Android OS's vulnerabilities. However, these studies are aimed at detection and use of malicious apps, and there are limitations in evaluating threats.

2.2 Cyber Battle Damage Assessments for Human

Most of the cyber-BDA studies that have been conducted so far focus on the damage to cyber assets that are more or less threatened. Typical examples include system paralysis caused by cyber attacks, recovery time, and amount of damage etc.

Research on damage assessment in cyberspace has been studied by various methods such as business model and attack tree. Horony proposed a damage assessment model using business modeling considering eight factors: recovery, education/training, business expense, productivity, data, lost revenue, reputation and human life [11]. Grimaila et al. presented a measure of damage through the relationship of work impacts. This study considers both the technical aspects of the damage assessment and the damage assessment of the cyber asset side. However, this study focuses only on the assessment of the damage of the technology, and there is a limit to the actual human impact [6]. Ostler proposed a framework for assessing damage by modeling the attack methodology of the enemy using CAMEL (Cyber Attack Method Exhaustive Listing) process and CAMAT (Cyber Attack Methodology Attack Tree) [21].

Most damage assessment studies are focused on cyberspace hardware, software, and applications. Recently, it has been expanding to personal injury such as ransomware, and attacks that cause social harm such as the Russian scandal and the Italian Hacking Team. Taking these changes into consideration, a damage assessment that affects the real world, as well as cyberspace, is needed.

3   Attack Scenario

In the concept of cyberspace layer, the cyber attack does not affect only one layer. This section describes cyber-influence attack scenarios based on the concept of cyberspace.

3.1   Cyberspace Layers

According to Joint Publication 3–12R Cyber Operation, the cyberspace explains that the physical layer, the logical layer, and the persona layer are connected in a complementary relationship. The physical layer is a layer composed of geographical and physical network elements. A logical layer is a network composed of physical or geographically connected logical connections between nodes. The persona layer is a layer that reflects human perception in a logically organized network [20].

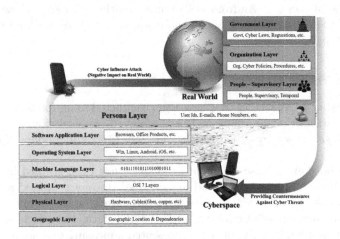

Fig. 1. The damage caused by cyber attacks can be caused by secondary damage to the real world connected with cyberspace, and the higher the availability of mobile devices, the more likely the damage will expand.

Clark subdivided the persona layer related to the real world into the information layer and the top layer-people 2 layer rather than the cyberspace layer of JP 3–12. The "Information Layer" is a layer that reflects the flow of information stored, transmitted, or converted in cyberspace. "Top Layer-People" is a group of people who participate in the cyber-experience and communicate and make decisions using services and the functions [1]. The cyber situational awareness model divides the three or four layers of the described cyberspace into six layers: social, people, persona, information, network, and the real world. This model emphasized the connectivity between cyberspace and the real world by constructing the "Top Layer-People" claimed by David Clark as Social, People, and Persona components [14].

The report, published by the US Department of Homeland Security in 2011, describes the "Enabling Distributed Security in Cyberspace", an extension of the cyberspace layer as a cyber ecosystem. In this report, the cyber ecosystem explained that private companies, nonprofit organizations, governments, individuals, processes, and devices (computers, software, and communication technologies etc) interacted for many purposes as well as natural ecosystems. The Cyber ecosystem consists of 15 layers that are connected to hardware, cables, people, buildings, all physical and physical items to solve the complex interactions of people, processes, and technologies. The development of this concept of cyberspace has been developed to emphasize the connection to the real world of human beings [23]. The concept of cyberspace is shown in Fig. 1.

3.2 Influence Attack Scenario Using Exploit for Mobile Device

For cyber-influence attacks using mobile devices, this research has set three hypotheses for mobile devices to attack targets.

Fig. 2. The cyber influence attack utilizes various layers considering cyberspace and the real world.

- Mobile devices have social networks apps such as Facebook, Twitter and Instagram etc
- Mobile devices with root privilege and smearing vulnerability
- The ultimate goal of the attacker is to manipulate public opinion during the election.

In this scenario, illegal information (a malicious rumor, fake news) generated through an attack on an Android device set a scenario from the viewpoint that it hinders human rational decision making. The attack scenario follows the procedure. First, the attacker performs a smear attack on the mobile device on which the Android OS is based. Second, the attacker produces illegal information, a malicious rumor, and fake news that are suitable for attack intent. Third, an authorized attacker continues to deploy false information produced through social networks apps. At this time, the attack on the mobile device corresponds to the logical layer in the cyberspace layer. Producing false information and spreading it through social networks apps is a persona layer. The procedure for this is shown in Fig. 2.

In order for such an attack to be possible, it must ultimately hinder human rational decision-making. To prevent such rational decision-making, it is necessary to produce information that is biased toward an emotional situation rather than a rational situation. According to Deacon and Firebaugh, the emotional state of humans is likely to be made in an impulsive or intuitive context. These rational decision-making vulnerabilities are "High Uncertainty", "Lack of Precedent", "Access Limited Information", "Lack of Decision Time" and "Number of Similar Alternatives". Table 1 shows the results [3].

Table 1. In order to manipulate the public opinion of cyberspace, it should hinder human rational decision making by using "High Uncertainty", "Lack of Precedent", "Access Limited Information", "Lack of Decision Time" and "Number of Similar Alternative".

Vulnerabilities	Role
High Uncertainty	Increase future uncertainty about choice
Lack of Precedent	A lack of additional information related to decision making
Access Limited Information	Absence of official announcement of government or organization, where access to information is restricted
Lack of Decision-Making Time	In decision-making, when time is lack
Number of Similar Alternatives	A situation where people could not choose a priority from a decision due to excessive or lack of information

3.3   Exploits in Attack Scenario

Influence attacks using a mobile device are performed by a browser or application exploits (malicious application installation) through smishing attacks. For this attack, an attacker must set a primary goal to obtain certain permissions or root privileges [7,8].

Smishing attacks are a combination of text messages (SMS) and phishing. This attack can induce users to install malicious apps with specific URL access regardless of their intentions, which can cause damage such as information hijacking and a small payment. Most smishing attacks involve sending URLs to the SMS of interest to induce malicious app installations with excessive privileges. There are two types of malicious applications using smishing. (i) a type that replaces frequently used apps with genuine apps, and (ii) a type that seizes and operates internal data. In fact, most of the cases found are forged on financial apps, but the scope is not limited.

The proposed scenario aims to spread false information through the application of social network through smishing attack on the mobile device based on Android OS. Vulnerabilities that could gain root privileges on Android OS-based mobile devices are CVE-2015-1085, CVE-2014–3153, and CVE-2015–3636. Recently, a vulnerability (CVE-2016-0819, CVE-2016-0805) was discovered that allowed routing to Android devices with Snapdragon processors. The exploits are shown in Table 2 [19].

Table 2. For cyber-influence attacks, the attackers must have the capability to exploit vulnerabilities that can gain root privileges on a mobile device.

Publish date	Type	CVE-ID	CVSS Score	Description
2016.3.12	CWE-264	CVE-2016-0819	9.3	The Qualcomm performance component allows attackers to gain privileges via a crafted application
2016.2.6	CWE-264	CVE-2016-0805	7.2	The performance event manager for Qualcomm ARM processors allows attackers to gain privileges via a crafted application
2015.8.5	CWE-416	CVE-2015–3636	4.9	The ping_unhash function does not initialize a certain list data structure during an unhash operation, which allows local users to gain privileges or cause a denial of service and then making a connect system call after a disconnect
2015.4.10	CWE-264	CVE-2015-1085	1.9	AppleKeyStore does not properly restrict a certain passcode-confirmation interface, which makes it easier for attackers to verify correct passcode guesses via a crafted app
2014.6.7	CWE-264	CVE-2014–3153	7.2	The futex_requeue function does not ensure that calls have two different futex addresses, which allows local users to gain privileges

CWE-264: Permissions, Privileges, and Access Control, **CWE-416**: Use After Free

Using the exploit shown in Table 2, it is possible to develop a malicious application that can launch false information through social networks (Facebook, Twitter and Instagram etc). The next section describes the damage assessment approach to applying the FAIR model to exploit attack scenarios.

4   Damage Assessment of Cyber Influence Attacks

This paper describes a cyber influence attack scenario using a mobile device based on Android OS. This section applies the FAI (Factor Analysis of Information Risk) model based on the proposed scenarios for damage assessment. The FAIR model is a risk measurement method that measures damage by classifying risk contributing factors into assets and threats. The reason for applying the FAIR model in this study is that the cyber influence attack occurs in various cyberspace layers so that it is possible to set the frequency and size of the event occurrence. In addition, it is possible to measure the incidental damage caused by influence attacks through primary loss and secondary loss. Because there are no cases that have an impact on the actual democracy system, this study assesses the damage through the 2016 US presidential election, where information leaks and fake news are most common.

4.1   Asset of Influence Attack Scenario

Based on the scenario, this research should set the approval rating of the electoral candidate as an asset. However, since the approval rating of the presidential election is measured by the polls, there is a limit to whether the influence attack has affected in real time. For the application of the FAIR model, the assets were selected as the Google Trend of the election candidates. The reason we chose assets with Google Trend is that it is connected with human interest. Also, since the goal of cyber-influence attacks in this scenario is to interfere with human rational decision-making, it is assumed that human interest can affect the approval rating.

During the election period, voters indirectly contact candidates through the media, such as the media or social networks. In this situation, factors influencing the candidate's approval rating are the residential area, education, age, property, and political orientation. However, interest in media actually affects assets more than these factors. For this reason, the study utilized the Google trend to compare the relative interest of public opinion on candidates, rather than the results of surveys provided by "HuffPost" [12]. In particular, since Google Trend is data based on the number of clicks (queries) of users in Internet browsing, it can estimate the degree of interest in candidates. Table 3 and Fig. 3 show the changes in the trend of the elections according to the election schedule during the 2016 US presidential election.

Table 3. The official schedule for the 2016 US presidential election began on the 18th of July, the Republican National Convention, and ended on 19th of the presidential election day.

Date	Schedule
July 18 - July 21	Republican National Convention
July 25 - July 28	Democratic National Convention
26 Sep	First US Presidential Election Debate
04 Oct	Bipartisan Vice Presidential Debate
09 Oct	Second US presidential election debate
19 Oct	Third US presidential election debate
08 Nov	Voting and Counting by Ordinary Voters
19 Dec	Voting by the Electoral College

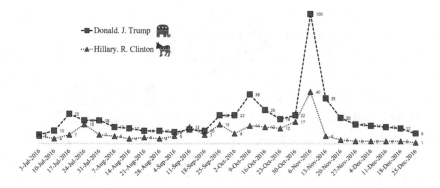

Fig. 3. Through the Google Trends during the 2016 US presidential election, it is possible to confirm that voters' interest in the candidates increases with the official schedule.

Donald Trump is predominantly in the Google Trends graph, but Hillary Clinton dominated on July 24, 2016, September 11–17, 2016. However, since then, it has shown a decline. Donald from October 2 to October 23. The trend for Trump has increased while the trend for Hillary Clinton has been relatively small. During this period, false information about Hillary Clinton (fake news, illegal information, malicious rumours, etc.) surged. Typical examples are fake news, such as Clinton's ISIS weapons sales [18]. In addition, the information of the Clinton election director leaked by the hacking group supported by the Russian government was spreading through WikiLeaks [15]. This phenomenon has increased as the voting date approaches.

As evidenced by the changes in Google trends, influence attacks such as fake news, illegal information and malicious rumors have some influence on the approval ratings of candidates. However, if we reflect the threat to cyberspace, the degree of damage that occurs in the real world could be evaluated differently.

4.2 Assessment Using FAIR

The risk to assets in this study represents the degree of damage. To measure this, FAIR models are classified into LEF (Loss Event Frequency) and LM (Loss Magnitude). LEF is a threat measure, consisting of Threat Event Frequency (TEF) and VUL (Vulnerabilities). VUL is composed of TCap (Threat Capability) indicating the threat agent's ability and CS (Control Strength) indicating the threat that the threat is difficult to act on the asset. LM is a factor indicating the damage of an asset, and it is composed of PL (Primary Loss) and SL (Secondary Loss). PL consists of PLM (Primary Loss Magnitude) and PLEF (Primary Loss Event Frequency). SL consists of SLM (Secondary Loss Magnitude) and SLEF (Secondary Loss Event Frequency). In this paper, SL is used as a factor to measure damage occurring in the real world. The FAIR model is shown in Fig. 4 [16].

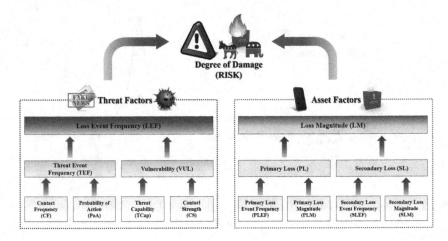

Fig. 4. The FAIR model consists of threat factor and asset factor. In this study, the threat factor reflects illegal information and vulnerabilities of Android os. And the asset factor reflected data that could affect the democratic system.

Along with these factors, in the FAIR model, it is necessary to set up a TCom (Threat Community) that can determine whether an attacker is an individual or a group. This study assumes that an attacker is a politically motivated group trying to intervene in democratic elections by spreading false information by attacking Android-based mobile devices. The profile for TCom is shown in Table 4.

LEF (Loss Event Frequency). LEF consists of TEF and VUL. In this study, TEF was measured based on fake news data provided by Kaggle. During the US presidential election period (October 10–July 31, 2014), a total of 1,274 fake news events occurred. Through this, the average daily occurrence of fake news was 41.2. TCap exploits CVSS (Common Vulnerability Scoring System), and the exploit corresponding to Tcap is shown in Table 2. TCap is expressed as CVSS score because it provides objective threat index for exploit until now. The impact of the exploit was measured by the time of the disclosure and the effect of the TEF and TCap was measured when the date of disclosure was the latest from 2014 to 2016. The TEF and TCap are shown in Table 5.

LM (Loss Magnitude). LM (Loss Magnitude) is measured through the primary and secondary losses that affect the outcome of the event. This study sets the primary loss as a politically-themed stock. The reason for this is that the pledges announced by the presidential candidates directly or indirectly affect the stocks involved. In the case of secondary loss, we used the national demographic index of 2016 provided by the Economist [5]. Fake news is a threat to democratic electoral systems because it hinders voters' rational decision-making. It is available for this analysis because the secondary stakeholder is potentially at risk. The frequency and magnitude of the loss are shown in Table 6.

Table 4. The study set up TCom as a state or enterprise in which an attacker is trying to achieve political intent.

Factor	Description
Motive	Social disorder
Primary intent	Obtain political gain, Acquisition of Economic Benefits
Sponsorship	Government, Company
Preferred general target characteristics	Interest in media (journalism)
Preferred targets	People with voting rights (Voter)
Capability	Threat of exploits about mobile device
Personal risk tolerance	Interference with a specific political event
Concern for collateral damage	Democratic society collapse, national security threat, etc

Table 5. Result of TEF (Threat Event Frequency) & TCap (Threat Capability)

TCom	TEF Min	TEF ML	TEF Max	TCap Min	TCap ML	TCap Max
Hostile Nation, Enterprise	6 (Once in 4 h)	6 (Once in 30 min)	142 (Once in 10 min)	0	6.8	10

Table 6. Result of LM (Loss Magnitude) & LEF (Loss Event Frequency)

Target	TCom	Threat type	Effect	Max LEF	Max SLM
Voters	Hostile Nation, Enterprise	Malicious	Availability	24	92,280

5 Result

This study normalized each factor for FAIR by dividing the existing data into 10 sections from 0 to 10 to decide on the threat. In addition, we assume that the weights for each element are equivalent. Among the normalized factors, TEF, PLM, and SLM have the same value in this study. In the case of TEF, it is the result showing the degree of production of fake news, and PLM is the degree of change in stock after the election. In addition, SLM has a constant value because it represents the democracy index of a country. According to the equation, the risk is calculated and the results are shown in Table 7 below. CVSS severity [19] of All CVEs in the table is "critical", so we set TEF as 10, and PLM and SLM used the share of the Android operating system [13] and democracy index of the United States [5] respectively.

$$VUL = Ave(TCap(CVSS) + Date(\frac{t_{current} - t_{discover}}{3}))$$

$$Damage = \sum_{i \in PL,SL} Ave(LM + Ave(TEF + VUL))$$

Table 7. The TEF is measured by the contact frequency (CF) and the probability of action (PoA), which takes action from the asset, but assuming that there is a limit to the measurement of actual activity and that a threat has occurred. However, as a result, when the threat of cyberspace reflects the damage of real world, the degree of damage is measured highly.

CVE-ID	TEF	Tcap	CS	VUL	PLEF	SLEF	PLM	SLM	PL	SL	Degree of Damage
2016-0819	10	9.3	7.31	8.3	9.15	8.23	8.5	7.98	8.83	8.11	8.45
2016-0805	10	7.2	6.99	7.09	8.54	7.77	8.5	7.98	8.52	7.88	8.2
2015-3636	10	4.9	5.3	5.1	7.55	6.42	8.5	7.98	8.03	7.2	7.62
2015-1085	10	1.9	4.23	3.06	6.53	5.38	8.5	7.98	7.52	6.68	7.1
2014-3153	10	7.2	1.43	4.31	7.15	4.29	8.5	7.98	7.83	6.14	6.98

The CVSS score is a score expressed as a score of cyber space risk. In contrast, relatively low-grade exploits have risen as a result of reflecting real-world variables such as fake news, politically-themed stocks, and democratic indicators. In other words, when the threat that occurs in cyberspace is extended to the real world, it also means that the damage can be increased as well.

6   Conclusion

As cyber attacks on mobile devices have increased in recent years, threats in general network space are expanding to mobile devices. Especially, malware using the vulnerability of mobile device is increasing rapidly. The increase in mobile threats also threatens the real world in which people live. A typical example of such an attack is obtaining root privileges through smishing. Secondary damage caused by this can occur in various ways. This study assumes a form of cyber attack that propagates false information through the acquisition of Android based mobile device privilege. As a result, it was confirmed that the degree of damage of the CVSS score for a relatively low grade may be different depending on the environment of the country. In other words, an attack on a mobile device means that there is a risk that it could have a negative effect on human or society.

PCs are designed for general use, but mobile devices are often made for specific purposes. Most of the recently released smart phones provide most of the functions of PCs, such as surfing the Web, SNS, and media playback, but they basically have to provide the call function like a mobile phone. As a result, human accessibility is higher than other devices. Since the types of mobile devices are so diverse (customized OS usage by manufacturers, type of hardware architecture, etc.), it is difficult to classify the analysis method and the product launch cycle is short, so there is a limit to analysis such as digital forensics do. This increases the vulnerability of mobile devices and increases the likelihood that they will be exploited as scenarios presented in the research [2].

Recently, cyber threat information such as Indicators of Compromise (IOC) has been actively studied for rapid and accurate response to increasing cyber threats and for organic communication among organizations. However, research on social damage and threat information or indicators linking them is limited due to political reasons. At the RSA Conference in 2017, US Department of Homeland Security (DHS) chief counsel Michael McCaul criticized the US government for responding to a 21st-century threat with 20th-century technology and 19th-century institutions. De-politicization of cyber security policies is required to respond to real-world threats such as cyber-influence attacks.

Acknowledgment. This work was supported by Defense Acquisition Program Administration and Agency for Defense Development under the contract (UD060048AD).

References

1. Clark, D.: Characterizing cyberspace: past, present and future. MIT CSAIL, Version 1, 2016–2028 (2010)
2. Daware, S., Dahake, S., Thakare, V.: Mobile forensics: overview of digital forensic, computer forensics vs. mobile forensics and tools. Int. J. Comput. Appl. 7–8 (2012)
3. Deacon, R.E., Firebaugh, F.M.: Family Resource Management: Principles and Applications. Allyn and Bacon, Boston (1981)
4. D'Orazio, C.J., Lu, R., Choo, K.K.R., Vasilakos, A.V.: A markov adversary model to detect vulnerable ios devices and vulnerabilities in IOS apps. Appl. Math. Comput. **293**, 523–544 (2017)
5. Economist, T.: The economist intelligence unit's democracy index (2016). https://infographics.economist.com/2017/DemocracyIndex/
6. Grimaila, M.R., Fortson, L.W.: Towards an information asset-based defensive cyber damage assessment process. In: 2007 IEEE Symposium on Computational Intelligence in Security and Defense Applications, CISDA 2007, pp. 206–212. IEEE (2007)
7. Guido, D.: The exploit intelligence project. PowerPoint presentation, iSEC Partners (2011)

8. Guido, D., Arpaia, M.: The mobile exploit intelligence project. Blackhat EU (2012)
9. Hern, A.: Hacking team hacked: firm sold spying tools to repressive regimes, documents claim (2015). https://www.theguardian.com/technology/2015/jul/06/hacking-team-hacked-firm-sold-spying-tools-to-repressive-regimes-documents-claim
10. Herr, T.: Prep: A framework for malware & cyber weapons. Browser Download This Paper (2013)
11. Horony, M.D.: Information system incidents: the development of a damage assessment model. Technical report, Air Force Institute of Technology, Wright-Patterson Air Force Base, Ohio (1999)
12. HUFFPOST: 2016 general election: Trump vs. clinton (2016). http://elections.huffingtonpost.com/pollster/2016-general-election-trump-vs-clinton
13. IDC: Smartphone os market share (2017). https://www.idc.com/promo/smartphone-market-share/os
14. Jajodia, S., Liu, P., Swarup, V., Wang, C.: Cyber Situational Awareness. Advances in Information Security, vol. 14. Springer, Boston (2010). https://doi.org/10.1007/978-1-4419-0140-8
15. Jim Sciutto, N.G., Browne, R.: Us finds growing evidence Russia feeding emails to wikileaks (2016). http://edition.cnn.com/2016/10/13/politics/russia-us-election/index.html
16. Jones, J.: An introduction to factor analysis of information risk (fair). Norwich J. Inf. Assur. **2**(1), 67 (2006)
17. Joshi, J., Parekh, C.: Android smartphone vulnerabilities: a survey. In: International Conference on Advances in Computing, Communication, & Automation (ICACCA)(Spring), pp. 1–5. IEEE (2016)
18. LaCapria, K.: As wikileaks released several batches of e-mails in october 2016, partisans claimed they confirmed hillary clinton sold weapons to ISIS (2016). http://www.snopes.com/wikileaks-cofirms-hillary-clinton-sold-weapons-to-isis/
19. NIST: National vulnerability database (2014–2016). https://nvd.nist.gov/
20. Cyberspace Operations: Joint publication 3–12 (r). Joint Chief of Staffs (2013)
21. Ostler, R.: Defensive cyber battle damage assessment through attack methodology modeling. Technical report, Air Force Institute of Technology, Wright-Patterson Air Force Base, Ohio (2011)
22. Pagliery, J.: Wikileaks claims to reveal how CIA hacks TVS and phones all over the world (2017). http://money.cnn.com/2017/03/07/technology/wikileaks-cia-hacking/index.html
23. Philip, R., et al.: Enabling distributed security in cyberspace. Department of Homeland Security (2011)
24. RSA: 2016:current state of cybercrime (2016). https://www.rsa.com/content/dam/rsa/PDF/2016/05/2016-current-state-of-cybercrime.pdf
25. Saenko, I., Lauta, O., Kotenko, I.: Analytical modeling of mobile banking attacks based on a stochastic network conversion technique (2016)
26. Shezan, F.H., Afroze, S.F., Iqbal, A.: Vulnerability detection in recent android apps: an empirical study. In: 2017 International Conference on Networking, Systems and Security (NSysS), pp. 55–63. IEEE (2017)

Method for Predicting Pixel Values in Background Areas in the Problem of Weighted Steganalysis in the Spatial Domain of Natural Images Under Small Payloads

Daniil A. Bashmakov[1]([⊠]) [iD], Anatoliy G. Korobeynikov[2] [iD],
Alexey V. Sivachev[1] [iD], Didier El Baz[1,3], and Dmitry Levshun[1]

[1] Saint Petersburg National Research University of Information Technologies,
Mechanics and Optics, (ITMO University), St. Petersburg 197101, Russia
bashmakov.dan@gmail.com
[2] Pushkov Institute of Terrestrial Magnetism, Ionosphere and Radio Wave
Propagation of the Russian Academy of Sciences St.-Petersburg Filial
(SPbF IZMIRAN), St. Petersburg 197101, Russia
[3] LAAS-CNRS, Universite de Toulouse, CNRS, Toulouse, France

Abstract. The problem of effective counteraction to the malicious data transfer channels is of importance in any area where data transfer is performed. One of the aspects of the Mobile Internet Security is detecting such channels, regardless the way these channels are organized. Steganography is one of the ways to interact without attracting attention, and still digital image is one of the most popular steganographic containers nowadays. The effectiveness of the weighted steganalysis of still digital images in the spatial domain in the task of determining the fact of embedding in the least significant bits of the images with a significant fraction of a homogeneous background is discussed. A definition of the concept of a homogeneous background of a natural digital image in the steganalysis problem is given. The connection of the fraction of a homogeneous background in the image with the efficiency of a weighted steganalysis of the image is shown. The connection between the accuracy of the prediction of the pixel values in the background areas of images and the effectiveness of steganalysis in such is shown. A method for predicting the pixel values of background images has been developed, which makes it possible to improve the efficiency of weighted steganalysis of images with a significant fraction of a homogeneous background by 3–8%. The data of numerical estimates of the increase in the effectiveness of steganalysis are presented using the proposed method for predicting pixel values in background areas.

Keywords: Steganography · Steganoimage · Steganalysis
Binary classification · Weighted steganalysis · Method of steganalysis
WeightedStegoImage · Background area of image · LSB-steganography
Least significant bit

I. You et al. (Eds.): MobiSec 2017, CCIS 971, pp. 65–82, 2019.
https://doi.org/10.1007/978-981-13-3732-1_5

1 Introduction

Nowadays, different methods are used to steal and disclose information in the World Wide Web using various techniques and communication channels. Effective counter-action to such threats is of big interest and value today [1]. Steganography using still digital images as a container is widely used both legally and for criminal purposes [2]. Along with any other ways to use steganography for criminal purposes, it can be widely used in the matter of industrial espionage, allowing to covertly taking infor-mation out of the security zone of the company, which is an actual threat now, when the great attention is paid to the insider threats [3]. This causes the relevance of steganalysis as a means of countering the steganography channels of information transmission in the matter of Mobile Internet Security, along with other security means and tools providing complex security toolkit [4]. Embedding of information in the least significant bit refers to the simplest and most accessible steganography methods that do not require the use of complex software and significant hardware resources [5]. Increasing traffic of digital images in the Internet makes possible to utilize small payloads rates in the matter of organization of steganography-based communication channel, which requires adequate detecting, as a part of adapting of security systems to the growing amount of data [6]. At the same time, the possibilities of modern ste-ganalysis algorithms for detecting the fact of embedding into LSB on small payloads rates do not allow to organize effective counteraction to the steganography channel that uses LSB-embedding [7].

The algorithm of WeightedStegoImage (WS) steganalysis [8] and a number of its modifications [9, 10] shows the best accuracy in detecting the fact of LSB-embedding [11]. At the same time, studies show that when analyzing images with a significant fraction of a homogeneous background, the WS algorithm works with reduced accu-racy [12]. The paper analyzes the reasons for the decreasing in the accuracy of the steganalysis using the WS method in the background areas of still digital images, analyzes the causes of the incorrect pixels prediction of the background areas. The accuracy of the pixels prediction of the background image area is estimated using various known prediction models. A method for predicting the pixel values in the background image area is proposed, which makes it possible to neutralize the declining in the accuracy of steganalysis in images with a significant fraction of a homogeneous background.

2 Method for Evaluating the Effectiveness of Steganalysis and the Concept of Homogeneous Background of Image

2.1 Homogeneous Background of Natural Image

The difference between the values of the neighbor pixels of the analyzed image is of importance in the steganalysis of the changes introduced into the plane of the least significant bit of the image (LSB) in the case of steganography embedding the LSB plane. Since the methods of steganalysis in this field set the goal of detecting anomalous changes in pixels by 1 in comparison with the expected, the areas where the difference in 1 compared with neighbor ones occurs more often, can be a problem in steganalysis. The method may face the problem of distinguishing the change in the pixel value by 1 as a result of a steganographic embedding and as a natural effect in a present image area. In areas where the average difference between neighbor pixels is large, a change by 1 compared to the expected value is considered to be an anomaly that can be easy identified by the method of steganalysis. Nevertheless, there is a common semantic area of the image, repeated on a large set of natural images - homogeneous background areas.

By homogeneous background areas are meant such areas of the image in which the values of neighbor pixels vary by no more than a certain amount on average for the area and no more than a certain amount from the average value of the pixels for the same area. A mathematically homogeneous background area is defined as follows: Assume I - is the variety of pixels of the image. Then the homogeneous background area B - is a set of such image areas, for each of which the following is performed:

$$\forall p \in B : |p - p_N| < T_N, |p - p_A| < T_A \tag{1}$$

where p - is the pixel brightness value, p_N - is the neighbor pixel brightness value, which is most differing in value among all neighbor pixels, p_A - is the average value of all the pixels belonging to the set, B, T_N, T_A - are the thresholds entered individually for each image.

The result of selecting a homogeneous background area in the image amongst the BOWS2 collection is shown in Fig. 1 for the threshold values 1 $T_N = 2, T_A = 10$. Figure 1a contains the original image. In Fig. 1b, the background areas are highlighted in dark gray.

a   b

Fig. 1. Homogeneous background of natural image

In natural images, homogeneous background areas are often found: as a rule, they correspond to the area of the sky, sea or an artificially created homogeneous background, for example, while studio photography.

The nature of the distortions introduced by embedding in the LSB determines the importance of the availability and proportion of background areas in the analyzed image. In background areas, where the difference between the values of neighbor pixels is small, the original nature of the distribution of pixel values is little different from the tracks of embedding in LSB. Thus, we can expect a decline in the effectiveness of steganalysis in images with a large proportion of a homogeneous background.

2.2   Procedure of the Experiment

Experiments are conducted on a variety of test images, which are digital photographs. Since the considered problem of the decline in accuracy is examined when analyzing images with a significant fraction of a homogeneous background, the set is subdivided into HB and LB samples (Highbackground, Lowbackground):

- The HB sample contains images in which fraction of the homogeneous background exceeds 40%;
- The LB sample contains images, in which fraction of homogeneous background exceeds 5%.

Images that do not fall into any of the samples are deleted from the test set.

After deleting images that are not included in the HB and LB samples, each of the samples is also subdivided into two subsamples – original images and steganograms. For steganograms, serial LSB-inlining at various payload volumes not exceeding 5% is simulated.

When analyzing an image, the accuracy of the pixel prediction is estimated by the analyzer underlying the WS algorithm. Original images and steganograms are analyzed by the WS algorithm to determine the accuracy of the classification separately in each of the samples. The obtained values are estimated numerically.

2.3   Factors for Conducting the Experiment

To create the initial set of test images, a collection of images collected from a series of reference samples is used: BOWS2 [13], BOSS [14], eTrim [15], Places [16], that are widely used as test samples for determining the effectiveness of steganalysis by various methods.

The capacity of the initial test sample is 27000 images of density from 300×400 to 4000×5000 pixels. After selecting HB and LB samples, the sample capacity is 7000 images.

Simulation of steganographic embedding in color images is performed separately for each color plane. The results obtained for the three color planes are averaged. If the image is originally presented in shades of gray, a single accessible color plane is used.

2.4 Methods for Evaluating of Steganalyis Efficiency

As the result of operation, the algorithm of WS statistical steganalysis considered in the article has an evaluation of message length embedded in LSB pixels [8]. When constructing systems for detecting the fact of steganographic embedding, binary classification is applied to the result of the algorithm operation. From the excess of the evaluated message length of a certain threshold, a conclusion is drawn of the presence or absence of the fact of steganographic embedding into the image.

The ideal classifier always defines original images as true (True Negative, TN), and modified ones with steganography as steganograms (True Positive, TP). In real conditions, the classifier can make errors, classifying the original images as steganograms (False Positive, FP), and modified images as original (False Negative, FN). The distribution of the classification percentage by categories depends on the correctness of the message length evaluation by the algorithm. As an evaluation of the effectiveness of steganalysis, the percentage of incorrect classification is used under a given percentage of correct classification.

When analyzing the accuracy of the pixel prediction function in background areas, the deviation of the predicted value from the actual value, averaged over the background image area as accuracy metric is used, and then, for all images of the sample.

3 Effect of a Decline in the Effectiveness of Weighted Steganalysis in Homogeneous Background Areas

3.1 Evaluation of the Degree of Decline in the Effectiveness of Steganalysis in Background Areas

The diagram in Fig. 2 shows the result of the experiment for a payload value of 1% for the WS method. It can be seen that a significant decline in the effectiveness of steganalysis is observed in the HB subsample. The same effect is observed on payload rate 3, 5 and 10%: The efficiency on the HB subsample is constantly lower than on the LB subsample.

Since the homogeneous background is a common and commonly occurring semantic area of the image, and its selection can be carried out automatically for imaging, the decline in the effectiveness of the steganalysis using the WS method when analyzing in the background areas makes it possible to organize an attack on the most effective method from the considered ones, integrating messages into background areas with suitable properties, thereby reducing the effectiveness of the analysis of container-like by WS method. Investigating the cause of the effectiveness declining when analyzing in the background areas and improving the WS algorithm for leveling the effect of the effectiveness decline when analyzing in the background area are considered to be currently important task.

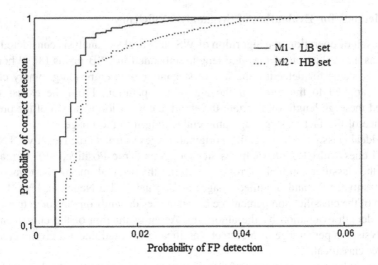

Fig. 2. The decline in the effectiveness of steganalysis while analyzing of images with a significant fraction of a homogeneous background

3.2   Analysis of Reasons of Decline of the Effectiveness of Weighted Steganalysis in Background Areas

When using the steganalysis by WS method, the length of the embedded message in the image is estimated. Further conclusion regarding the presence or absence of the embedded message depends on the selected threshold. Nevertheless, the accuracy of the evaluation of the message length directly affects the accuracy of the final classification.

The effect of a decline in the accuracy of steganalysis when working on images with a significant proportion of a homogeneous background is shown above. The article presents the final effect, which can be caused by two factors:

- When considering the system as a binary analyzer - by overstating the rate of positive or negative false triggering of the algorithm when working on a HB sample;
- When considering the algorithm evaluating the length of the inline message - due to systemic overstating or underestimation of the evaluated message length on the HB sample as compared to that of the LB sample.

To determine the proportion of positive and false negative detection, the proportion of positive and false negative classifications is estimated among all classifications on subsamples of original images only and steganograms respectively. The accuracy was evaluated separately for HB and LB samples. The payload of the embedding is 3%. The results are shown in Table 1.

To evaluate the displacement of the length of the predicted message, the algorithm is run on a sub-sampling of steganograms with the same payload and the absolute length of the embedded message separately for HB and LB samples. To ensure a constant absolute length of the embedded message with a constant payload, only

Table 1. The proportion of false detection, depending on the proportion of a homogeneous background in the image.

Sampling/Sub-sampling	HB	LB
Original images (FP percentage)	22,4%	13,1%
Steganograms (FN percentage)	10,0%	9,5%

images of the same resolution are used. The deviation of the predicted message length was estimated as a percentage of the actual message length (positive percentage means overstating of the length, negative - understatement).

The results are shown in Table 2.

Table 2. The deviation of the predicted message length from the real one, depending on the proportion of the background area of the image

Load/Sub-sampling	HB	LB
5%	21,0%	8,3%
3%	26,8%	10,7%
1%	34,9%	15,4%

As can be seen from Tables 1 and 2, the decline in the accuracy of the steganalysis is provided practically by completely increased proportion of false positive detection. In its turn, the increased proportion of FP is provided by overestimating the evaluated length of the embedded message in comparison with the actual length. To increase the accuracy of steganalysis in background areas, it is required to increase the accuracy of evaluating the length of the embedded message.

The histogram in Fig. 3 clearly shows that the decline in the effectiveness of steganalysis in images with a significant percentage of a homogeneous background is caused by increase in the proportion of false positive detection, with percentage of false negative detection at about a constant level.

To understand the reason for overestimating of the evaluated length, one should refer to the total formula for the length of the message given in [9]:

$$M = 2 \sum_{i=1}^{N} (s_i - \hat{c}_i)(s_i - \bar{s}_i) \qquad (2)$$

Where M – is the total prediction of the length of the embedded message, N – is the image size in pixels, s_i – is the actual value of the brightness level of the analyzed pixel, $\bar{s}_i$ – is the actual value of the brightness level of the analyzed pixel with the inverted least significant bit, $\hat{c}_i$ – is the value of pixel brightness level, evaluated from the prediction formula of the pixel value.

From the formula it is obvious that the total message length is composed of the difference between the predicted and the actual pixel of the steganograms image. The factor $s_i - \bar{s}_i$ does not depend on anything other than one single pixel of the image for each summand of total sum, and therefore the distribution of its values obviously does

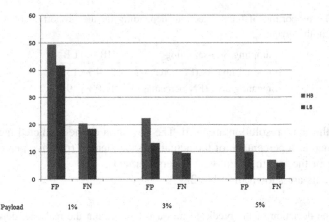

Fig. 3. Contribution of various types of incorrect classification to the total decline in the effectiveness of steganalysis

not depend on the background percentage in the analyzed image. Taking into account that the percentage of false positive detection grows, that is, the effect is observed even in the analysis of only original images, it can be assumed that in the background areas the predicted value of the pixel is systematically overestimated with respect to the real value in those cases when $s_i - \bar{s}_i = 1$. To verify this assumption, the algorithm on a sub-sampling of original images separately for HB and LB samples is run. The diagram in Fig. 4 shows the distribution of the difference between the predicted and real pixel value $s_i - \hat{c}_i$ for $s_i - \bar{s}_i = 1$ for two samples.

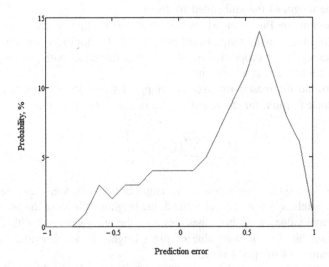

Fig. 4. The probability of the pixel prediction error distribution in the background area

The diagram in Fig. 4 shows that when analyzing images with a significant percentage of the background, the predicted value does have a probability peak in the overstating zone. This explains the high percentage of false positive detections.

The diagram in Fig. 4 shows the overstating of the predicted pixel value using the standard prediction model proposed by the authors of the method in [9]. The pixel prediction model is simple and is described by the formula:

$$\hat{c}_F(i,j) = \frac{c(i+1,j) + c(i-1,j) + c(i,j+1) + c(i,j-1)}{4} \tag{3}$$

where $\hat{c}_F(i,j)$ – is the estimated pixel value at position $[i, j]$ in the spatial distribution matrix of the image, $c\ (i, j)$ is the actual pixel value at position $[i, j]$.

From the aforementioned it is clear that indicated model of the prediction of the pixel value in the background areas leads to an accumulation of the error and an overstating of the percentage of false positive detection.

4 A Method for Predicting Pixel Values in a Background Area of an Image

4.1 Justification of the Approach

The well-known regularity of the consistency of the pixel values adjacent to the predicted one can be extended specifically for the background areas of the images in order to involve more pixels adjacent to the data for a more accurate prediction of the pixel value.

The prediction method for pixel tuples (hereinafter - the tuple method) aims to increase the forecast accuracy in the background areas by using more extensive information about the surrounding pixels of the image in the background area.

The method is based on the assumption of the presence of repeated sequences of pixels in the background area - pixel tuple. By collecting information on the tuples of the background area of the image prior to the beginning of the steganoanalysis, it is possible to predict the brightness values of the pixels that satisfy the tuple during the steganoanalysis. If you can select a tuple for an image that repeats a significant number of times, the prediction by tuple can be more accurate than the prediction by surrounding pixels.

The assumption of the presence of repeating tuples in background areas is made on the basis of the following facts:

- The total number of possible pixel values of the color layer of the image in this model is small and amounts to 255 values.
- The background area, based on its definition, is characterized by a slight change in the values of neighbor pixels.

It is possible to estimate the probability of occurrence in the background area of an image of repeating tupels of pixels and to give a formula for estimating the expected number of repetitions of a tuple for a given pixel value.

Based on the problem of predicting a pixel value with an error ranging from 0.5 to 1.5, it is obvious that the values of neighbor pixels should not differ from the predicted value by more than 2. Based on the assumption that there are no jumps in pixel values in the background area, the number of possible tuples for a given pixel is estimated as the number of possible values of the sequence of neighboring pixels in a certain direction. If there is an allowable pixel difference with neighbors in 0, 1 and 2, the number of unique tuples n is estimated to be:

$$U = 3^n \tag{4}$$

Without loss of generality, for simplicity, consider a square image with a side of a pixels. The total number of pixels in the image in the RGB color model is estimated as $3a^2$. Considering only the background area of the image, you should enter the ratio of the background of the image r. Thus, for a square image with a background r of size a in the RGB color model with a color depth of 8 bits, the expected number of repetitions of the unique tuple n in the background image area is estimated as follows:

$$k = r\frac{3a^2}{3^n} = r\frac{a^2}{3^{n-1}} \tag{5}$$

The surface graph in Fig. 5 shows the order of magnitude of the expected values of the number of repeating gradient tuples for images ranging in size from 1000 to 2000 pixels (the range is taken based on the working resolution of a modern monitor of 1920×1080 pixels) and the length of tuples from 3 to 5 assuming a fraction of a homogeneous background in the image of 40% (threshold for assigning an image to the sample HB).

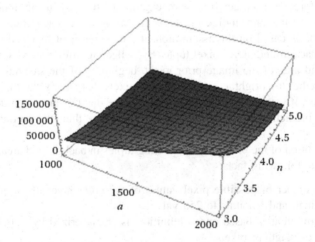

Fig. 5. The order of magnitude of the expected number of repeating tuples for a pixel

Based on the estimate available from the graph in Fig. 5, you can expect a significant number of repeating tuples for a given pixel in areas where the WS steganalysis method has difficulty predicting pixel values.

The method is based on the assumption of the existence among a set of repeating tuples for a given pixel value such that are provided with features of representing consecutive pixel values in the spatial region of the image. The required features can be caused by the details of the imaging implementation of the image by means of photography and the features of the distribution of pixel values in the images during their subsequent processing.

4.2 Determination of the Method of Pixel Prediction

The method involves preliminary processing of the analyzed image before the start of the steganoanalysis. Preprocessing consists in constructing a matrix of tuples of pixels in the background area.

Let I (1) is an analyzed image whose spatial distribution element is defined as $I[i,j]$, where i,j are the pixel coordinates. Then the n-tuple for the pixel $I[i,j]$ is the tuple $I[i \pm 1,j]...I[i \pm n,j]$. Thus, the n-tuple for a pixel is an ordered set of n neighbor pixels in a certain direction. Depending on the direction, such tuples are denoted by nL, nR, nT and nB (respectively, for directions to the left, right, up and down).

Figure 6 illustrates four tuples of pixels for a given analyzed in a spatial distribution of the image. In the example in Fig. 6, the length of the tuples is 4. Thus, the 4L, 4R, 4T, and 4B pixel tuples are represented.

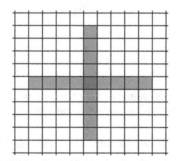

Fig. 6. 4L, 4R, 4T, and 4B pixel tuples

After the construction of all four tuples for each pixel of the image, for each unique tuple, the number of pixels for which it was built is determined. The uniqueness of the tuple is determined by its length in pixels, the brightness level of the pixels that make up it and its direction. The most common pixel for a given tuple is the predicted pixel. The set of pairs "tuple-predicted pixel" is a matrix of pixels tuples. When predicting the pixel value of the analyzed image, the n-tuple will end up for it. If such an n-tuple is present in the matrix of pixels tuples, the pixel value is taken from the matrix for the given tuple. If there is no tuple, the value is predicted as the average of four neighbor pixels.

The concept of strength of a tuple is introduced. The strength of this tuple for a given pixel value is the number of times the tuple was constructed for the given pixel when this image is preprocessed. Thus, the strength as a characteristic does not belong to the tuple, but to the pair "tuple - pixel", that is, to the element of the tuple matrix. The strength is included in the matrix of pixels tuples.

When preprocessing an image for one pixel value, more than one unique tuple can be constructed. After constructing all tuples for all pixels, the matrix of tuples is filtered according to the following rules.

If more than one tuple is constructed for one pixel value, and the strength of tuples of this pixel is different - the tuple of the highest strength remains in the matrix, the others are excluded from the matrix. This filtering step is designed to exclude random, non-systemic pixel tuples that do not occur in the image a large number of times.

If more than one tuple is constructed for one pixel value, and several tuples of the maximum and the same strength are present, the tuple of the largest length remains in the matrix, the others are excluded from the matrix. This step is designed to exclude short chains that occur a significant number of times due to the limited options for the brightness values of the pixels of the analyzed image.

Thus, after filtering, one tuple corresponds to each unique pixel value in the matrix.

The confidence thresholds of the pixel neighborhood matrix are entered. When constructing a matrix on an image without explicit structural patterns, the matrix can produce inadequate results, which can negatively affect the efficiency of the analysis. For sample size K images, thresholds are entered for each tuple, t is relative, and a is absolute:

$$t = \frac{N_m}{N_s} \tag{6}$$

$$a = \frac{N_m}{K} \tag{7}$$

where N_m is the number of appearance of the predicted pixel for a given tuple, N_s is the number of appearance of the given tuple for the entire sample, K is the number of images in the sample.

By changing the thresholds of confidence, one can vary the range of application of the pixel neighborhood matrix and the analysis on adjacent pixels.

Figure 7 is a visualization of the portion of the matrix of tuples of pixels obtained during preprocessing.

Different matrices of pixel neighborhood are used both in statistical steganoanalysis and in steganoanalysis based on machine learning. As a rule, the neighborhood matrices of pixels are built on the training sample, and then applied to the analysis of the test sample (in particular, this approach is used in the method of stegan analysis of fixed digital images SPAM). In general, the method does not have a training sample, only an image intended for analysis. To apply the method in this case, you can use the analyzed image itself as a learning image. This is possible if the method is applied for small values of the payload. Given that in this case the value of the payload rate is small, the distortions introduced into the image by steganographic embedding are not

Prediction	Direction	Length	Tuple				Rate
92	L	4	88	71	90	91	10451
17	U	4	17	17	16	18	7003
38	D	3	39	40	39		81056

Fig. 7. Visualization of a part of a matrix of pixel tuple

enough to introduce a significant error in the regularity of the location of pixels in the background areas, taking into account the use of absolute and relative thresholds of confidence in the matrix.

The matrix should be applied and taught only in the background areas of the image. In non-background areas, due to the greater number of variants of changing the value of the neighbor pixel in comparison with the current one, the number of repeating tuples for a given pixel is much smaller (as shown in p. 3.2.1, the average strength of the tuple for a given pixel is characterized by an inverse exponential dependence on the number of variants of changing the pixel value compared to the current one).

In special cases, significant changes in the pixel value in comparison with the neighboring one are also possible in the background area. The background interval B is entered - the maximum difference between the pixel value and the peak value at which the pixel is considered to belong to the background. The background area is the one for which for at least two of the three color planes the difference between the pixel value and the peak for the given color plane does not exceed B.

Thus, the final set of parameters of the improved algorithm includes confidence thresholds a, t and a background interval B.

The improved model of the pixel prediction is given by the following equation:

$$pr[i,j] = \begin{cases} m[i,j], |pr[i,j] - P| > B \\ m[i,j], |pr[i,j] - P| < B, \nexists M(C(p[i,j]), a, t, B) \\ M(C(p[i,j]), a, t, B), |pr[i,j] - P| < B, \exists M(C(p[i,j]), a, t, B) \end{cases} \qquad (8)$$

where $p[i,j]$ is the pixel of the image being analyzed, $pr[i,j]$ is the prediction of the pixel value, $m[i,j]$ is the value predicted from the average surrounding pixels, P is the peak value of the histogram for the color layer, M is the operation of taking the predicted value from the matrix tuples, C is the operation of computing a tuple for a pixel.

5 Practical Evaluation of the Effectiveness of the Proposed Method

5.1 Effect of the Method on the Pixel Prediction Error in the Background Image Areas

The tuple prediction method aims to reduce the error in predicting the pixel value in the background areas of the images.

Figures 8 and 9 show the probability distribution of the pixel prediction error in the background areas for the HB and LB collections, respectively. On the graphs, the PLAIN curve shows the probability distribution for the prediction for the average neighbor pixels. The CHAIN curve shows the probability distribution when using the prediction of tuples of pixels.

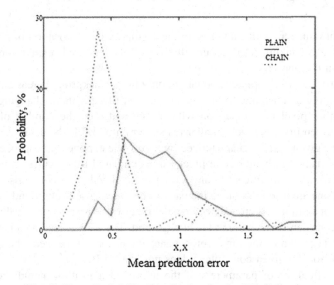

Fig. 8. Error Probability Distribution for the HB Collection

Samples and the method of their formation is similar to that described in p. 3.1. The following thresholds are used: $t = 0.9$, $a = 200$.

Table 3 contains numerical estimates of the average error in the pixel prediction for various collections and prediction methods.

From the graphs in Figs. 8, 9 and the data in Table 3, it can be seen that the tuple prediction method can significantly reduce the error of the pixel prediction in the background areas, yielding the maximum of the probability distribution over the interval $[0.5; 1.5]$.

The assumption that the fact of steganographic embedding does not have a significant effect on the statistics of tuples also needs experimental confirmation.

The graph in Fig. 10 shows the average error in the tuple forecast, depending on the value of the payload.

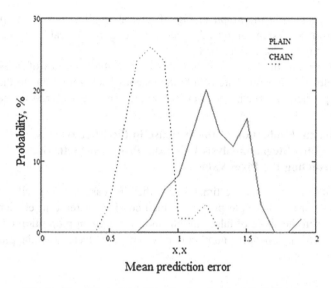

Fig. 9. Error Probability Distribution for the LB Collection

Table 3. Pixel prediction error for the original and proposed pixel prediction method

Method/Collection	HB	LB
Original	1.22	1.74
Proposed	0.74	0.96

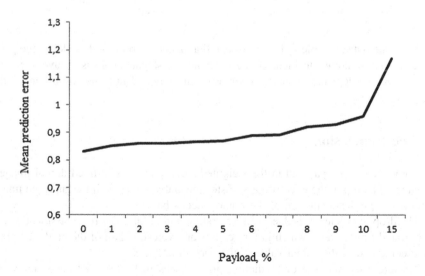

Fig. 10. The average error of the tuple prediction, depending on the value of the payload rate

It can be seen from the graph in Fig. 10 that at small values of the payload the prediction error grows insignificantly, demonstrating a noticeable increase only at values of the payload exceeding 10%.

The prediction method of tuples allows to increase the efficiency of steganoanalysis in images with a significant share of a homogeneous background due to the reduction of the pixel prediction error in the background areas of the analyzed image.

5.2 A Practical Evaluation of the Increase in the Effectiveness of Weighted Steganoanalysis Using the Proposed Method for Predicting the Pixel Value

Table 4 contains numerical estimates of the increase in the effectiveness of steganoanalysis using the tuple prediction method. The increase in efficiency is estimated as a fall in the share of false classification for a given proportion of the correct classification (95%). A positive number corresponds to a decrease in the probability of incorrect classification.

Table 4. Increase in the effectiveness of steganoanalysis due to the use of the proposed method for predicting the pixel value

Load/Resolution	800×800	1500×1500	2400×2400	Average
1%	9.75%	9.1%	6.95%	8.6%
2%	8.65%	7.6%	5.75%	7.3%
3%	5.6%	5.45%	5%	5.4%
4%	4.1%	4.05%	4.0%	4.03%
5%	3.8%	3.7%	3.3%	3.6%

From the data in Table 4, it can be seen that using the proposed model of the pixel value prediction allows to increase the efficiency of steganoanalysis on average from 3.6% to 8.6%, depending on the volume of the payload and the resolution of the analyzed image.

6 The Conclusion

At low values of the payload in the weighted steganoanalysis of fixed digital images, the effect of a drop in the effectiveness of steganoanalysis appears if the analyzed image contains a significant fraction of the homogeneous background.

The drop in efficiency is due to an overestimation of false positive classifications in background image areas, which in turn causes an overestimation of the predicted pixel value compared to the actual value in the background areas.

The proposed method of predicting pixel values in background areas allows to reduce the prediction error and to achieve a 3–8% increase in the effectiveness of steganoanalysis at low values of the payload (up to 5%).

The considered method is the simplest method of expanding the region of pixel neighborhood with the predicted one under the condition of avoiding the "curse of dimensionality". Further research in this direction may include the analysis and suggestion of more complex pixel structures adjacent to the data, the use of which in the background areas can lead to a further reduction in the prediction error of the pixel values.

Acknowledgements. This work was supported by Government of Russian Federation (Grant 08-08).

References

1. Kolomeec, M., Checulin, A., Pronoza, A., Kotenko, I.: Technique of data visualization: example of network topology display for security monitoring. J. Wirel. Mob. Netw. Ubiquitous Comput. Dependable Appl. (JoWUA) **7**(1), 58–78 (2016)
2. FBI: Spies hid secret messages on public websites. https://www.wired.com/2010/06/alleged-spies-hid-secret-messages-on-public-websites
3. Hashem, Y., Takabi, H., GhasemiGol, M., Dantu, R.: Inside the mind of the insider: towards insider threat detection using psychophysiological signals. J. Internet Serv. Inf. Secur. (JISIS) **6**(1), 20–36 (2016)
4. Bordel, B., Alcarria, R., Manso, M.A., Jara, A.: Building enhanced environmental traceability solutions: from thing-to-thing communications to generalized cyber-physical systems. J. Internet Serv. Inf. Secur (JISIS) **7**(3), 17–33 (2017)
5. Gayathri, C., Kalpana, V.: Study on image steganography techniques. Int. J. Eng. Technol. (IJET) **5**, 572–577 (2013)
6. Kotenko, I., Saenko, I., Kushnerevich, A.: Parallel big data processing system for security monitoring in Internet of Things networks. J. Wirel. Mob. Netw. Ubiquitous Comput. Dependable Appl. (JoWUA) **8**(4), 60–74 (2017)
7. Prokhozhev, N., Mikhailichenko, O., Sivachev, A., Bashmakov, D., Korobeynikov, A.: Passive steganalysis evaluation: reliabilities of modern quantitative steganalysis algorithms. In: Abraham, A., Kovalev, S., Tarassov, V., Snášel, V. (eds.) Proceedings of the First International Scientific Conference "Intelligent Information Technologies for Industry" (IITI 2016). AISC, vol. 451, pp. 89–94. Springer, Cham (2016). https://doi.org/10.1007/978-3-319-33816-3_9
8. Fridrich, J., Goljan, M.: On estimation of secret message length in LSB steganography in spatial domain. In: Proceedings of SPIE, Security, Steganography, and Watermarking of Multimedia Contents VI, vol. 5306 (2004). https://doi.org/10.1117/12.521350
9. Ker, A.: A Weighted stego image detector for sequential LSB replacement. In: Proceedings - IAS 2007 3rd International Symposium on Information Assurance and Security, pp. 453–456 (2007). https://doi.org/10.1109/ias.2007.71
10. Ker, A., Böhme, R.: Revisiting weighted stego-image steganalysis. In: Proceedings of SPIE, Security, Forensics, Steganography, and Watermarking of Multimedia Contents X, vol. 6819 (2008). https://doi.org/10.1117/12.766820
11. Yu, X., Babaguchi, N.: Weighted stego-Image based steganalysis in multiple least significant bits. In: 2008 IEEE International Conference on Multimedia and Expo, Hannover, pp. 265–268 (2008)

12. Bashmakov, D.: Adaptive pixel pixel prediction in gradient areas to improve the accuracy of steganoanalysis in still digital images. Cybern. Program. (2), 83–93 (2018). https://doi.org/10.25136/2306-4196.2018.2.25514
13. Break Our Watermarking System (BOWS) image database. http://bows2.ec-lille.fr
14. Break Our Steganographic System (BOSS) image database. http://agents.fel.cvut.cz/boss/index.php?mode=VIEW&tmpl=materials
15. E-Trim Image database. http://www.ipb.uni-bonn.de/projects/etrims_db/
16. Places image database. http://places2.csail.mit.edu/

Steganalysis Method for Detecting Embedded Coefficients of Discrete-Wavelet Image Transformation into High-Frequency Domains

Alexey V. Sivachev[1]([✉]) [ID], Daniil A. Bashmakov[1] [ID],
Olga V. Mikhailishenko[1] [ID], Anatoliy G. Korobeynikov[2] [ID],
and Roland Rieke[1,3] [ID]

[1] Saint Petersburg National Research University of Information Technologies,
Mechanics and Optics (ITMO University), St. Petersburg 197101, Russia
sivachev239@mail.ru
[2] Pushkov Institute of Terrestrial Magnetism, Ionosphere and Radio Wave
Propagation of the Russian Academy of Sciences St.-Petersburg Filial,
St. Petersburg 197101, Russia
[3] Fraunhofer-Institute for Secure Information Technology SIT,
Darmstadt, Germany

Abstract. The paper deals with a research aimed at providing the highest performance of detection of an embedding into a wavelet-domain image, in particular in LH and HL subbands, due to the combined use of several methods proposed by the authors. The paper discusses various methods for enhancing detection of the embedding into a wavelet-domain image as proposed by the authors for their possible combined use in order to ensure the best possible performance of detecting the embedding into a wavelet-domain image. These methods use the features of the wavelet's transform, interrelations of various domains of the coefficients obtained by the wavelet transform of the image, or peculiar features or frequency domain of images. By the results of this research, a steganalysis method is proposed, based on the combined use of the above-described methods for increasing the steganalysis efficiency, which allows providing a better performance of detection of a wavelet-domain image embedding compared with existing methods of the steganalysis. The proposed methods of increasing the efficiency of steganalysis will improve the effectiveness of the steganalysis of information embedded in the LH and HL subbands by 4–7% in comparison with the already existing methods. The proposed method is based on combining them and allows you to get an additional increase in efficiency by 1–3%. The results of the given research can be useful for the experts, dealing with the information security problems while detecting and counteracting with the hidden data channel, based on the use of steganography, including in the mobile Internet. The obtained results can be used in the development of steganalysis systems.

Keywords: Steganography · Stego image · Steganalysis · Binary classification
The Haar wavelet · Discrete wavelet transform (DWT)
Image frequency domain · Discrete cosine transformation (DCT)
Discrete sine transformation (DST)

© Springer Nature Singapore Pte Ltd. 2019
I. You et al. (Eds.): MobiSec 2017, CCIS 971, pp. 83–95, 2019.
https://doi.org/10.1007/978-981-13-3732-1_6

1 Introduction

In the modern world, steganography can be used for hidden communication. That may be applied in organization of hidden communication channels and for communication for terrorists and other illegal activities [1, 2, 8]. This is especially true in connection with the spread of mobile Internet [9]. Today the steganography techniques are widely used to embedding information in digital images [3]. Embedding information in the domain of a discrete wavelet transform (DWT) of image is of a special interest today. It is associated with the distribution of JPEG2000 format based on the use of DWT, which is used in various kinds of data [5]. An illegal use of steganography makes it an important problem to detect cases of steganographic embedding for detection and closing down of the unauthorized communication channels [6].

To detect the fact of embedding, various steganalysis methods are developed that allow the detection of the embedding case, including into the digital images [4]. As shown by recent studies, the modern methods of steganalysis do not allow detecting the fact of embedding information in the area of DWT images for sure. In particular, the efficiency of detection of the embedding case in the DWT image area is highly dependent on the current subband (LL, LH, HL and HH) used for the embedding of information, the most problematic in terms of detection, accordingly [14] are the subbands LL, LH and HL.

The impossibility to reliably detect the fact of embedding into the DWT image domain makes the current research on efficiency improvement for detection of embedding in the DWT image domain a crucial one. The given paper deals with the combined use of several methods to increase the efficiency of the steganalysis proposed by the authors, to ensure a higher performance of detection of the embedding cases for the subbands LH and HL in comparison with existing methods of the steganalysis.

2 The Study Domain

The given chapter describes the methods of increasing the steganalysis efficiency of the embedding into the DWT image domain, in particular in the LH and HL subbands, by analyzing various characteristics of the image proposed by the authors.

2.1 The First Method

The first method of increasing the steganalysis efficiency is based on the use of the DWT image features. This method is based on the following two regularities:

- The wavelet applied for the DWT image has a significant influence on how the parameter values of subbands LH and HL (particularly statistical moments) are used in steganalysis of an image using machine learning methods, in consequence of embedding information into the DWT image domain.
- Values of the parameters for LH and HL subbands, used for the image steganalysis, obtained using different wavelets are also interconnected by the parameter value obtained using a single wavelet, and we can estimate the parameter values obtained using another wavelet.

The idea to use the given patterns to detect the embedding into the DWT image domain has been proposed by the authors in [7].

Figure 1 shows a histogram of values for one of the image parameters for the scope of the original and stego images obtained using Haar wavelet and a random wavelet. According the histograms it is clearly seen that by using the Haar wavelet the difference between the scopes of values for the original image and stego images is more noticeable.

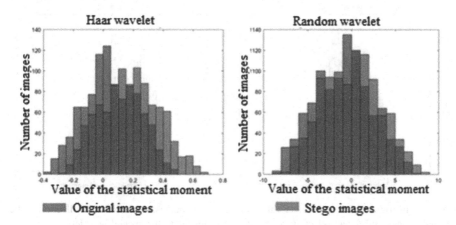

Fig. 1. A histogram of the parameter value of the image obtained using a Haar wavelet and using a random wavelet.

In the proposed method, the given patterns are applied to evaluate a number of parameter values of LH and HL subbands, such as statistical moments, in the original images. It can allow to clearly recognizing the change of these parameter values due to embedding of information into the LH and HL subbands. To measure the parameter values of LH and HL subbands domains a specially-found wavelet is used with the low and high frequency coefficients:

$$Lo = \{0.417, 0.916, 0.011, 0.389, 0.579, 0.527, 1.007\}$$
$$Hi = \{0.417, 0.916, 0.011, -0.389, 0.579, -0.527, -1.007\}$$

For the given wavelet the following aspects are characteristic:

- values of LH and HL subbands' parameters, in particular the statistical moments obtained using this special wavelet practically are not changed when embedding the information in the LH and HL subbands, produced using another wavelet, particularly the Haar wavelet.
- between parameter values of LH and HL subbands (particularly statistical moments), which are obtained by using this special wavelet and parameter values obtained by using the Haar wavelet, there is an interrelation which allows predicting a parameter value obtained using another wavelet by the parameter value obtained using a single wavelet.

Figures 2 and 3 demonstrate properties of the special wavelet. Figure 2 shows the value of one of image parameters obtained for the collection of original images and for the collection of stego images obtained using this special wavelet. Figure 3 demonstrates the interrelation of one of the parameters of the image obtained using the Haar wavelet and obtained using this special wavelet.

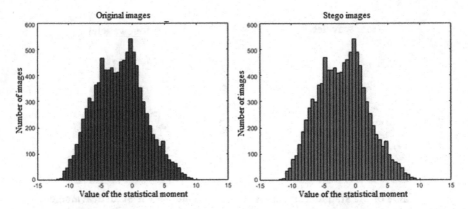

Fig. 2. A histogram of the parameter values of one of the images, obtained for a collection of the original images and for a collection of the stego images using the special wavelet.

As a result, for image steganalysis the first method uses the following parameters:

- 1, 2, 3 and 4 statistical moments obtained for each of the subbands (LL, HL, LH and HH) when we use a two-dimensional DWT image, used by other methods - 16 parameters in total;
- 1, 2, 3 and 4 statistical moments for the subbands of LL, HL, LH, HH, obtained by the described special wavelet - 16 parameters in total.

The first group of these parameters is sensitive to information embedding in the LH and HL subbands, and the values of these parameters are changed when embedding the information in the LH and HL subbands of the DWT images that allows machine learning techniques to classify the image as the original image or stego image. The second group of these parameters is used to predict the first group parameter values of the original image which allowing a machine learning method to more accurately detect the fact of changes in parameter values for the first group due to the embedding into the LH and HL domains.

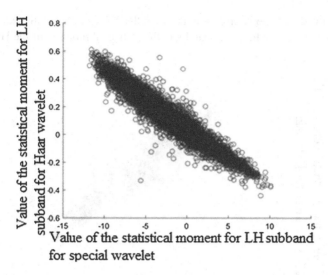

Fig. 3. A graph of values correlation for one of the parameters of an image obtained using the Haar wavelet and using the special wavelet.

2.2 The Second Method

The second method of increasing the steganalysis efficiency is based on correlation of different subbands parameters obtained by DWT image [15]. This method is based on the following patterns:

- low frequency L subband, obtained with one-dimensional DWT image, interconnected with a high-frequency HL subband, obtained by the two-dimensional DWT image;
- a low frequency H subband obtained at DWT single-dimensional image is correlated with high frequency LH subband, obtained by the two-dimensional DWT image;

The idea to use the given regularities to detect the embedding of the DWT image domain has been proposed by the authors in [6].

The method is based on the fact that the data regularities can predict certain parameters of the high frequency subbands of LH and HL of a bidimensional DWT image in the original image based on L and H subbands of a single-dimensional DWT image. That will allow to more accurately detect these parameters' change due to embedded information in the LH and HL subbands. In particular, one can predict the value of the statistical moments of LH and HL subbands based on "difference array", calculated for the L and H subbands according to the following formulas:

$$Dif_x(X) = X(x+1,y) - X(x,y)$$
$$Dif_y(X) = X(x,y+1) - X(x,y)$$

88   A. V. Sivachev et al.

Figure 4 illustrates the interrelation between the values of the statistical moment of the "difference array" for the L subband and the statistical moment of the HL subband.

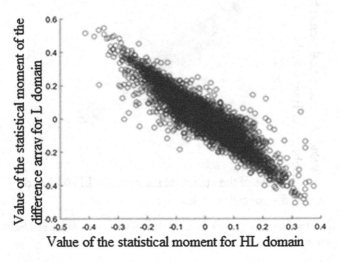

Fig. 4. Graph of dependence of the values of one of the statistical moments of the «difference arrays» for the L subband the statistical moment of the HL subband.

Thus, the embedding into the LH subband has no obvious effect on the parameters of the H subband, in particular on the values of the statistical moments of the "difference arrays" for the given subband. And accordingly, the embedding into the HL subband has no obvious effect on the parameters of the L subband. Figure 5 contains a graph of statistical moment values of the "difference array" - the graph clearly shows that the values of this statistical moment in the original image and the stego image are equal, because the graph is a straight line.

As a result, for steganalysis of images the second method involves the following parameters:

- 1, 2, 3 and 4 statistical moments for the subbands LL, HL, LH, HH, used by the other methods of steganalysis - 16 parameters in total;
- 1, 2, 3 and 4 statistical moments obtained for vertical and horizontal "difference arrays" obtained from the subbands L and H of a single-dimensional DWT image - 8 parameters in total.

The first part of these parameters is sensitive to the embedding of information in the subbands LH and HL and the values of these parameters vary significantly when embedding the information in the LH and HL subbands of DWT images, which allows the machine learning methods to classify the image into the original image or the stego image. The second part of these parameters is used to predict the parameter values of the first group in the original image, which allows a method of machine learning to more clearly detect the fact of change in the parameter values of the first group due to the embedding into the LH and HL subbands.

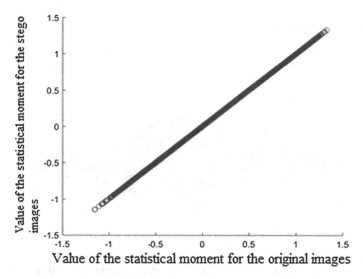

Fig. 5. A graph with the dependence of values of one of the statistical moments of the "difference array" in the original image on the statistical moment of the "difference array" in the stego image.

2.3 The Third Method

The third method for increasing the steganalysis efficiency is based on the use of frequency domain characteristic features of an image obtained by discrete cosine transform (DCT) or discrete sine transform (DST). This method is based on the following regularity: while processing an image, for example, by adding a Gaussian noise into the image, in the frequency domain of an image there occur certain coefficient changes that characterize the type of the image processing.

The idea to use this regularity to detect an embedding into the DWT image domain has been first proposed by the authors in [16].

Figure 6 represents a graph of the coefficient difference of the image frequency domain obtained by the DCT, between the values of the frequency domain of the original image and the stego image, containing the embedding in the DWT domain of image.

According to this graph it is clearly seen that the changes in the majority of the frequency domain coefficients with embedding the information into an image ranges from −2 to +2. At the same time the values of specific image domain frequency coefficients, in particular angular coefficients, vary significantly more. This method is based on the use of highly sensitive frequency domain coefficients for improving the efficiency of embedding detection in DWT domain of image.

Figure 7 shows a histogram of the values for one of the angular coefficients of the image frequency domain resulting from a DCT image for the array of original images and stego images. According to the graph shown in the Fig. 7, it is clearly seen that the value of this ratio can be determined whether this is an original image or a stego image for a significant number of images.

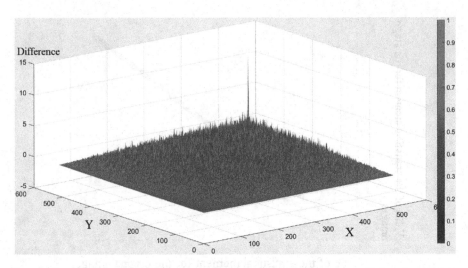

Fig. 6. Graph illustrating the difference of the image domain frequency coefficients between the values of the original image and stego image coefficients.

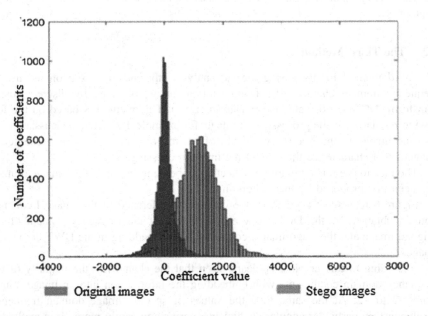

Fig. 7. The values histogram for one of the angular image domain frequency coefficients for the array of original images and the stego-images.

As a result, for the steganalysis of images the third method applies the following parameters:

- 1, 2, 3 and 4 the statistical moments for subbands LL, LH, HL, HH, used by other methods of steganalysis - 16 parameters in total;

- angular coefficients of the coefficients matrix obtained by bi-dimensional DCT image - the total number of 4 parameters;
- angular coefficients of the coefficients matrix obtained by the bi-dimensional DST image - total number of 4 parameters.

The first part of these parameters to be sensitive to embedding information in subbands LH and HL. Values of these parameters vary significantly when embedding the information in the LH and HL subbands of DWT images that allows the machine learning methods to classify the image into the original image or the stego image. The second and third groups of these parameters are also significantly changed in case of embedding the information into the LH and HL subbands of the DWT images, which enables the method of machine learning to more clearly detect the fact of changes in the parameter values of the first group due to the embedding into the LH and HL subbands.

2.4   The Possibility of Combined Application of These Methods

All the three methods of increasing the efficiency of steganalysis using machine-learning techniques. These methods are based on the formation of a set of parameters that allow to detect the fact of information embedding into a DWT image domain. All the three methods of efficiency increase will help you to achieve a higher performance when detecting the embedding into the LH and HL subbands, but they apply different image parameters for this. Accordingly, at the shared use of parameters proposed by the given methods, there may occur a cumulative effect that allows obtaining a higher efficiency than the one provided by any of these three methods.

3   Description of the Proposed Method

The steganalysis method proposed in the given paper allow gaining the steganalysis efficiency for the domains of LH and HL. This method based on the combined use of the above-mentioned methods to increase the efficiency of steganalysis. Each of these methods taken separately provides an increased efficiency in detection of embedding in certain coefficients of the DWT image domains. To ensure a maximal efficiency of the steganalysis it is proposed to use the proposed methods in combination which allows increasing of the steganalysis efficiency. Thus, the proposed steganalysis method is based on the following set of parameters:

- 1, 2, 3 and 4 statistical moments of LL, LH, HL, HH subbands, used by other methods of the steganalysis [10–13];
- 1, 2, 3 and 4 statistical moments of LL, HL, LH, HH subbands, obtained by the described special wavelet;
- 1, 2, 3 and 4 statistical moments obtained for the vertical and horizontal "difference arrays" obtained from L and H subbands of a single-dimensional DWT image;
- angular coefficients of the matrix coefficients obtained at the bi-dimensional DCT image;
- angular coefficients of the matrix coefficients obtained at the bi-dimensional DST image.

This set of parameters is supplied at the input for the image classification as for embedding.

4 Conditions and Methods of Carrying Out Experiments

To evaluate the efficacy of the steganalysis methods there was used a collection of images consisting of 9500 image resolution of 640 × 480 pixels. To be able to compare the effectiveness of the proposed method compared with other modern steganalysis methods, the following best known and most frequently cited methods proposed were selected:

- Kumar et al. [10];
- Farid [11];
- Liu et al. [12];
- Shi et al. [13].

Also, the effectiveness of the proposed method is compared to the above-mentioned techniques to improve the efficiency of the steganalysis.

Modeling of steganographic impact was carried out by values modification for penultimate significant bits of the coefficients of one of the subband (LH or HL), obtained by a single bi-dimensional DWT image.

On the basis of the given collection of images, there were formed collections of stego images containing the embedding in 20% of the maximum payload in one of subband of DWT domain (LL, LH, HL and HH).

For the image classification the support vector machine was used; a set of image samples was used consisting of 20% of the collection of original images and 20% of the collection of stego images to train the machine. The remaining 80% of each of these collections were used for testing the quality of a support vector machine learning - in particular the ratio of the number of images that were classified as true negative, true positive, false negative and false positive.

5 A Way to Evaluate Effectiveness of Steganalysis Methods

As a result of support vector machine's activity using the sets of parameters proposed in the methods [12–15], we obtain a binary image classification: an original image or a stego image. Ideally, the steganalysis method should accurately detect the presence of the embedded information in the image, i.e., to be classified 100% of original images as the ones not containing any embedded information, and all 100% stego images to be classified as an images containing embedded information, and the percentage of images wrongly determined should be zero. The closer the result of a real method is to the ideal - the more accurate the method is considered to be.

6   Results of the Experiment

The results of experiments evaluating the effectiveness of the proposed steganalysis method are presented as a TN ratio graphs (true negative); TP (true positive); FP (false positive); FN (false negative); T (the total number of images correctly classified, T = TN + TP); F (the total number of images not correctly classified, F = FN + FP) in the Figs. 8.1 and 8.2.

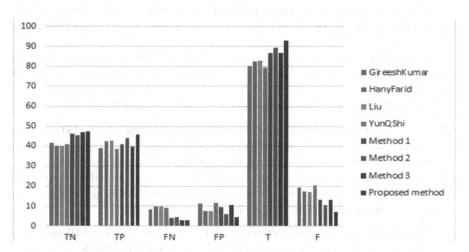

Fig. 8.1. Graph of the ratio of TN, TP, FN, FP, T, N for detecting embedding into the domain of LH.

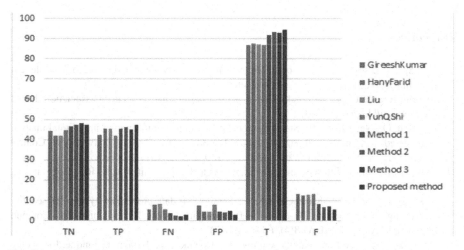

Fig. 8.2. Graph of the ratio of TN, TP, FN, FP, T, N for detecting of embedding into the domain of HL.

7   Conclusion

Best shown efficacy in the existing methods of steganalysis was:

- 82.88% of correctly classified when detecting the embedding into the LH subband, obtained at DWT image, for the method [12];
- 87.46% of correctly classified when detecting the embedding into the HL subband, obtained at DWT image, for the method [11].

The methods of increasing the steganalysis efficiency when detecting the embedding into the LH and HL subbands proposed by the authors can improve efficiency by 4–7%%.

The method proposed in the article, which is based on the combined use of these methods of increasing the efficiency of steganalysis, can further improve the efficiency by 1–3%%.

As a result, the effectiveness of the proposed method is as follows:

- 92.91% of correctly classified when detecting the embedding into the LH subband, which is 10.03% more than that of the method [12], and 3.42% higher than when using only one method of increasing the steganalysis efficiency;
- 94.48% of correctly classified when detecting the embedding into the HL subband, which is 7.02% higher than that of the method [11], and 1.06% higher than when using only one method of increasing the steganalysis efficiency.

The proposed method is effective in detecting embedding in LH and HL subbands and gives an increase in efficiency in comparison with existing methods.

Acknowledgements. This work was supported by Government of Russian Federation (Grant 08-08).

References

1. FBI: Spies hid secret messages on public websites. https://www.wired.com/2010/06/alleged-spies-hid-secret-messages-on-public-websites/
2. Security foresignt: Steganography: BISA: Business information security association. http://bis-expert.ru/blog/660/56301
3. Evsyutin, O., Negacheva, E.: Steganographic embedding of information into digital images, compressed using block cellular automaton. Reports of Tomsk State University of Control Systems and Radioelectronics, no. 4(30), pp. 130–135 (2013)
4. Vyas, A., Dudul, S.: Study of image steganalysis techniques. Int. J. Adv. Res. Comput. Sci. 6(8), 7–11 (2015)
5. Kotenko, I., Saenko, I., Kushnerevich, A.: Parallel big data processing system for security monitoring in Internet of Things networks. J. Wirel. Mob. Netw. Ubiquitous Comput. Dependable Appl. (JoWUA) 8(4), 60–74 (2017)
6. Desnitsky, V., Levshun, D., Chechulin, A., Kotenko, I.: Design technique for secure embedded devices: application for creation of integrated cyber-physical security system. J. Wirel. Mob. Netw. Ubiquitous Comput. Dependable Appl. (JoWUA) 7(2), 60–80 (2016)

7. Sivachev, A., Prokhozhev, N., Mikhaylichenko, O.: Improving of steganalysis accuracy by optimizing parameters of wavelet transformation methods. Sci. Tech. Newsl. Inf. Technol. Mech. Optics **1**, 113–121 (2018)
8. Kolomeec, M., Chechulin, A., Pronoza, A., Kotenko, I.: Technique of data visualization: example of network topology display for security monitoring. J. Wirel. Mob. Netw. Ubiquitous Comput. Dependable Appl. (JoWUA) **7**(1), 58–78 (2016)
9. Hashem, Y., Takabi, H., GhasemiGol, M., Dantu, R.: Inside the mind of the insider: towards insider threat detection using psychophysiological signals. J. Internet Serv. Inf. Secur. (JISIS) **6**(1), 20–36 (2016)
10. Kumar, G., Jithin, R., Deepa, D.: Shankar feature based steganalysis using wavelet decomposition and magnitude statistics. In: Advances in Computer Engineering (ACE), pp. 298–300 (2010)
11. Farid, H.: Detecting Steganographic Messages in Digital Images. Technical report TR2001-412, Dartmouth College, Computer Science Department (2001)
12. Liu, C., Ouyang, C., Guo, M., Chen, H.: Image steganalysis based on spatial domain and DWT domain features. In: Proceedings of the 2010 Second International Conference on Networks Security, Wireless Communications and Trusted Computing, vol. 01, pp. 329–331 (2010)
13. Shi, Y., et al.: Effective steganalysis based on statistical moments of wavelet characteristic function. In: IEEE Conference on Information Technology: Coding and Computation (ITCC05), Las Vegas, Nevada, USA (2005)
14. Sivachev, A., Prokhozhev, N., Mikhailichenko, O., Bashmakov, D.: Efficiency of steganalysis based on machine learning methods. Sci. Tech. Newsl. Inf. Technol. Mech. Opt. **17**(3), 457–466 (2017)
15. Sivachev, A., Mikhaylichenko, O., Prokhozhev, N., Bashmakov, D.: Improved accuracy in DWT steganalysis by using the correlation between domains of bi-dimensional and single-dimensional decompositions. Cybern. Program. **2**, 78–87 (2017)
16. Sivachev, A.: Increase of steganalysis efficiency of DWT image domain by analyzing the image domain frequency parameters. Cybern. Program. **2**, 29–37 (2018)

Voronoi Maps for Planar Sensor Networks Visualization

Maxim Kolomeets[1,2] , Andrey Chechulin[1,2(✉)] ,
Igor Kotenko[2] , and Martin Strecker[2,3]

[1] St. Petersburg Institute for Informatics and Automation of the Russian
Academy of Sciences, Saint-Petersburg 199178, Russia
{kolomeec, chechulin}@comsec.spb.ru
[2] ITMO University, Saint-Petersburg 197101, Russia
ivkote@comsec.spb.ru, martin.strecker@irit.fr
[3] Paul Sabatier University, Toulouse, France

Abstract. The paper describes Voronoi Maps – a new technique for visualizing
sensor networks that can reduced to planar graph. Visualization in the form of
Voronoi Maps as well as TreeMaps provides a great use of screen space, and at
the same time allows us to visualize planar non-hierarchical decentralized
topology. The paper provides an overview of existing techniques of information
security visualization, the Voronoi Maps concept, Voronoi Maps mapping
technique, Voronoi Maps cell area resizing technique and Voronoi Map usage
examples for visualization of sensor network analysis processes.

Keywords: Security data visualization · Sensor networks
Security analysis of sensor networks · Voronoi Maps · TreeMaps
Graph structures

1 Introduction

Nowadays due to the complexity of current attacks, the detection and reaction process
requires additional tools to help security analysts in the decision-making process. For
faster and better analysis and visual monitoring of information, analysts have to take
into account the three basic needs. The first it's breadth of graphical model for the
ability to visualize data from different sources and security sensors. The second is a
graphical model`s capacity of security metrics. And the third is simplicity of data
perception. Graphs and TreeMaps (in the case of hierarchical structures) are usually
used for visualization of security network data that has dependencies (linked data), for
example network topology. The TreeMaps were further developed in the form of the
Voronoi TreeMaps, which are based on the Voronoi Diagram. TreeMaps and Voronoi
TreeMaps more effectively display metrics in comparison with graphs, but they have
two main drawbacks that significantly limit their usage: (1) they can display only the
leaf metrics of the tree if the metrics of the nodes don't depend on each other; (2) they
can only display a hierarchical topology.

In this paper, we propose the development of Voronoi Maps graphical model for
security analysis of sensor networks that can be presented as planar structure. Voronoi

I. You et al. (Eds.): MobiSec 2017, CCIS 971, pp. 96–109, 2019.
https://doi.org/10.1007/978-981-13-3732-1_7

Maps can display the metrics of sensors, as well as planar topologies, using the same area attributes as the TreeMaps and Voronoi TreeMaps. We suppose that the use of Voronoi Maps will allow us to enhance performance of visual analysis and monitoring of information security data that have planar structure. We also give example sensor network visualization for analysis of sensors' charge level.

The novelty of the paper is the application of Voronoi Maps to visualize the sensor network analysis and its evaluation. The contribution of this paper is a description of the generation and polymorphism techniques for the Voronoi Maps graphical model.

The paper consists of the following sections. First section shows relevance of this paper for improvement the effectiveness of visual analytics of sensor networks security. Second section shows existing security visualization models, their possibilities and limitations. Third section shows the concept of Voronoi Maps and technique of generation – in the form of algorithms, we outline how to generate Voronoi Maps and what problems arise during polymorphism of cells. Fourth section describes how the prototype was implemented, what libraries were used, and shows Voronoi Maps use case: sensor network visualization for analysis of sensors' charge level. In fifth section we compare the proposed model with analogs, evaluate its capabilities and describe plans for further research. The last section summarizes the results.

2   Review of Visualization Techniques

When analyzing security data, two types of models are usually used: geometrical [1] (to calculate the impact of cyber events or select countermeasures) and graphical [2] (to analyze the topology or other linked security data). Great difficulty is represented by linked security data structures, such as computer networks [3, 4], attack trees [5], service dependencies [6] and other.

Sensor networks topology can be represented as a linked data too. Also, sensor networks can be represented as graphs with reduced planar topology, that used to conserve energy and reduce interference. Let us look which visualization techniques of security network visualization can be used for visual representation and analysis of planar sensor networks.

One of the most common ways to visualize dependent or related structures are graphs. Graphs are the best option to analyze the topology and common way for visualization of networks security [7]. Advantage of graphs is that they can visualize any type of sensor network topology. At the same time, they can't effectively visualize link metrics (as communication channels) and object metrics (as sensors).

TreeMaps [8] are used to visualize the metrics of objects that are linked hierarchically in form of tree. So TreeMaps can be used for visualization for multilevel centralized sensor networks. At the same time, TreeMaps have disadvantages. First, the area of the rectangle-ancestor is equal to the sum of the rectangles-descendants. As a consequence, we can visualize only the metrics of the leaves of a tree. In many cases, the visualization of "not leaves" metrics is not required.

For example, when leaves in multilevel centralized sensor networks are presented as physical sensors and other nodes are presented as hubs that helps to process and to transport data to central host, we need to visualize only metrics of leaves-sensors. On the other hand, when sensors act as hubs, we need to visualize metrics of leaves-sensors and nodes-sensors that cannot be done using TreeMaps. Secondly, TreeMaps can only display hierarchical structures and in case of decentralized sensor network they can't be used.

TreeMaps were further developed in the form of the Voronoi TreeMaps [9], which are based on the Voronoi Diagram [10]. The Voronoi diagram is generated on the basis of points and represents a partition of a plane or space into polygons. The distance from any dot inside the polygon to the point (on the basis of which the given polygon was generated) always less than to the other point.

For example, Voronoi diagrams can be used to analyze the movement of a person on the signal of his cell phone (see Fig. 1). By exploiting the SS7 vulnerability [11], one can obtain the base station number to which the phone is connected. Having formed the Voronoi Diagram on the basis of the coordinates of the base stations, one can find out the area in which the person is located.

Voronoi TreeMaps [9] (Fig. 2) are interpreted differently from Voronoi diagram. Like the TreeMaps, Voronoi TreeMaps consist of nested areas that can be specified in color, size, and opacity. By using polygons, it is easier to analyze the data and recognize the nesting.

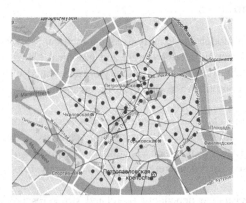
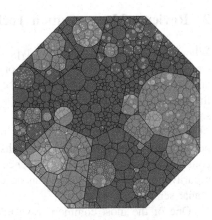

Fig. 1. The Voronoi diagram based on the mobile base stations in St. Petersburg.   **Fig. 2.** Voronoi TreeMaps.

Each visualization model has its own advantages of application and can be used for visualization of sensor networks with limitations. Therefore, they are usually used together (according to the multiple-view paradigm [12]) in order to increase situational awareness.

However, the limitations of the TreeMaps and the Voronoi TreeMaps don't allow them to be used for non-hierarchical sensor networks. At the same time, limitations of the graphs don't allow them to be used for effective analysis of metrics of sensors and communication channels.

The proposed approach allows us to visualize sensor networks on principles that are similar to the graphs and Voronoi TreeMaps, thereby inheriting their advantages.

3 Proposed Graphical Model

Conceptually, Voronoi Map is a structure of related objects with a planar topology in which the object is represented by a polygon, and the connections between objects are edges between polygons. In this structure, delimiters can also arise – some edges can separate objects. Voronoi Map is built on the basis of a planar graph. The graph and the corresponding Voronoi Map are shown in Fig. 3.

Fig. 3. The Voronoi Map and the corresponding graph.

This way of visualization of graph structures is conceptually different from the Voronoi diagram and Voronoi TreeMaps. The Voronoi diagram is a partition of the space and does not contain related structures. Voronoi TreeMaps are extension of the TreeMaps, and they can display only hierarchical topology. Thus, the resemblance to Voronoi diagram and Voronoi TreeMaps is only visual.

A good analogy of the Voronoi Maps is a labyrinth. Each cell of the map (object – sensor) is a room of the labyrinth, some edges of cells (connections between objects – connections between sensors) are doors, and other edges-separators of cells (no relations between objects – no connection between sensors) are walls. The topology of the structure is perceived as the ability to move between rooms, while the various indicators of rooms and doors (colors, sizes, position) perceive the attributes of objects (sensors' data) and their relationships.

Voronoi Maps have the ability to display metrics with the help of cells and edges: the size, color, transparency or saturation of the cell; as well as color, thickness and transparency or saturation of the edge. In security monitoring Voronoi Maps can be used to analyze metrics and topologies. Objects of visualization can be not only sensor networks, but also any planar structure: premises; computer networks on the physical layer of the OSI model; graphs and attack trees; file systems, etc. The basis of Voronoi Maps generations is the correspondence of the Delaunay triangulation and the Voronoi diagram. The algorithm consists of four stages and is realized on the basis of a planar graph.

The first stage is to place the existing graph (Fig. 4) inside a shape of an arbitrary shape (Fig. 5). In this case, the convex hull of the resulting vertex set should not contain vertices belonging to the graph.

The second stage involves a restricted Delaunay triangulation (Fig. 6). Unlike triangulation based on vertices, restricted triangulation takes into account the existing edges of the graph and the edges of the outer figure. As a result, the resulting partitioning contains both edges added as a result of the triangulation, as are the original edges of the graph and the outer shape.

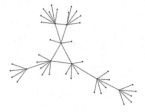 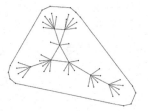 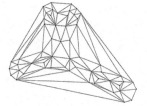

Fig. 4. Input graph.　　**Fig. 5.** Graph inside figure similar to graph's convex hull.　　**Fig. 6.** Result of restricted delaunay triangulation.

At the third stage Voronoi diagram is generated on the basis of Delaunay triangulation. This can be done in several ways. To uniquely match the vertices of the graph to the cells of the diagram, we propose to form cells of the Voronoi diagram on the basis of the weight centers of the triangles (Fig. 7): for each vertex of the original graph, a set of triangles is determined from the Delaunay triangulation in such a way that each triangle contains a given vertex.

Having determined the weight centers of these vertices, connect them clockwise or counterclockwise relative to the top of the graph. The resultant polygon is the cell of the Voronoi diagram, which uniquely corresponds to the vertex of the graph on the basis of which it was constructed. The set of polygons (Fig. 8) forms a Voronoi diagram whose cells correspond to the original graph.

At the fourth stage, it is necessary to create a Voronoi Map by designating a topology based on the original graph. Each edge, except the outer, belongs simultaneously to two cells of the diagram. Since the cells correspond to the vertices of the

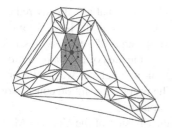

Fig. 7. Cells are formed from the centers of triangles around the graph vertexes.

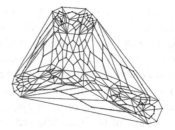

Fig. 8. Result of Voronoi Maps forming.

original graph, they can be compared. If there is no edge between two vertices on the graph, and there is an edge on the map belonging to two corresponding cells, the edge of the cells must be replaced by a separator. Also, on the dividers, all edges that belong exclusively to one cell - all external edges - should be replaced.

In order to put sensors' metrics in the area of cells, we have to implement a polymorphism algorithm that will allow us to change the cell areas to the required ones. The problem of polymorphism is a consequence of the dependence of cell areas on each other. Since the points and edges (except for the outer edges) are common for at least two cells, changing one cell leads to a change in the neighboring cells.

So, if one reduce the area of cell 1 (see Fig. 9) in the map by moving the blue dot along the arrow shown, this will increase the cell 2 and reduce cell 3. After the cell polymorphism, one can block its points in order to keep the required size, but if the bypassing order of cells is incorrect, one can get cell in which all points are blocked in case of blocking of points of previous cells. Consider the example with the map shown

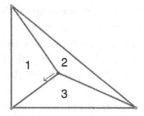

Fig. 9. Dot moving change cells area. (Color figure online)

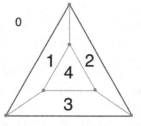

Fig. 10. Example of cell lock.

in Fig. 10 and the order of the bypass 1-2-3-4.

After polymorphism of cell 2, all map points are blocked. On the third cell, one can create new points on the edges 4/3 or 3/0 and continue their movement. However, after, cell 4 is blocked – it does not have free points, and the creation and movement of points on the edges 4/1, 4/2, 4/3 will violate the area of other cells that are already reduced to the required size. With a different order of traversal, for example 1-4-2-3, only after changing cell 2 all the points are blocked, but the change of cell 3 is possible, by creating a 3/0 point, since its movement will not affect the area of cells already formed.

Potentially, polymorphism can be implemented in a variety of ways. We propose a solution based on the movement of cell points. The proposed solution consists of two parts: cells bypassing order and sequential polymorphism.

The basis of the bypassing order algorithm is the division of the Voronoi Map into layers with finding in each layer of the Hamiltonian path. The result of the algorithm is an ordered sequence of cells.

Each layer is defined by cells that contain edges belonging to only one cell after removing the edges of the previous layer. In fact, in this way, the outer cells of the map

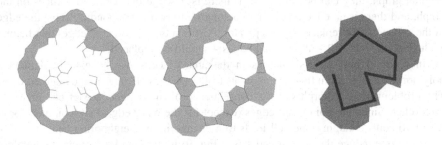

Fig. 11. First, second and third (with Hamiltonian path) layer of Voronoi Map. (Color figure online)

are defined by its hull. The selected set is a separate layer. The first layer of the map is highlighted in Fig. 11 as blue.

In the second stage, Hamiltonian paths are selected for each layer, on the basis of which a sequence of cells bypassing will be singled out. Each layer consisting of their cells can be represented in the form of a graph in which the vertices of the graph are the cells of the map, and the edges of the graph are the common edges of the cells. In the graph on the basis of the layer, it is necessary to single out the Hamiltonian path. The path found by the Hamiltonian is the desired sequence of cells, the bypass of which will not lead to locks in the process of polymorphism.

If the Hamiltonian path in the layer-graph does not exist (see Fig. 12), the layer must be broken down into several layers. This can be done by adding a graph to virtual vertices (see Figs. 13 and 14) that are linked to all vertices except virtual ones, until there is a Hamiltonian path (see Fig. 15). If we divide the resulting Hamiltonian path in places where the vertices are virtual edges (see Fig. 16), the resulting sequences will be sublayers of the layer, each of which forms a Hamiltonian path (see Fig. 17) whose sequence does not lead to locks in the process of polymorphism.

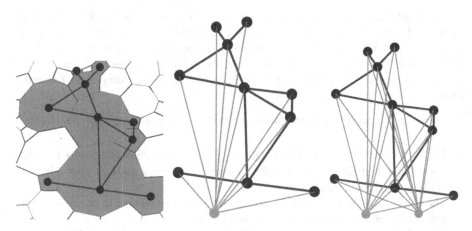

Fig. 12. Orange layer that doesn't have a Hamiltonian path. (Color figure online)

Fig. 13. Adding of virtual node for finding Hamiltonian path.

Fig. 14. Adding another virtual node for finding Hamiltonian path.

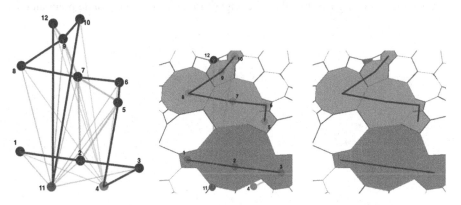

Fig. 15. Hamiltonian path exists in that configuration.

Fig. 16. Cut Hamiltonian path by virtual nodes.

Fig. 17. Forming Voronoi slices.

As a result, there is an order of layers, each of which contains the Hamiltonian path - the order of the cells. To start the bypassing follows from the last layer, according to the sequence of cells defined as a result of finding the Hamiltonian path.

After determining the bypassing order, we have to implement polymorphism of each cell. Each cell is given a numerical metric. Metrics are normalized in such a way that the largest value of the metric from the set becomes equal to the area of the smallest cell. Thus, the cells need only be reduced, bypassing their increase.

Reducing the cells occurs by moving the polygon points according to the following rules:

1. Cells are subjected to polymorphism by moving points of a polygon that forms a cell;
2. Polymorphism is complete if $LieFactor = \left|\frac{required\,area}{current\,area}\right|$ of cell is less than 1.1 – it has been experimentally established that a person perceives cells as approximately equal, even if their area differs by 10%;
3. The points move in turn clockwise or counterclockwise relative to the center of the cell, which ensures uniformity of the cell decrease;
4. The points move along the bisector of the angle formed from the movable point and the neighboring ones, so the movement of the point will not violate the planarity of the cell.
5. Points move to a distance equal to 1% of the distance when moving to which the planarity of the figure is violated provided that the angle on the left is greater and the angle on the right is less than the angle formed from the movable point and the

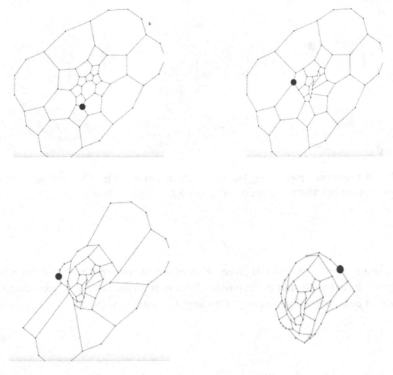

Fig. 18. Four snapshots of the polymorphism algorithm. (Color figure online)

neighboring ones; 3% if the right and left angles are greater; by 0.5% if the right and left angles are less; experimentally, it is established that such a combination is optimal for smoothing acute angles and bringing the cell to a symmetrical form;

6. After one circle of motion (one iteration over all points of the cell), the curve from the movable points is normalized in such a way that the faces of the curve have the same length; this does not allow the edges to be reduced so much, so their length can't be distinguish by user.

7. If the point is close to the violation of planarity, it stops, and the neighboring edges break up into 2, thus forming 2 additional points; this makes it possible to reduce complex nonconvex figures when a small number of points can move.

The result of the algorithm at various stages is shown in Fig. 18. The locked points are highlighted in red and blue represent point that is moving at the moment.

4 Voronoi Maps Implementation and Examples of Application

To perform experiments on visualization with the use of Voronoi Maps, we implemented a prototype using Java, which consists of three modules: generation, rendering, and polymorphism.

At the input of the generation module, a topology structure is provided in the form of a planar graph or a matrix of tree contiguities, as well as a set of metrics for visualizing links and objects. The module calculates the coordinates of polygon, edge, and delimiter points, and returns them as a structure.

The rendering module is designed to render the resulting structure. Rendering is performed using JavaScript D3.js. The polymorphism module allows one to resize the cells. The following libraries and modules are used in the prototype: GraphViz [13] – transforms the matrices of contiguities into planar structures; Triangle [14] – performs a restricted Delaunay triangulation and finding a convex hull; D3.js [15] – rendering of the Voronoi Map.

This prototype is used to monitor statement of sensor networks. Also, it can be used to visualize any security processes that are represented as planar graphs.

4.1 Example Based on Decentralized Sensor Network

In the experiment we used the data about decentralized sensor network that consist of autonomous devices [16–18]. Devices have multiple sensors; some of them are located outdoor and have remote charging systems, including solar panels for charging. The network of these devices can be shown as a graph or a Voronoi Map (Fig. 19).

Each device has criticality level that have been calculated based on the criticality of assets which are located in this area. Therefore, the loss of the sensor will mean the loss of monitoring of these assets. Since the devices are autonomous, they are discharging, but they can be charged using solar panels.

Sensor network in form of Voronoi Map with metrics is shown in Fig. 20.

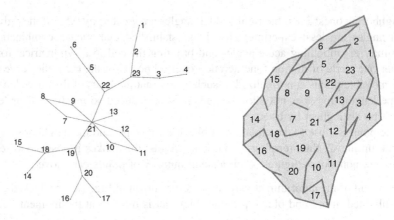

Fig. 19. Sensor network in form of graph (in the left) and in form of Voronoi Map (in the right).

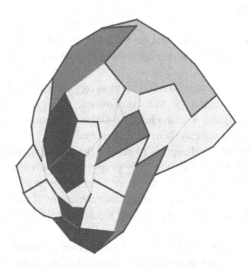

Fig. 20. Sensor network in form of Voronoi Map with metrics. (Color figure online)

Cell size shows the criticality of sensor. Grey color shows that in the last 24 h sensor gets more energy than used up. Blue color shows that in the last 24 h sensor used up more energy than get, but they still have enough power. Red color shows that more than in the last 24 h sensor used up more energy than get, and now they don't have enough power and will disconnect soon. Opacity shows speed of charging or discharging.

Table 1. Capabilities of Voronoi Maps and other graphical models

	Graphs	TreeMaps (TM), Voronoi TM	Matrices	Voronoi Maps
Topology support	Any topology	Trees only (multi-level centralized networks)	Any topology	Planar only (including reduces to planar)
Objects Visualization	All objects	Leafs only	Not support	All objects
Links Visualization	All links	Not support	All links	All links
Objects Metrics	Size, color, opacity	Size (+), color (+), opacity	Not support	Size (+), color (+), opacity
Links Metrics	Size, color, opacity	Not support	Color (+), opacity	Size, color, opacity
Applying	Topology analysis	Sensors' metrics analysis, Analysis of tree structures	Connections Analysis	Sensors' metrics analysis, Analysis of planar structures
Complexity of implementation	Low	Medium	Low	High

5   Discussion

To assess the possibilities of using Voronoi Maps for visualization of sensor networks, we compare the capabilities of Voronoi Maps and the most used models of visualization of linked data: Graphs, TreeMaps/Voronoi TreeMaps (have the same indicators), Matrices. The results of the comparison are presented in Table 1.

The table contains seven fields for comparison. Topology support (1) shows which sensor network's topology can visualize the model. Visualization of objects (2) and links (3) shows what types of objects and relationships the model can visualize. In the rows of "object metrics" (4) and "link metrics" (5), graphical ways of visualizing metrics of sensor by models are listed. In the same fields, the " + " sign indicates the most effective ways to visualize metrics. Application (6) – areas of application in which the model most effectively manifests itself. The complexity of the implementation (7) shows the complexity of the algorithms used in constructing the model. Also, the worst indicators in the table field are highlighted in red, and the best in blue. The remaining indicators, as well as indicators whose results are not obvious, are highlighted in yellow.

On the basis of Table 1, it can be concluded that Voronoi Maps can be an alternative when visualizing sensor networks with a planar topology. This is due to the fact that they effectively display metrics due to the size and color of the elements. Visualization of metrics is necessary for making decisions in many information security processes. If previously the most appropriate model for visualizing metrics were TreeMaps, Voronoi Maps are an alternative that can visualize not only hierarchical structures. At the same time, if TreeMaps are able to visualize only the metrics of leaves that can be used in multilevel centralized sensor networks, Voronoi Maps can visualize the parent elements of the tree, thereby providing more analysis capabilities and expanding application possibilities including capability of visualization of centralized and decentralized planar sensor networks.

From the obvious drawbacks, one can single out the possibility of constructing the Voronoi Map only for sensor networks with a planar topology, while graphs and matrices do not have such limitations. Another drawback is the complexity of the construction and the even greater complexity of the polymorphism of Voronoi cells in comparison with graphs, TreeMaps and matrices. It is important to node, that Voronoi Maps can be used to visualize any structures and processes that can be represented in the form of a planar graph. Thus, the potential of using Voronoi Maps goes far beyond information security.

6   Conclusion

This paper describes a new way to visualize sensors network which can be represented as a planar graph. Visualization in the form of Voronoi Maps provides effective visualization of metrics due to the use of screen space and allows one to visualize data with a planar non-hierarchical and hierarchical structure for centralized and reduced to planar decentralized sensor networks. An overview was given of the existing methods to visualize sensors networks, such as graphs, TreeMaps, Voronoi diagrams and Voronoi TreeMaps. The Voronoi Map concept is presented, explaining the way of its interpretation. The technique for constructing the Voronoi Map from a planar graph in the form of algorithms is given. The technique of resizing the cells of the Voronoi Map in the form of algorithms is presented. Example of visualization of sensor network in form of the Voronoi Map is given. The polymorphism algorithm presented in this paper is only one of the potential ways of converting cells to the required size.

Future work will be devoted to the possibility of using approaches based on other principles for polymorphism. For example, the size of the cells of the Voronoi Map depends on the graph vertices positions. It is necessary to consider the approach to setting the configuration parameters of power drawing (vertex charge, strength and tensile strength of the ribs) or other "physical" structure to bring the size of the cells to a given size. Also, the potential has an approach to setting cell sizes by means of an S-decomposition of the Voronoi Map.

Acknowledgements. This work was partially supported by grants of RFBR (projects No. 16-29-09482, 18-07-01488), by the budget (the project No. AAAA-A16-116033110102-5), and by Government of Russian Federation (Grant 08-08).

References

1. Granadillo, G.G., Garcia-Alfaro, J., Debar, H.: Using a 3D geometrical model to improve accuracy in the evaluation and selection of countermeasures against complex cyber attacks. In: Thuraisingham, B., Wang, X., Yegneswaran, V. (eds.) SecureComm 2015. LNICST, vol. 164, pp. 538–555. Springer, Cham (2015). https://doi.org/10.1007/978-3-319-28865-9_29

2. Kolomeec, M., et al.: Choosing models for security metrics visualization. In: Rak, J., Bay, J., Kotenko, I., Popyack, L., Skormin, V., Szczypiorski, K. (eds.) MMM-ACNS 2017. LNCS, vol. 10446, pp. 75–87. Springer, Cham (2017). https://doi.org/10.1007/978-3-319-65127-9_7
3. Marty, R.: Applied Security Visualization. Addison-Wesley, Upper Saddle River (2009)
4. Kolomeec, M., Chechulin, A., Pronoza, A., Kotenko, I.: Technique of data visualization: example of network topology display for security monitoring. J. Wirel. Mobile Netw. Ubiquit. Comput. Dependable Appl. (JoWUA) 7(1), 58–78 (2016)
5. Chechulin, A., Kotenko, I.: Attack tree-based approach for real-time security event processing. Autom. Control Comput. Sci. 49, 701–704 (2015)
6. Kotenko, I., Doynikova, E.: Selection of countermeasures against network attacks based on dynamical calculation of security metrics. J. Defense Model. Simul. Appl. Methodol. Technol. 15, 181–204 (2017)
7. McGuffin, M.: Simple algorithms for network visualization: a tutorial. Tsinghua Sci. Technol. 17, 383–398 (2012)
8. Harrison, L., Spahn, R., Iannacone, M., Downing, E., Goodall, J.: NV: Nessus vulnerability visualization for the web. In: Proceedings of the Ninth International Symposium on Visualization for Cyber Security - VizSec 2012 (2012)
9. Balzer, M., Deussen, O., Lewerentz, C.: Voronoi treemaps for the visualization of software metrics. In: Proceedings of the 2005 ACM symposium on Software visualization - SoftVis 2005 (2005)
10. Aziz, N., Mohemmed, A., Alias, M.: A wireless sensor network coverage optimization algorithm based on particle swarm optimization and Voronoi diagram. In: 2009 International Conference on Networking, Sensing and Control (2009)
11. Signaling system 7 (SS7) security report. https://www.ptsecurity.com/upload/iblock/083/08391102d2bd30c5fe234145877ebcc0.pdf
12. Roberts, J.: Guest editor's introduction: special issue on coordinated and multiple views in exploratory visualization. Inf. Vis. 2, 199–200 (2003)
13. GraphViz Library. http://www.graphviz.org
14. Triangle Library. https://www.cs.cmu.edu/~quake/triangle.html
15. D3.js Library. https://d3js.org
16. Desnitsky, V., Levshun, D., Chechulin, A., Kotenko, I.: Design technique for secure embedded devices: application for creation of integrated cyber-physical security system. J. Wirel. Mobile Netw. Ubiquit. Comput. Dependable Appl. (JoWUA) 7(2), 60–80 (2016)
17. Aram, S., Shirvani, R.A., Pasero, E.G., Chouikha, M.F.: Implantable medical devices; networking security survey. J. Internet Serv. Inf. Secur. (JISIS) 6(3), 40–60 (2016)
18. Bordel, B., Alcarria, R., Manso, M.A., Jara, A.: Building enhanced environmental traceability solutions: from thing-to-thing communications to generalized cyber-physical systems. J. Internet Serv. Inf. Secur. (JISIS). 7(3), 17–33 (2017)

Secure Data and Services Management in Distributed Structures and in the Cloud with Application of Blockchain Technologies

Marek R. Ogiela[1(✉)] and Lidia Ogiela[2]

[1] Cryptography and Cognitive Informatics Research Group, AGH University of Science and Technology, 30 Mickiewicza Avenue, 30-059 Kraków, Poland
mogiela@agh.edu.pl
[2] Pedagogical University of Cracow, Podchorążych 2 Street, 30-084 Kraków, Poland
lidia.ogiela@gmail.com

Abstract. In this paper will be presented new ideas of application of security procedures for data and services management in distributed computer infrastructures, and in Cloud Computing. Services management in Cloud Computing will be connected with application of secure cognitive information systems supporting management activities and securing data using blockchain technologies and distributed ledger. Application of distributed ledger enables the development of decentralized management protocols, which allow verification of all performed operations by all authorized parties. Such protocols give the opportunity to create secure and efficient data sharing protocols in structures, where all authorized entities are equal and can independently verify the type of operations, and instances that process such data.

Keywords: Distributed ledger · Blockchain technology · Data sharing
Information management

1 Introduction

One of the most important topics in security applications is possibilities of using distributed ledger and blockchain technologies for secure digital data distribution and management [1, 2]. Distributed ledger with blockchain solutions were proposed in late 70s as a type of protocols for verification of operations performed on the data. Starting from 2008, the blockchain technology has met with a significant increase in interest, due to the occurrence of the cryptocurrencies like bitcoin. It allows verification of all operations carried out under a specific protocol, and can be also used for digital data management tasks [3].

The current data management systems are oriented on using classic techniques for collecting, transmitting or managing data (e.g. databases, queries, semantic relations) [4, 5]. Such solutions are not fully sufficient, because they do not take into consideration complicated data structures, or user rights that can be defined in extended management structures (e.g. hierarchical structures) [6, 7]. For such structures we will try to develop new management protocols that will allow completely decentralized data

I. You et al. (Eds.): MobiSec 2017, CCIS 971, pp. 110–119, 2019.
https://doi.org/10.1007/978-981-13-3732-1_8

management tasks, performed by authorized instances on different levels in management structures.

One of the most important examples of application of distributed ledgers in security protocols, can be connected with security procedures for Fog-Cloud infrastructure [8]. Such solutions are very promising in development of modern security protocols dedicated for different distributed services and data management tasks. Many resources of strategic data or core information may be stored in Cloud infrastructures with possible access by authorized users working in the independent way, at different levels or end nodes of this big infrastructure [9]. For such information distribution protocol we can use linguistic and biometric secret division procedures [10] handled by trusted instances at Fog level. This allows division of any resources with cognitive cryptography approaches [11–13] and set the reconstruction abilities for particular users, with the same level of security grants. Divided information may be distributed among different groups of users, depending on different distribution keys. In this procedure, the globally encrypted data can be decrypted when a group of trusted persons compiles theirs secret parts into one original information [14].

2   Data Management with Distributed Ledger

Presently we haven't universal data management systems based on blockchain technologies, which enables the implementation of various information management tasks in independent manner, and supervise of all operations carried out by all participating in management processes [15]. It is especially important for various management structures, which can be observed in Fog and Cloud computing and also in management sciences [5].

In general computer-based management techniques based on blockchain technologies can be dedicated to management activities on various independent levels, i.e. they will be able to process data depending on the authority of units at a given level, and manage data independently of different locations. Implementation of blockchain-based management protocols is aimed mainly at determining the possibilities of efficient application of blockchain technology to create protocols for digital data management, as well as creation of algorithms aimed at fully independent control and verifiability of operations by all parties authorized to carry them out.

Creation of management protocols with such requirements should provide efficient and sharing protocols for secure data management, which can be performed in the big or distributed data structures. Application of distributed ledgers also should enable the new security features in such classes of management procedures, and increase security levels.

Protocols, which can use blockchain technologies and distributed ledgers, will be goaled at creating fully decentralized data management protocols in layered and hierarchical structures.

Below will be presented two different protocols dedicated for data sharing based on distributed ledgers, use for verification and secret data status monitoring.

2.1 Protocol for Layered Structures

In layered structures we can find several different, and independent layers, which haven't connections and cannot transfer data between them. In such structures it is possible to distribute secret information in independent manner for different layers. It is also possible to share the same secret information divided in different manners for particular level.

We can consider such special case, in which we'll try to distribute the same data in different manners depending on the layer. For such distribution and status verification a distributed ledger can be used. The general idea of such protocol is presented in Fig. 1.

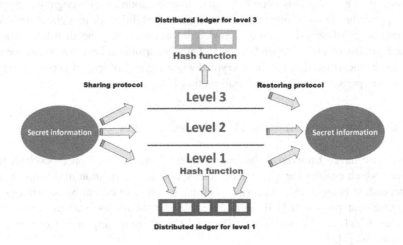

Fig. 1. Data distribution in layered structure using distributed ledger.

In plain layered structures information may be divided independently for any number of participants at particular layers. On each layer the number of trusted persons can be different, so the same secret data can be divided using different threshold procedures or input parameters.

Finally on each layer, it is possible to restore of original data after collecting of required number of secret parts. Application of distributed ledger in such distribution protocol requires that for each layer and each participant during sharing procedure should be evaluated a hash value for obtained secret part. When the secret remain divided at particular level, each participants can compare his hash value with other hashes stored at the same level. If the values are different that proves that secret has not been restored at this level, even by other qualified group of trusted persons. In case of secret reconstruction at particular level, for all participants can be evaluated new hash value represents original restored data and place in distributed ledger. In such situation each person can determine that secret was restored even if it was done without his participation. Finally in layered structures, distributed ledger allow to monitor all activities performed at particular level. In case of any information changes or data revealing, distributed ledger reflect all activities immediately, and shows to all other participants that secret was restored.

2.2 Distributed Ledger in Hierarchical Structures

The second protocol is oriented on management in hierarchical structures. In hierarchical structures we can find several layers, with many connections between layers. Layers are not fully independent, and can transfer information between adjacent levels. In such structures on the top levels are placed instances or participants with stronger privileges in accessing for secret data. Management task in such structures can be connected with sharing the same data in various manners depending on the layers, and considering number of trusted persons on particular level. In Fig. 2 is presented management pyramid, which reflects hierarchical structure containing several layers.

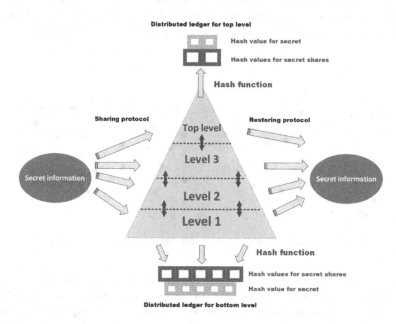

Fig. 2. Data distribution in hierarchical structure using double distributed ledger.

Application of distributed ledger in hierarchical structures are slightly more different that in layered ones. Here we should define two ledgers. One for monitoring global activities in management pyramid, and second for local activities at different levels. Local ledgers works in the same way as in layered structures, and change hash values when the secret is restored. In such situation any participants can check restoring activities and gain confirmation of data revealing at particular level.

Global ledger should monitor secret revealing task for precedent and subordinate layers, showing such activities for layer in the middle level. To guarantee such possibilities we need to use the second hash value in ledger structures, which will be a kind of flag, showing reconstruction activities on the higher or lower structure. When the information is not restored, both legers will contain the same values. But when at particular level the secret is revealed, on the ledgers connected with higher and lower levels, are also placed hash values representing the original data.

3 Universal Protocol for Data Management

In previous section have been presented dedicated protocols oriented for secure data distribution in layered and hierarchical structures. However in real application beside such type of structures we can also consider situation in which doesn't exist any constraints for information fusion and possible connections between layers. In most general situation we can also define a decentralized structures without any layers and dependencies, in which each participant may have unlimited connections for data transmissions with any other instances. Below will be presented the generalized protocol for secure data sharing and distribution especially for such general structures (Fig. 3).

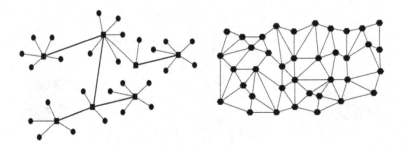

Fig. 3. Examples of decentralized structures with irregular topology.

Because in such structures we cannot determine any layers, this means that we don't need to define ledgers for each layer. In these structures we can define twin ledger similar to hierarchical structures, but here one of them will be responsible to tracing operations, which can be performed by neighbors of particular node (instance), and the second one will be responsible for tracing (marking) operation performed by other nodes (not connected with considering one).

In decentralized structures we can share an important information in fuzzy mode. This means that particular secret can be divided using different procedures or different parameters for the same algorithms, but distribution of obtained secret parts can be performed with different keys (strategy) considering local connections and accessing privileges. This means that particular node may possess different parts of the same secret, which were generated by different procedures. Secret reconstruction using such parts will be possible considering different sets of nodes (instances) which also possess other shares important for secret reconstruction.

In such topology we can define twin distributed ledgers which will be connected with each node in such manner that each instance should have two ledger tables. One will be connected with operations which may occurs within all nodes connected with considering one (local operations with neighbors). Divided secret can be restored only by connected group of peers, which may be located in different positions of the whole communication grid. With such group of connected nodes the ledger should reflect only possible secret reconstructions, which may be done by any trusted subgroup of participants. After reconstruction of information all ledgers (local parts) connected with particular node will be filled with hash value of restored information, what allow to show that information was restored for any other nodes connected with the considering one.

Because information can be distributed over the whole connection network. From particular node of view it can be also reconstructed by instanced not connected with this one, so in such cases it is necessary to use the ledger table associated with particular node, which should reflect such operation by changing its content to secret hash value.

Finally twin ledgers connected with particular node, allow to monitor secret reconstruction procedures, which can be performed by direct neighbors of particular node, as well as by peers not connected directly, but also available in the network infrastructures.

In Fig. 4 is presented examples infrastructures with twin ledgers responsible for secret sharing and data reconstruction.

In Fig. 4 is presented general situation with irregular connections in small grid. The central node is considered as a processing peer for which ledgers can be created. As mentioned before any secret data can be distributed in local area i.e. all direct neighbors having connections with processing node. And for such local structure may be used one table of ledgers, which will contain hash values for generated secret parts. In case of secret revealing by any subset of nodes all ledger parts should be changed for hash value generated for the whole secret data. This will mark for all other connected nodes (instances) that restoration has been done. This procedure works with or without participation of central considered instance.

In Fig. 4 is also marked a small group of nodes not directly connected with the central one. Secret data may be also distributed between such nodes, and it is necessary to introduce also the second ledger layer, which allow to reflect any operation in global manner. Finally from central node point of view this second layer shows any activities which can be done a far away from central node, and show not only the reconstruction activities, but also the set of trusted instances which participated in such reconstruction procedure.

4   Knowledge-Based Management Protocols

Presented in previous sections protocols, allow to implement management task based only hash values stored in distributed ledgers. Such solutions are universal and open for connecting with other security protocols like cognitive cryptography procedures [12, 13].

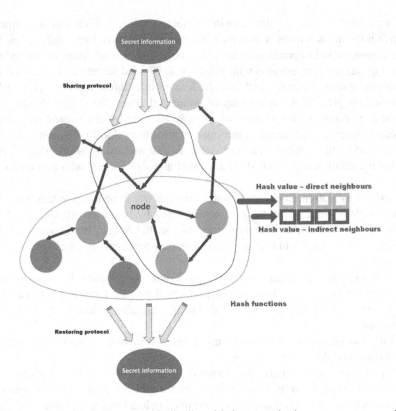

Fig. 4. Decentralized structure with distributed ledgers monitoring secret reconstruction.

In this section will be described an extension of such protocols with authentication stage, which is based on using specific, expert knowledge possessed by participants [16–18]. Verification procedure using such knowledge-based protocols can be performed in any irregular distributed computer infrastructures with different accessing levels. In such knowledge-based verification procedures it is possible to gain access to data or computer systems, after proper selection of required information or answers for particular questions. Inappropriate selection or answers during verification can prevent the access to data or requested services. In this solution, it is necessary to correctly select the semantic combination of answers, which fulfil particular requirements or have a specific meaning. Such protocols during verification procedure, may require specific knowledge from different areas. It may be connected with medicine, engineering, history, technology, art, earth sciences, sport, music, cinema etc. In Fig. 5 is presented an example of such solution, based on mineral structures.

The meaning of presented visual codes can be different when using other visual content, but for presented example the proper answer for authenticating users can be connected with selection of images which show particular mineral, or mineral having particular color, chemical formula, crystal system, or even occurrence in particular

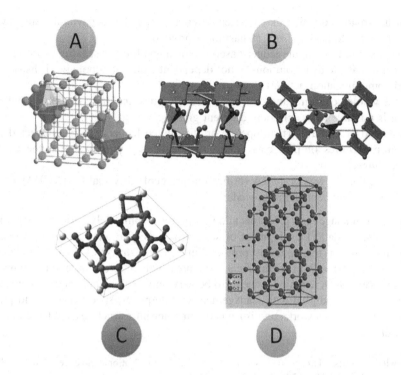

Fig. 5. Example of expert knowledge authentication which required chemical or geological knowledge. Presented minerals: A - halite, B - chalcantite, C - malachite, D - calcite

place on Earth. The proper answer in such cases can be find only by trusted people having experiences or expert knowledge from this particular area [19].

Such semantic codes can be added to management protocols which operate on distributed ledgers, and all operation reflected in such blockchain structure can be dependent on user activities, connected with authentication unit using described semantic or knowledge-based protocols [20–23].

5 Conclusions

Application of distributed ledgers in management systems are very efficient and universal, especially in solutions oriented for particular trusted users or group of authorized persons. These procedures have following features:

- Protocols are secure from cryptographic point of view, due to the application of cryptographic algorithms for secret sharing and application of blockchain technologies.
- Protocols are efficient, and complexity of presented algorithms remain at the level as the complexity of division procedures.

- For information division may be used different personal or behavioral features what allow to create personalized management protocol.
- It is possible to combine ledger-based protocols with other security procedures.
- General management solutions is not dependent from the topology of distribution and communication networks.
- In the whole communication infrastructure all nodes may have the same privileges or it is possible to assign them different grants.
- Described procedures which operate on distributed ledgers can be connected with other procedures or protocols dedicated for security purposes or authentication procedures.
- In particular knowledge-based verification protocols or visual CAPTCHAs can be included for authentication procedures.

Proposed management protocols allow to perform completely verifiable operations on the collected data. Development of such protocols give the opportunity to create secure information management protocol in layered structures (where authorized entities are equal) and in hierarchical structures with different accessing grants for different levels. Such techniques seems to be very universal in applications, and can be applied in areas of digital data management in enterprises, state agencies and public administration sectors works on distributed computer infrastructures and Cloud or Fog Computing.

Acknowledgements. This work has been supported by the National Science Centre, Poland, under project number DEC-2016/23/B/HS4/00616.

References

1. Larios-Hernández, G.J.: Blockchain entrepreneurship opportunity in the practices of the unbanked. Bus. Horiz. **60**, 865–874 (2017)
2. Li, J., Wu, J., Chen, L.: Block-secure: blockchain based scheme for secure P2P cloud storage. Inf. Sci. **465**, 219–231 (2018)
3. Jallow, A.K., Demian, P., Anumba, Ch.J., Baldwin, A.N.: An enterprise architecture framework for electronic requirements information management. Int. J. Inf. Manag. **37**, 455–472 (2017)
4. Ogiela, L.: Cognitive information systems in management sciences. Elsevier, Academic Press (2017)
5. Ogiela, L., Ogiela, M.R. Management Information Systems. LNEE, vol. 331, pp. 449–456 (2015)
6. Ogiela, M.R., Ogiela, U.: Grammar encoding in DNA-like secret sharing infrastructure. In: Kim, T.-h., Adeli, H. (eds.) ACN/AST/ISA/UCMA -2010. LNCS, vol. 6059, pp. 175–182. Springer, Heidelberg (2010). https://doi.org/10.1007/978-3-642-13577-4_15
7. Ogiela, M.R., Ogiela, U.: Secure information management in hierarchical structures. In: Kim, T.-h., Adeli, H., Robles, R.J., Balitanas, M. (eds.) AST 2011. CCIS, vol. 195, pp. 31–35. Springer, Heidelberg (2011). https://doi.org/10.1007/978-3-642-24267-0_5
8. Kshetri, N.: Blockchain's roles in strengthening cybersecurity and protecting privacy. Telecommun. Policy **41**(10), 1027–1038 (2017)

9. Gregg, M., Schneider, B.: Security Practitioner and Cryptography Handbook and Study Guide Set. Wiley, Hoboken (2014)
10. Ogiela, L., Ogiela, M.R.: Data mining and semantic inference in cognitive systems. In: Xhafa, F., Barolli, L., Palmieri, F., et al. (eds.) 2014 International Conference on Intelligent Networking and Collaborative Systems (IEEE INCoS 2014), Italy, pp. 257–261 (2014)
11. Ogiela, L.: Towards cognitive economy. Soft. Comput. **18**, 1675–1683 (2014)
12. Ogiela, M.R., Ogiela, L.: On using cognitive models in cryptography. In: IEEE AINA 2016 - The IEEE 30th International Conference on Advanced Information Networking and Applications, Crans-Montana, Switzerland, pp. 1055–1058 (2016). https://doi.org/10.1109/aina.2016.159
13. Ogiela, M.R., Ogiela, L.: Cognitive keys in personalized cryptography. In: IEEE AINA 2017 - The 31st IEEE International Conference on Advanced Information Networking and Applications, Taipei, Taiwan, pp. 1050–1054 (2017). https://doi.org/10.1109/aina.2017.164
14. Hahn, Ch., Hur, J.: Efficient and privacy-preserving biometric identification in cloud. ICT Express **2**, 135–139 (2016)
15. Reyna, A., Martín, C., Chen, J., Soler, E., Díaz, M.: On blockchain and its integration with IoT. Challenges and opportunities. Futur. Gener. Comput. Syst. **88**, 173–190 (2018)
16. Alsuhibany, S.: Evaluating the usability of optimizing text-based CAPTCHA generation. Int. J. Adv. Comput. Sci. Appl. **7**(8), 164–169 (2016)
17. Bursztein, E., Bethard, S., Fabry, C., Mitchell, J., Jurafsky, D.: How good are humans at solving CAPTCHAs? A large scale evaluation. In: Proceedings - IEEE Symposium on Security and Privacy, pp. 399–413 (2010)
18. Krzyworzeka, N., Ogiela, L.: Visual CAPTCHA for data understanding and cognitive management. In: Barolli, L., Xhafa, F., Conesa, J. (eds.) BWCCA 2017. LNDECT, vol. 12, pp. 249–255. Springer, Cham (2018). https://doi.org/10.1007/978-3-319-69811-3_22
19. Ogiela, L.: Cognitive computational intelligence in medical pattern semantic understanding. In: Guo, M.Z., Zhao, L., Wang, L.P. (eds.) ICNC 2008: Fourth International Conference on Natural Computation, vol. 6, Proceedings, Jian, Peoples R China, 18–20 October, pp. 245–247 (2008)
20. Ogiela, L., Ogiela, M.R.: Insider threats and cryptographic techniques in secure information management. IEEE Syst. J. **11**, 405–414 (2017)
21. Osadchy, M., Hernandez-Castro, J., Gibson, S., Dunkelman, O., Perez-Cabo, D.: No bot expects the DeepCAPTCHA! Introducing immutable adversarial examples, with applications to CAPTCHA generation. IEEE Trans. Inf. Forensics Secur. **12**(11), 2640–2653 (2017)
22. Carniani, E., Costantino, G., Marino, F., Martinelli, F., Mori, P.: Enhancing video surveillance with usage control and privacy-preserving solutions. J. Wirel. Mob. Netw. Ubiquitous Comput. Dependable Appl. **7**(4), 20–40 (2016)
23. Kim, J.S., Pan, S.B.: A study on EMG-based biometrics. J. Internet Serv. Inf. Secur. (JISIS) **7**(2), 19–31 (2017)

Using iBeacon Technology with Nearest Neighbor Algorithm to Area Positioning Systems

Chia-Hsin Cheng[(⊠)] and Chia-Yao Hu

Department of Electrical Engineering,
National Formosa University, Huwei, Taiwan
chcheng@nfu.edu.tw

Abstract. With the advances in information and communication technologies, indoor Location Based Service (LBS) has been a hot topic of research. In a wireless positioning system, signals would be distorted and attenuated by the environment during the signal transmission. In the case, the distorted signals would degrade positioning accuracy. In order to reduce positioning errors due to bad signals, this paper uses a pattern matching approach to build environmental model. This method can reduce positioning error due to the unstable signals. We used iBeacon to build positioning environment in Wireless Sensor Networks. The K Nearest Neighbor (KNN) algorithm is used to compare the accuracy of area positioning with various environments.

Keywords: iBeacon · Positioning system · Pattern matching
Wireless sensor networks

1 Introduction

In recent years, there have been rapid developments in the communication technology. A significant number of studies have been done in positioning moving targets with sensor wireless sensor networks (WANs). Positioning could have two different types, one is outdoor positioning system and the other is indoor positioning system. The outdoor positioning system is based on Global Positioning System (GPS), which combined the geographic information and applied various field such as traffic navigation, military warfare, logistics systems. However, GPS is not suitable for indoor positioning due to buildings and walls that serve as obstacle to the satellite's signals leading to poor communication quality [1, 2]. The requisition accuracy of indoor positioning is higher than that of outdoor positioning. It needs combine inside building of geographic information. Indoor positioning system could have two different types, one is area positioning and the other is accuracy coordinated positioning. Area positioning is a plane map which is divided into a number of small areas, the region does not specify the scope and shape. Positioning system would anticipate where the target location, when the target in the small area. Accuracy coordinated positioning is different form area positioning. This method is precise to know where the coordinate of target location.

I. You et al. (Eds.): MobiSec 2017, CCIS 971, pp. 120–130, 2019.
https://doi.org/10.1007/978-981-13-3732-1_9

Most indoor positioning system uses short distance wireless communication technology such as Wi-Fi, Bluetooth and ZigBee. In recent years, Wi-Fi devices become more and more common such as smart phone, laptop and tablet. It is a good way to use the wireless network for positioning. The advantage of Wi-Fi is long distance propagation and fast transmission rate; however, it has a lot of cost for power consumption. Wi-Fi cannot achieve the basic requirement of wireless sensor networks. The power consumption and cost of Bluetooth is lower than that of Wi-Fi and ZigBee. The iBeacon of Bluetooth is a protocol developed by Apple and introduced at the Apple Worldwide Developers Conference in 2013 [3].

The iBeacon device be applied to an indoor positioning system based on Bluetooth Low Energy (BLE) technology [4]. This wireless technology has become a recent alternative for Wi-Fi, especially in Internet of Things (IoT) devices and apps. It can help smartphones determine their approximate location or context. Moreover, its low power consumption, low cost and protocol are more suitable for use as a home care positioning system than other technologies [5]. In indoor positioning, wireless signal of Received Signal Strength Indicator (RSSI) would be influenced by different environments. RSSI would have unstable signals in the same distance in different environments. This will increase the difficulty of positioning. Therefore, this paper uses the pattern matching to establish the signal characteristics of positioning environmental samples. This method would compare the RSSI values which collect by target and the training points in the sample database rather than estimate distance between the target and the reference points. Since each position would receive the various RSSI values of reference points, it could reduce positioning error from unstable RSSI [6, 7]. The positioning feature of the environment allows the positioning algorithm to establish the positioning model for the environment. Two common positioning algorithms are Nearest Neighbor in Signal Strength (NNSS) and Probability-based algorithms, which are low complex, no input hypothesis and not sensitive to abnormal values. The positioning is good in the ideal positioning environment; however, but the positioning is bad in the reality positioning environment.

In recent years, many investigators have discussed the machine learning. K-Nearest Neighbor (KNN) is a non-parametric and lazy learning algorithm used for classification and regression [8]. Its purpose is to use a database in which the data points are separated into several classes to predict the classification of a new sample point. Today, KNN is a versatile algorithm and is used in a huge number of fields. There are some methods for wireless LAN based indoor positioning using RSSI with the deterministic K Nearest Neighbors (KNN) that considers Euclidean distance for the estimation of user location [9, 10]. This paper is an extended version of a paper presented at proceedings of the MobiSec 2017 [11]. In this paper, we propose the indoor positioning system by Bluetooth Finger print technique based on KNN algorithm. Therefore, this paper would discuss the environmental parameters of the KNN and compare with the various environments in area positioning accuracy.

2 Background

2.1 Wireless Sensor Networks

In recent years, wireless communication, microcontroller unit and battery technology advance to make Wireless Sensor Networks technology growth. WSN have some features such as low cost, small size, low power, easy to build the network, which apply in different filed. WSNs are made up of many sensor nodes. Sensor could detect the physical of the environment such as gas, temperature, luminosity. Nodes could utilize wireless communication to communicate one another in communication range. Sensor would return the data which sensor is collected data to the sink or base station [12, 13].

2.2 Bluetooth iBeacon Technology

Bluetooth Low Energy (BLE) signals from battery driven beacons are at the core of the indoor location technology. It's one of the latest technologies that has emerged and become an industry standard available on most devices today. It uses so called BLE beacons (or iBeacons) that are inexpensive, small, have a long battery life and do not require an external energy source. The device detects the signal from the beacon and can calculate roughly the distance to the beacon and hence estimate the location. At the most simple form, an iBeacon is a Bluetooth low energy device emitting advertisement following a strict format, that being an Apple defined iBeacon prefix, followed by a variable UUID, and a major, minor pair [14]. Figure 1 shows the iBeacon data format.

iBeacon prefix (9 bytes)	Proximity UUID (16 bytes)	Major (2 bytes)	Minor (2 bytes)	TX power (1 byte)

Fig. 1. iBeacon data format

2.3 Pattern Matching

Pattern matching process has two parts including offline training phase and online matching phase. For pattern matching methods of the localization, the device-carrying individual needs to build a radio map at every possible location before the localization of the real-time operation, a method known as RSSI profiling. The time of map building, when the links between all anchor nodes and the radio device in a network are recorded, is referred to as the offline training phase. The new RSSI obtained from the measurements from all of the links is then compared against the radio map, so as to select the RSSI location with the closest matching as the localization result, a process referred to as the online matching phase.

2.4 Nearest Neighbor Algorithm

Nearest Neighbor in Signal Strength (NNSS) uses the online RSSI to search for the closest match stored in the radio map during the offline phase. According to the nearest data classify the unknown data. NNSS utilizes Euclidean Distance to calculate the data similarity (1).

$$\|X - Y\| = \sqrt{(x_1 - y_1)^2 + (x_2 - y_2)^2 + \cdots + (x_n - y_n)^2} \tag{1}$$

In (1), $X = x_1, x_2, \ldots, x_n$ and $Y = y_1, y_2, \ldots, y_n$ are represented two coordinate points in n-dimension space. The smaller the distance, the higher the similarity of the data. Show in Fig. 2. The classified information may be attributable to Class A.

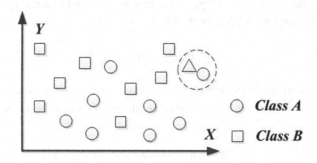

Fig. 2. Nearest Neighbor algorithm classification

3 K-Nearest Neighbor Positioning Algorithm

In this paper, indoor positioning system based on pattern matching to locate the target. The flow graph shows in Fig. 3. First, total n reference points are deployed on the map and we select the coordinates of the several training positions. The RSSI of the positioning reference points were collected at each training point and stored in the sample database. After the training phase, the sample database would have a lot of records with $(x, y)_{1,2,\ldots,m,\ldots M}\big|_{(s_1, s_2, \ldots, s_N)}$, where x and y are the training position coordinates and s_n is the RSSI where the nth reference point is received at this training position, M is the number of training data for the training position. According to the data in the positioning database to establish positioning model. When system received the target of signal, target would be calculated in the positioning model and then estimated the target position. But even though using the same map sample, different positioning model would have different area positioning accuracy. Therefore. The model would be used to compare the KNN with various environments for area positioning accuracy.

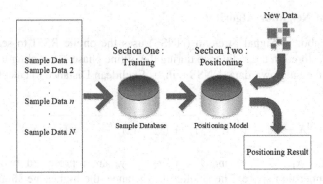

Fig. 3. Flow of pattern matching.

According the pattern matching, all training points would be set up characteristic vector in the positioning model, as shown in (2).

$$C_i = \left(c_1^i, c_2^i, \ldots, c_j^i, \ldots c_N^i\right) \tag{2}$$

where c_j^i represents the RSSI where the reference point n is received at the training point i. In the same time, the target's characteristic vector would be set up as shown in (3).

$$S = (s_1, s_2, \ldots, s_n, \ldots, s_N) \tag{3}$$

where s_n represents the target's RSSI where received at nth positioning reference point. Finally calculate the Euclidean Distance between characteristic vector of target and each training point, as shown in (4).

$$E_i = \|S, C_i\| = \sqrt{\sum_{j=1}^{N} \left(s_j - c_j^i\right)^2} \tag{4}$$

According to Euclidean Distance would find training point which is the nearest target. In KNN, K is a constant. If K is 4, it represents to find 4 the nearest training points to estimate the target positioning and then utilized average coordinate to find the target where is in the area, as shown in (5).

$$(x, y) = \frac{1}{K} \sum_{n=1}^{K} (x_n, y_n) \tag{5}$$

where the (x, y) is the estimation position of mobile node, the (x_n, y_n) is the coordinate of this reference node and the (x, y) is the estimation position of mobile node.

For Weighted KNN (WKNN), the BLE BEACON system will choose K-nearest reference nodes to calculate the unknown position of the mobile node by

$$(x, y) = \sum_{n}^{K} w_n(x_n, y_n) \tag{6}$$

The weight that depends on the k-nearest reference nodes' Euclidean distance of the mobile node is defined as:

$$w_n = 1/E_n / \sum_{n=1}^{K} \frac{1}{E_n} \tag{7}$$

4 System Architecture

In this paper, the system architecture is shown in Fig. 4. System architecture could be mainly divided into two parts. The first part is PC side and the second part is user side. The main function of the PC side to receive each reference node's RSSI value information via Bluetooth to 4.0 from the user node. Then, we would use the algorithms to calculate the location information and display the user's location information by Visual C# computer man-machine interface. We can store the user's room location, date and time, etc. into the back-end MySQL database. At the same time, we can see the user location from back-end MySQL database in human-machine interface. The main function of the user side has an iBeacon receiver on the user and it has the capability to receive the RSSI signal of the iBeacon positioning reference node in the environment.

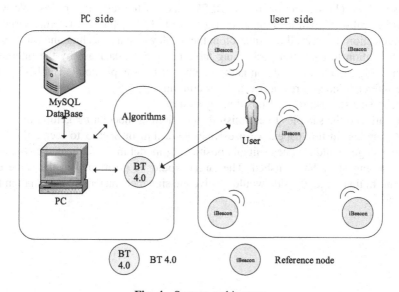

Fig. 4. System architecture

The user-side's microcontroller would integrate the received RSSI values and return to the PC-side via the Bluetooth 4.0. PC side would use the information to locate user's location and display on the man-machine interface.

The proposed indoor positioning system has three main functions of indoor positioning system which are positioning algorithm, environment monitoring, and man-machine interface. Positioning algorithm utilized the pattern matching that have offline training phase and online positioning phase. First, we utilized offline training phase to get signal characteristic sample. This paper utilized HM-10 BLE Modules as Low-Cost iBeacons for user node and reference nodes and used iBeacon mode to collect data that would be stored in the back-end MySQL positioning database. The offline training phase is divided into three steps which are the collection step, the storage step and the establishment of the positioning model step. And the collected signal feature sample data is stored in the back-end MySQL database.

Step (1): Collect the positioning signal samples

Fig. 5. The content of iBeacon packet format

The user node searches the neighboring iBeacon device and acquires the broadcast packet from the surrounding iBeacon device. The content of the iBeacon packet format used in this paper is shown in Fig. 5. The setting of the UUID is shown in Table 1.

Step (2): Storage positioning signal samples

Using Step (1), we can obtain the RSSI values of the reference nodes. We would pass RSSI value of each location reference node to PC by BT 4.0. Use the serial port communication to show all information in the display of man-machine interface. Stores the information to back-end positioning table in MySQL database by the Internet, as shown in Fig. 6. The first column is the number of the sample point. The RSSI values of the reference nodes are shown in other columns.

Step (3): Establishment of positioning model:

We utilized the samples to establish the positioning model after getting the map of signal samples. In this paper, we use KNN algorithm in Sect. 3 to locate the target. Training stage would produce suitable positioning model in the dedicated environment when training stage had finished. The target would be positioned in the same environment. In this stage, PC side would receive the signal characteristic information from the user.

Table 1. Parameters of experiment

Location reference node	UUID
Node 1	1
Node 2	2
Node 3	3
Node 4	4
Node 5	5

point	node1	rssi1	node2	rssi2	node3	rssi3	node4	rssi4	node5	rssi5
2	1	-47	2	-63	3	-66	4	-68	5	-58
3	1	-54	2	-58	3	-65	4	-68	5	-56
4	1	-60	2	-55	3	-68	4	-65	5	-56
5	1	-65	2	-45	3	-71	4	-66	5	-60
6	1	-67	2	-47	3	-73	4	-65	5	-62
7	1	-50	2	-66	3	-62	4	-68	5	-61
8	1	-46	2	-64	3	-62	4	-69	5	-57

Fig. 6. The content of positioning signal samples

5 Experiment and Result

5.1 Environment of Experiment

We used 5 positioning reference nodes, 36 positioning training nodes in all positioning map. The map was divided into 25 regions, each region in the division of four small areas as a positioning test point and the total positioning test points are 100. The map size shows in Fig. 7, where N is map length and width, where n is small area length and width. Due to the characteristics of the channel, we set N to 3 meters and n is set to 60 cm, as shown Table 2. There are two experimental environments in our positioning system. One is complex environment and the other one is open environment, as shown in Figs. 8 and 9, respectively. Two maps are used to experiment with the regional recognition rate of different algorithms. The target object is placed on the positioning test point. When the identification area is the same as the actual area, it is the correct regional recognition.

5.2 Experiment Result

The following is the experimental results for each positioning model. We compared various positioning algorithms which are KNN and WKNN with the regional recognition rate. The experiment results with various positioning algorithms are shown in Table 3.

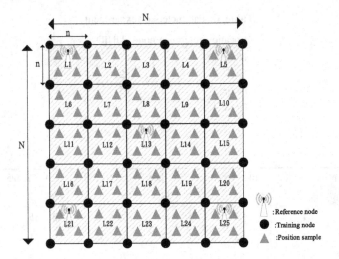

Fig. 7. Experiment map

Table 2. Parameters of the MAP

Map	Environment	N	n
Map A	open	3 m	0.6 m
Map B	complex	3 m	0.6 m

Fig. 8. Map A: Open environment

Since the KNN is an inductive algorithm, when the environment data is not very well, the KNN algorithm could not be adjusted by weighting. The WKNN is a supervised learning algorithm, so WKNN can learn the built map environment to adjust the weighting. The WKNN would effectively improve positioning accuracy when the environment is not very well. And in terms of complexity, the WKNN algorithm is similar to the KNN.

Fig. 9. Map B: Complex environment

Table 3. Comparison of positioning algorithms in regional recognition rate

Algorithm	Map A	Map B
NNSS (K = 1)	46%	41%
KNN (K = 3)	60%	52%
WKNN (K = 3)	66%	55%
KNN (K = 4)	65%	47%
WKNN (K = 4)	72%	52%
KNN (K = 5)	62%	49%
WKNN (K = 5)	68%	53%

6 Conclusion

In this paper, we utilized iBeacon technology to implement the indoor positioning system. We also design a man-machine interface by Microsoft Visual Studio C# to show user's location information. In the system, the target object to be positioned passes through the RSSI between the positioning reference nodes to know each other's distance. Since RSSI would be with the environment changes and become unstable, this paper used the pattern matching to get the signal characteristic of the environment in the positioning systems. We compared the positioning accuracy of the KNN and WKNN algorithms in the complex and open environmental maps. In the two positioning maps, the experimental results show that KNN also could adjust weighting to improve the positioning error. Compare with KNN, the positioning area accuracy of WKNN (K = 4) is better 7% and 5% than that of KNN ((K = 4) in our experimental complex and open environments, respectively. In the future, we hope to use this technology in the applications of Location based service.

References

1. Chen, L.H., Wu, E.H.K., Jin, M.H., Chen, G.H.: Intelligent fusion of Wi-Fi and inertial sensor-based positioning systems for indoor pedestrian navigation. IEEE Sens. J. **14**(11), 4034–4042 (2014)
2. Fang, M., Li, L., Huang, W.: Research of hybrid positioning based vehicle interactive navigation system. In: MINES, pp. 478–485 (2010)
3. Apple, iOS: Understanding iBeacon. https://support.apple.com/en-gb/HT202880. Accessed 5 Aug 2017
4. Zafari, F., Papapanagiotou, I.K., Devetsikiotis, M., Hacker, T.J.: An iBeacon based Proximity and Indoor Localization System. Computing Research Repository, pp. 1–14 (2017)
5. Apple iBeacons Explained: Smart Home Occupancy Sensing Solved? http://www. automatedhome.co.uk/apple/apple-ibeacons-explained-smart-home-occupancy-sensing-solved.html. Accessed 3 Oct 2013
6. Guowei, Z., Zhan, X., Dan, L.: Research and improvement on indoor localization based on RSSI fingerprint database and K-Nearest neighbor points. In: ICCCAS, pp. 68–71 (2013)
7. Hossain, S., Ariffin, S.H.S., Fisal, N., Neng, C.K., Hassan N.S.A., Latiff, L.A.: Accuracy enhancement of fingerprint indoor positioning system. In: ISMS, pp. 600–605 (2012)
8. Altman, N.S.: An introduction to kernel and nearest-neighbor nonparametric regression. Am. Stat. **46**(3), 175–185 (1992)
9. Duda, R.O., Hart, P.E., Stork, D.G.: Pattern classification, 2nd edn. Wiley, NY (2000)
10. Bahl, P., Padmanabhan, V.N.: RADAR: An in-building RF-based user location and tracking system. IEEE INFOCOM **2**, 775–784 (2000)
11. Cheng, C.H., Hu C.Y., Wang, T.P., Wu, F.C.: Using iBeacon technology with a back propagation neural network to positioning systems. In: MobiSec, pp. 1–9 (2017)
12. Lin, S., Liu, J., Fang, Y.: ZigBee based wireless sensor networks and its applications in industrial. In: CASE, pp. 1979–1983 (2007)
13. Zhang, J., Song, G., Wang H., Meng, T.: Design of a wireless sensor network based monitoring system for home automation. In: ICFCSA, pp. 57–60 (2011)
14. What is iBeacon? A guide to iBeacon. http://www.ibeacon.com/what-is-ibeacon-a-guide-to-beacons. Accessed 20 Apr 2014

An Efficient Facebook Place Information Extraction Strategy

Jong-Shin Chen[1], Chuan-Bi Lin[1], Cheng-Ying Yang[2],
and Yung-Fa Huang[1(✉)]

[1] Department of Information and Communication Engineering,
Chaoyang University of Technology,
Wufeng, Taichung 41349, Taiwan, R.O.C.
yfahuang@cyut.edu.tw
[2] Department of Computer Science, University of Taipei,
Taipei 10048, Taiwan, R.O.C.

Abstract. Facebook is an online social media and social networking service, which is most popular in the world. Location-based Facebook check-in service is a hot topic. Facebook users go to their interested check-in places and check in there. Numerous check-in behaviors at these places can form public options, for example hot places, high density regions. Therefore, information extraction of Facebook places can provide significant meanings such as business market decision or population traffic. However, few studies are based on it as the research field. These studies always are based on Foursquare as the research field. One of the major reasons is that Facebook platform only allows limited data access. Numerous places and check-in behaviors at these places can form public options for example hot places, high-density regions of places. In this study, we present a method to collect the big data of Facebook check-in places. Facebook penetration rate in Taiwan is the highest in the world. Moreover, there are many Facebook places in Taiwan are created related to delicacy food. Taiwanese "beef noodle", Japanese "Sushi", and Korean "Kimchi" all are popular in the world and in Taiwan. Accordingly, in this study, we use these as example to find out the related places, individually.

Keywords: Facebook place · Check-in · Public option · Beef noodle
Kimchi

1 Introduction

Facebook penetration rate in Taiwan is the highest in the world, until July 2015 in Taiwan, the number of daily users reached 13 million for approximately 23 million population. Check-in for places is a location-based function of Facebook. Facebook user can go to some famous scenic spots (Facebook places) or participate some activity and check in on the Facebook to show that the user participate some activities [1]. If there are no suitable name for the Facebook place, Facebook user can create a new place for the scenic spot. In the rest of this article, 'place' is referred to as 'Facebook place' simply and "…" is used to present a name of a specific Facebook place. After several years, there are numerous places and numerous check-in behaviors at these

© Springer Nature Singapore Pte Ltd. 2019
I. You et al. (Eds.): MobiSec 2017, CCIS 971, pp. 131–139, 2019.
https://doi.org/10.1007/978-981-13-3732-1_10

places in Taiwan. In this study, we attend to explore the public option from Facebook places for a special topic.

Taiwan beef noodle exists in variety of forms throughout East Asia and Southeast Asia. Beef noodle soup was first created by the Hui people (a Chinese Muslim ethnic group) during the Tang Dynasty of China. The red braised beef noodle soup was invented by the veterans in Kaoshiung, Taiwan who fled from mainland China during the Chinese civil war. In Taiwan it is considered a national dish and Taipei City holds several times of International Beef Noodle Festival, where variety of chefs and restaurants compete for the 'best beef noodle' title in Taiwan. 2011 Taipei International Beef Festival has been Taiwan beef noodle translated as "New Row Mian". The naming imitates Japanese Sushi as or Korean Kimchi that translated from the local language literal translation, highlighting the unique characteristics [2]. Sushi is the Japanese preparation and serving of specially prepared vinegared rice (sushi-meshi) combined with varied ingredients (neta) such as chiefly seafood (often uncooked), vegetables, and occasionally tropical fruits. Styles of sushi and its presentation vary widely, but the key ingredient is sushi rice, also referred to as shari, or sumeshi [3]. Kimchi, a staple in Korean cuisine, is a traditional side dish made from salted and fermented vegetables, most commonly napa cabbage and Korean radishes, with a variety of seasonings including chili powder, scallions, garlic, ginger, and jeotgal (salted seafood) [4]. Accordingly, we selected "New Row Mian", "Sushi", and "Kimchi" as the topic to explore related places from Facebook social network.

The rest of this article is organized as follows. In Sect. 2, related works are introduced. Next, the subject strategy is presented in Sect. 3. The demonstrations that take places in Taiwan are given in Sect. 4. Finally, we conclude this work and discuss the future work.

2 Related Work

The current research of check-in on social networks is divided into two types. The first type is based on big data that uses some technologies of Geographic Information Science [5–8, 11, 12, 15]. The other type is based on Ethnography-style study. The big-data [13, 14] based check-in studies generally depend on open Application Programming Interfaces (APIs), to acquire data from open social networking platforms and then do data mining and analyzing. The disadvantage of this method is that it cannot be discussed in depth with the focused persons.

These studies always are based on Foursquare as the research field. Facebook is the most popular check-in platform in the world. However few studies are based on it as the research field. One of the major reasons is that Facebook platform only allows limited data access. The other reason is that Facebook API often changes. Therefore, it is difficult to acquire mass data from Facebook platform by programming. Foursquare is another platform that user can do check-in at places. A Foursquare user dose check-in at a place and the information simultaneously display on Twitter. All of the information on Twitter is open. Accordingly, the mass data related to Foursquare can be acquired from Twitter platform.

3 Place Information Extraction Strategy

The data of Facebook places is open data. According to an access token ak, a developer can acquire the data from Facebook servers. The ak of a developer can be requested from the web page with url "https://developers.facebook.com". Each Facebook place has a unique identification, termed as id. A developer can acquire several identifications in a geographical area C according to Hypertext Transfer Protocol Secure (https) protocol by sending a request to Facebook server. The format of this request is as shown in (1), where c is a latitude and longitude coordinate, r is a distance, and n is a limit number. When a Facebook server acquired this request, it returns at most n identifications at a geographical circle-area C with center c and radius r. If the number of places at C is larger than n, the responded data will contain a next url. According to this url, Facebook sever will again provide other identifications at C. Similar process will be performed again and again until no next url is returned from Facebook server. The url of (2) is a request example, the returned data from Facebook server is shown in Fig. 1. The data is according JSON format and in encoded as UTF-8 format [9, 10]. Notably, JSON, i.e., JavaScript Object Notation, is an open-standard file format that uses human-readable text to transmit data objects consisting of attribute–value pairs and array data types (or any other serializable value). It is a very common data format used for asynchronous browser/server communication, including as a replacement for XML in some AJAX-style systems. UTF-8 is a character encoding capable of encoding all 1,112,064 valid code points in Unicode using one to four 8-bit bytes. The encoding is defined by the Unicode standard. The name is derived from Unicode (or Universal Coded Character Set) Transformation Format. After Facebook identifications are collected, for each id, the detailed data of id can be acquired by sending url, like (3), to Facebook server. Then, Facebook server will send the detailed data back. As shown in Fig. 2, a Facebook place with identification 1789770481248040 is presented.

$$\text{https://graph.facebook.com/search?type=place\&center=}c\text{\&distance=}r\text{\&access\_token=}ak\text{\&limit=}n \tag{1}$$

$$\text{https://graph.facebook.com/search?type=place\&center=24.069093, 120.7127943\&distance=150\&access\_token=1368411763}*****|\text{k95dZzlRoYVqg9I9NF\_QxU}*****\text{\&limit=2} \tag{2}$$

$$\text{https://graph.facebook.com/}id\text{/?access\_token=1368411763}*****|\text{k95dZzlRoYVqg9I9NF\_QxU}***** \tag{3}$$

For convenience, $C(c, r)$ is used to present a unit area with center c and radius r and Facebook server can provide the places in C each time. Simply, C_i, for $i = 1, 2, \ldots$, is used to index a unit area i and the visualization of C is represented using a hexagonal cell with radius r. A k circuit-area of a cell C, denoted as $CA(k, C)$, is the area of k-layer neighborhood cells with center cell C. As shown in Fig. 3, k-layer circuit-area

```
{
    "data": [
        {
            "category": "Religious Organization",
            "category_list": [
                {
                    "id": "187714557925874",
                    "name": "Religious Organization"
                },
                {
                    "id": "369730359717478",
                    "name": "Other"
                }
            ],
            "location": {
                "city": "Xinbei",
                "country": "Taiwan",
                "latitude": 25.06856,
                "longitude": 121.65773,
                "street": "\u6c50\u6b62\u5340\u4e2d\u6b63\u8def239\u865f",
                "zip": "221"
            },
            "name": "\u6c50\u6b62\u6fdf\u5fb7\u5bae\uff08\u6c50\u6b62\u5abd\u7956\u5edf\uff09",
            "id": "1789770481248040"
        },
        {
            "category": "Local Business",
            "category_list": [
                {
                    "id": "2500",
                    "name": "Local Business"
                }
            ],
            "location": {
                "city": "Xinbei",
                "country": "Taiwan",
                "latitude": 25.0688,
                "longitude": 121.65779,
                "street":
"\u65b0\u5317\u5e02\u6c50\u6b62\u5340\u4e2d\u6b63\u8def236\u865f\uff08\u5abd\u7956\u5edf\u5c0d\u9762\uff09",
                "zip": "22166"
            },
            "name": "\u5ed6\u5bb6\u7d05\u9f9c\u5e97",
            "id": "1099728306769986"
        }
    ],
    "paging": {
        "cursors": {
            "after": "MQZDZD"
        },
        "next":
"https://graph.facebook.com/v2.3/search?access_token=136841176381985\u00257Ck95dZzlRoYVqg9I9N
F_QxUDIciM&pretty=1&type=place&center=25.06856123\u00252C121.6577321&distance=150&limit=2
&after=MQZDZD"
    }
}
```

Fig. 1. Facebook identifications acquired from Facebook server

architecture of C is presented. In Fig. 3(a), the 1 circuit-area of C, i.e., $CA(1, C)$, contains only C. In Fig. 3(b), the 2 circuit-area of C, i.e., $CA(2, C)$, contains 7cells, including C and its neighboring 6 cells. Then, as shown in Fig. 3(c) and (d), $CA(3, C)$ and $CA(4, C)$ respectively contain 19 cells and 37 cells.

```
{
  "id": "1789770481248040",
  "can_post": false,
  "category": "Religious Organization",
  "category_list": [
    {
      "id": "187714557925874",
      "name": "Religious Organization"
    },
    {
      "id": "369730359717478",
      "name": "Other"
    }
  ],
  "check-ins ": 919,
  "cover": {
    "cover_id": "1872638582961229",
    "offset_x": 0,
    "offset_y": 42,
    "source":"https://scontent.xx.fbcdn.net/v/t1.0-
9/11885370_1872638582961229_6730984875519684127_n.jpg?oh=fe1683e85c46e0a388b35a93c62b203d&oe=59B
DFF52",
    "id": "1872638582961229"
  },
  "has_added_app": false,
  "hours": {
    "mon_1_open": "06:00",
    "mon_1_close": "20:00",
    "tue_1_open": "06:00",
    "tue_1_close": "20:00",
    "wed_1_open": "06:00",
    "wed_1_close": "20:00",
    "thu_1_open": "06:00",
    "thu_1_close": "20:00",
    "fri_1_open": "06:00",
    "fri_1_close": "20:00",
    "sat_1_open": "06:00",
    "sat_1_close": "20:00",
    "sun_1_open": "06:00",
    "sun_1_close": "20:00"
  },
  "is_community_page": false,
  "is_published": true,
  "likes": 903,
  "link":          "https://www.facebook.com/\u6c50\u6b62\u6fdf\u5fb7\u5bae\u6c50\u6b62\u5abd\u7956\u5edf-
1789770481248040/",
  "location": {
    "city": "Xinbei",
    "country": "Taiwan",
    "latitude": 25.06856,
    "longitude": 121.65773,
    "street": "\u6c50\u6b62\u5340\u4e2d\u6b63\u8def239\u865f",
    "zip": "221"
  },
  "name": "\u6c50\u6b62\u6fdf\u5fb7\u5bae\uff08\u6c50\u6b62\u5abd\u7956\u5edf\uff09",
  "name_with_location_descriptor":
"\u6c50\u6b62\u6fdf\u5fb7\u5bae\uff08\u6c50\u6b62\u5abd\u7956\u5edf\uff09",
  "phone": "\t02 2641 1362",
  "talking_about_count": 974,
  "website": "http://www.facebook.com.tw",
  "were_here_count": 919
}
```

Fig. 2. The detailed data of a Facebook place, taking 1789770481248040 for example

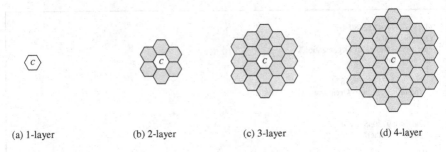

(a) 1-layer   (b) 2-layer   (c) 3-layer   (d) 4-layer

Fig. 3. Circuit-area architecture

The boundary B of a geographical area G is defined as in (4), where (x_i, y_i) is a latitude and longitude coordinate for $i = 0, 1, \ldots, n$. The boundary is formed from (x_0, y_0) to (x_1, y_1), (x_1, y_1) to $(x_2, y_2), \ldots, (x_{n-1}, y_{n-1})$ to (x_n, y_n) and (x_n, y_n) to (x_0, y_0). A node (x_t, y_t) is extended to a line $L(x_t, y_t)$ as in (5). If the extended line $L(x_t, y_t)$ meets the boundary B odd times, (x_t, y_t) is in G. Otherwise, (x_t, y_t) is not in G.

$$B = \{(x_0, y_0), (x_1, y_1), \ldots, (x_n, y_n)\} \tag{4}$$

$$L(x_t, y_t) = \{(x_k, y_t) | x_k \geq x_t\} \tag{5}$$

The method to find out the Facebook places in a specific area is to determine a unit area set of $\{C_1, C_2, \ldots, C_n\}$ where this specific area can fully be covered by C_1, $C_2, \ldots, C_n$.

For a geographical area G with its boundary B, the following steps are performed.

Step 1.   Evaluate $CA(n, C)$, where G can fully be covered by $CA(n, C)$.

Step 2.   Evaluate $CA_{in}(n, C)$, where $CA_{in}(n, C)$ contains all the cells in $CA(n, C)$ and these cells are in B.

Step 3.   For each cell $C_i(c_i, r)$ in $CA_{in}(n, C)$, according (1) can acquire the identifications using center c_i and radius r. Let ID be the set of the collected identifications

Step 4.   For each id in ID, according (3) can acquire the detailed data of place id

4 Demonstration

In this study, we take places in the island of Taiwan for example. The island of Taiwan lies some 180 km (110 mi) off the southeastern coast of mainland China, which lies across the Taiwan Strait, and has an area of 35,883 km^2. In our data, there are 1112188 places and 958799234 check-ins with average is 862.08 check-ins. For geography, averagely there are 39.99 places and there are 26720.15 check-ins per square kilometer. The population in Taiwan is more than 23.55 million until 2017. Therefore, each people averagely have 0.47 places and have done 40.71 check-ins. The 10 hot places, which the check-ins is larger than 1.4 million, are shown in Table 1. A hot

Facebook place almost is a geographical area in real world. A place id whose check-in count larger than 1.4 million means there are numerous Facebook users that have been here. You can visit the web page of this place on https://www.facebook.com/id. Some information, includes comments, of this place can be found out from the web page.

Table 1. 10 hot Facebook places in Taiwan

Id	Name	Check-in
110765362279102	Taipei City	6252154
143093992439556	Big City	2465689
412982505416602	Taoyuan International Airport	2317439
114511591898165	Kaohsiung City	2243388
110922325599480	Taichung City	1995932
109972075699000	Tainan City	1838131
162736400406103	Shilin Night Market	1644471
155192654517685	National Taiwan Normal University	1482522
128382387229505	Luo Dong Night Market	1477123
103765676329074	Taiwan	1446962

As shown in Fig. 4, cells covered to 4 specified Districts in Taipei City are presented. Each cell is a unit for acquiring Facebook places. Accordingly, to acquire the Facebook places in Xinyi District needs sending 1117 requests to Facebook server.

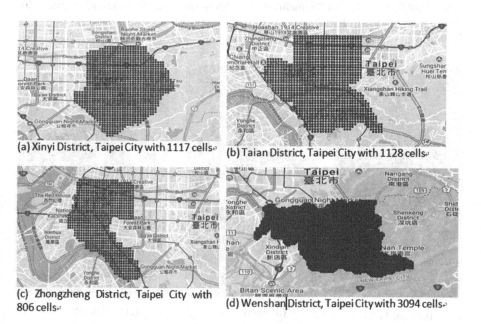

(a) Xinyi District, Taipei City with 1117 cells

(b) Taian District, Taipei City with 1128 cells

(c) Zhongzheng District, Taipei City with 806 cells

(d) Wenshan District, Taipei City with 3094 cells

Fig. 4. Cells covered specified districts in Taipei City, Taiwan

Moreover, Taian District needs 1128 requests, Zhongzheng Distric needs 806 requests, and Wenshan District needs 3094 requests. After acquiring Facebook identifications, using the method of (3) can acquire the detailed data of places.

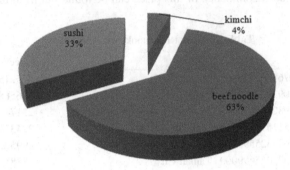

Fig. 5. Percentage of "beef noodle", "Sushi", and "Kimchi" places

The acquired Facebook data is stored using MySQL system. MySQL is an open-source database management systems through SQL (Structured Query Language) can extract information from places. As follows, "beef noodle", "Sushi", and "Kimchi" are taken for example. These places related "beef noodle", "Sushi", and "Kimchi" are to search the date of places which the name fields contain keywords "牛肉麵", "壽司", and "泡菜", respectively. Totally there are 5981 related places including 252 Kimchi places, 1978 Sushi places, and 3751Beef-Noodle places. As shown in Fig. 5, it presents the percentage of "beef noodle", "Sushi", and "Kimchi" places that "beef noodle" is 63%, "sushi" is 33%, and "Kimchi" is 4%. Moreover, the visualization of place distributions is shown in Fig. 6.

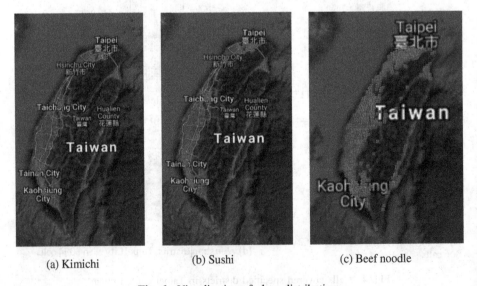

(a) Kimichi   (b) Sushi   (c) Beef noodle

Fig. 6. Visualization of place distributions

5 Conclusions

In this study, we proposed an efficient Facebook place information extraction strategy and taken "beef noodle", "Sushi", and "Kimchi" in Taiwan for example. A Facebook place is a location in real world. The web page of this place contains the Facebook users that have been there and comments that posted by Facebook users after attending some specific activities at this place. For Ethnography-style study, our study can help to find out the hot regions, the hot locations, and the Facebook users related to these regions for some topics. In our life, there are many important activities or things. However, they are very difficult to reveal the influences scientifically such as folk religion. To find out the effects of some folk religions on our life is our future work.

References

1. Wikipedia (2017). https://zh.wikipedia.org/wiki/Facebook. Accessed 5 Mar 2017
2. Wikipedia. https://zh.wikipedia.org/wiki/Beef_noodle_soup. Accessed 5 Mar 2017
3. Wikipedia. https://zh.wikipedia.org/wiki/Sushi. Accessed 5 Mar 2017
4. Wikipedia. https://zh.wikipedia.org/wiki/Kimchi. Accessed 5 Mar 2017
5. Bawa-Cavia, A.: Sensing the urban: using location-based social network data in urban analysis. In: First Workshop on Pervasive Urban Applications (PURBA), San Francisco (2010)
6. Cheng, Z., Caverlee, J., Lee, K., Sui, D.: Exploring millions of footprints in location sharing services. In: Proceedings of the Fifth International AAAI Conference on Weblogs and Social Media, Barcelona (2011)
7. Crandall, D.J., Backstrom, L., Cosley, D., Suri, S., Huttenlocher, D., Kleinberg, J.: Inferring social ties from geographic coincidences. Proc. Natl. Acad. Sci. 107(52), 22436–22441 (2010)
8. Cranshaw, J., Schwartz, R., Hong, J., Sadeh, N.: The livehoods project: utilizing social media to understand the dynamics of a city. In: Proceedings of the Sixth International AAAI Conference on Weblogs and Social Media, Dublin (2012)
9. RFC 4627. https://www.ietf.org/rfc/rfc4627.txt
10. RFC 3629. https://tools.ietf.org/html/rfc3629
11. Chen, J.S., et al.: Public option analysis for hot check-in places at Taiwan. In: International Conference on Advanced Information Technologies, pp. 745–755, Taiwan (2017)
12. Kotenko, I., Kolomeets, M., Chechulin, A., Chevalier, Y.: A visual analytics approach for the cyber forensics based on different views of the network traffic. J. Wirel. Mob. Netw. Ubiquitous Comput. Dependable Appl. (JoWUA) 9(2), 57–73 (2018)
13. Kotenko, I., Saenko, I., Kushnerevich, A.: Parallel big data processing system for security monitoring in Internet of Things networks. J. Wirel. Mob. Netw. Ubiquitous Comput. Dependable Appl. (JoWUA) 8(4), 60–74 (2017)
14. Kotenko, I., Saenko, I., Branitskiy, A.: Applying big data processing and machine learning methods for mobile internet of things security monitoring. J. Internet Services Inf. Secur. (JISIS) 8(3), 54–63 (2018)
15. Lim, K., Jeong, Y., Cho, S.-J., Park, M., Han, S.: An android application protection scheme against dynamic reverse engineering attacks. J. Wirel. Mob. Netw. Ubiquitous Comput. Dependable Appl. (JoWUA) 7(3), 40–52 (2016)

Performance of Sub-optimal Searching Algorithms on PTS Phase Selections for PAPR Reduction

Jyh-Horng Wen[1], Fang-Yu Chang[2], Yung-Fa Huang[3(⊠)],
Hsing-Chung Chen[4(⊠)], and Zon-Yin Shae[4]

[1] Department of Electrical Engineering, Tunghai University,
Taichung 407, Taiwan
jhwen@thu.edu.tw
[2] Department of Electrical Engineering, National Chung Cheng University,
Chiayi 62102, Taiwan
shamu.chang@gmail.com
[3] Department of Information and Communication Engineering,
Chaoyang University of Technology, Taichung 41349, Taiwan
yfahuang@cyut.edu.tw
[4] Department of Computer Science and Information Engineering,
Asia University, Taichung 413, Taiwan
{cdma2000,zshael}@asia.edu.tw

Abstract. The conventional partial transmit sequence (PTS) technique can provide good peak-to-average power ratio (PAPR) reduction performance for orthogonal frequency division multiplexing (OFDM) signals; however, determining the optimal phase factors requires an exhaustive search over all possible sets of phase factors, the search complexity of the original PTS method increases exponentially with the number of the sub-blocks and is extremely high for a larger number of sub-blocks. In this paper, we defined a new phase factor, and then proposed two algorithms to reduce search complexity and to improve the performance.

Keywords: OFDM · Peak-to-average power ratio · Partial transmit sequence Phase factor · Search complexity

1 Introduction

Orthogonal frequency division multiplexing (OFDM) is an attractive technique for achieving high-bit-rate wireless data communication [1, 9–13]. It has been received a lot of attentions especially in the field of wireless communications been adopted as the standard transmission technique in the wireless LAN systems and the terrestrial digital broadcasting system.

In order to reduce the one of the major drawback of the OFDM system, the high peak-to-average power ratio (PAPR), several techniques have been proposed [2–5]. Among these methods, the partial transmit sequence (PTS) is the most attractive scheme because of good PAPR reduction performance [5]. However, in PTS method

© Springer Nature Singapore Pte Ltd. 2019
I. You et al. (Eds.): MobiSec 2017, CCIS 971, pp. 140–150, 2019.
https://doi.org/10.1007/978-981-13-3732-1_11

the exhaustive search algorithm (ESA) employed to find the best phase factor suffers the exponentially complexity with the number of sub-blocks and is too high for implementation [5]. Moreover, all of the proposed searching methods for extensions of PTS, either the PAPR reduction is suboptimal or the complexity is still high [6, 7].

2 PAPR and PTS Methods

2.1 PAPR of OFDM Systems

In an OFDM system, we denote $\mathbf{X} = [X_0, X_1, \ldots, X_{N-1}]$ as the input data block of length N. Then the complex baseband OFDM signal consisting of N subcarriers is given by

$$x(t) = \frac{1}{\sqrt{N}} \sum_{n=0}^{N-1} X_n \cdot e^{j2\pi\Delta ft}, \ 0 \le t < NT \tag{1}$$

where $j = \sqrt{-1}$, Δf denotes the subcarrier spacing, and NT denotes the useful data sequence period, X_n denotes the modulated symbols. Then the peak-to-average ratio (PAPR) of continuous-time signal $x(t)$ is defined as the ratio of maximum instantaneous power and average power, given by

$$PAPR = \frac{\max_{0 \le t < NT} |x(t)|^2}{E\left[|x(t)|^2\right]} \tag{2}$$

where $E[\bullet]$ denote expectation. We can also calculate PAPR of discrete time signal.

$$PAPR = \frac{\max_{0 \le k < N} |x_k|^2}{E\left[|x_k|^2\right]} \tag{3}$$

2.2 OFDM Systems with PTS to Reduce the PAPR

The PTS method will be explained as follow and the structure is shown in Fig. 1. The input data $\mathbf{X}$ is partitioned into M disjoint sets, each $\tilde{X}_i$ is the sub-block with length N, where $i = 1, 2, \ldots, M$, i.e.:

$$\mathbf{X} = \sum_{i=1}^{M} \tilde{X}_{i.} \tag{4}$$

In general, for PTS scheme, the known sub-block partitioning methods can be

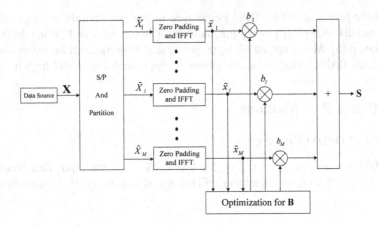

Fig. 1. The diagram of PTS structure.

classified into three categories: adjacent partition, interleaved partition and pseudo-random partition. In this paper, we use adjacent partition. Then, each $\tilde{X}_i$ passes IFFT. We assume

$$\tilde{x}_i = IFFT\{\tilde{X}_i\}, \forall i. \tag{5}$$

Let

$$
\begin{aligned}
\tilde{\mathbf{x}} &= \begin{bmatrix} \tilde{x}_1 & \tilde{x}_2 & \cdots & \tilde{x}_M \end{bmatrix}^T \\
&= \begin{bmatrix} \tilde{x}_1 \\ \tilde{x}_2 \\ \vdots \\ \tilde{x}_M \end{bmatrix} = IFFT \left\{ \begin{bmatrix} \tilde{X}_1 \\ \tilde{X}_2 \\ \vdots \\ \tilde{X}_M \end{bmatrix} \right\} = \begin{bmatrix} IFFT\{\tilde{X}_1\} \\ IFFT\{\tilde{X}_2\} \\ \vdots \\ IFFT\{\tilde{X}_M\} \end{bmatrix} = \begin{bmatrix} \tilde{x}_{1,0} & \tilde{x}_{1,1} & \cdots & \tilde{x}_{1,N-1} \\ \tilde{x}_{2,0} & \tilde{x}_{2,1} & \cdots & \tilde{x}_{2,N-1} \\ \vdots & \vdots & \vdots & \vdots \\ \tilde{x}_{M,0} & \tilde{x}_{M,1} & \cdots & \tilde{x}_{M,N-1} \end{bmatrix}.
\end{aligned}
\tag{6}
$$

and

$$
\mathbf{B} = \begin{bmatrix} b_1 \\ b_2 \\ \vdots \\ b_M \end{bmatrix} = \begin{bmatrix} e^{j\theta_1} \\ e^{j\theta_2} \\ \vdots \\ e^{j\theta_M} \end{bmatrix}, \tag{7}
$$

where θ_i is a phase factor and $\theta_i \in [0, 2\pi)$.

The output signal $\mathbf{S}$ is the combination of $\tilde{\mathbf{x}}$ and $\mathbf{B}$. The form of $\mathbf{S}$ is:

$$
\begin{aligned}
S &= \tilde{x}^T * B \\
&= \begin{bmatrix}
\tilde{x}_{1,0} & \tilde{x}_{1,1} & \cdots & \tilde{x}_{1,N-1} \\
\tilde{x}_{2,0} & \tilde{x}_{2,1} & \cdots & \tilde{x}_{2,N-1} \\
\vdots & \vdots & \vdots & \vdots \\
\tilde{x}_{M,0} & \tilde{x}_{M,1} & \cdots & \tilde{x}_{M,N-1}
\end{bmatrix}^T
* \begin{bmatrix}
e^{j\theta_1} \\
e^{j\theta_2} \\
\vdots \\
e^{j\theta_M}
\end{bmatrix}.
\end{aligned}
\tag{8}
$$

Assume $\boldsymbol{\theta} = [\,\theta_1 \quad \theta_2 \quad \cdots \quad \theta_M\,]^T$ is the optimal phase vector for input signal. $\boldsymbol{\theta}$ must satisfy:

$$
\hat{\theta} = \begin{bmatrix}
\hat{\theta}_1 \\
\hat{\theta}_2 \\
\vdots \\
\hat{\theta}_M
\end{bmatrix}
= \arg \min_{\theta_i \in [0,2\pi)} \max_{\ell = 0,1,\ldots,N-1}
\left\{ \frac{\left| \sum_{i=1}^{M} \tilde{x}_{i,\ell} e^{j\theta_i} \right|^2}{\frac{1}{N} \sum_{k=0}^{N-1} \left| \sum_{i=1}^{M} \tilde{x}_{i,k} e^{j\theta_i} \right|^2} \right\}
\tag{9}
$$

where $e^{j\hat{\theta}_i}$ is the optimum rotation of sub-block i.

As $\theta \in [0, 2\pi)$, so we become very difficult to find the optimal phase vector. Typically, the phase factors are constrained to a finite set. If we use the phase set $\theta_i \in \{0, \frac{\pi}{2}, \pi, \frac{3\pi}{2}\}$, we only find suboptimal phase vector $\hat{\theta}_{sub}$. $\hat{\theta}_{sub}$ can be expresses as

$$
\hat{\theta}_{sub} = \begin{bmatrix}
\hat{\theta}_1 \\
\hat{\theta}_2 \\
\vdots \\
\hat{\theta}_M
\end{bmatrix}
= \arg \min_{\theta_{sub_i} \in [0, \frac{\pi}{2}, \pi, \frac{3\pi}{2}]} \max_{\ell = 0,1,\ldots,N-1}
\left\{ \frac{\left| \sum_{i=1}^{M} \tilde{x}_{i,\ell} e^{j\theta_{sub_i}} \right|^2}{\frac{1}{N} \sum_{k=0}^{N-1} \left| \sum_{i=1}^{M} \tilde{x}_{i,k} e^{j\theta_{sub_i}} \right|^2} \right\}
\tag{10}
$$

Then, the optimum transmitted signal $\hat{\mathbf{S}} = \tilde{\mathbf{x}}^T * \hat{\mathbf{B}}$, i.e.:

$$
\hat{S}_k = \sum_{i=1}^{M} \tilde{x}_{i,k} e^{j\hat{\theta}_i}, k = 0, 2, \ldots, N-1.
\tag{11}
$$

In Eq. (10), it is obvious that finding a best phase factor set is a complex and difficult problem; therefore, in the next section, we propose a suboptimal search algorithm for PTS phase selection.

3 Proposed Algorithms

3.1 Observation and Definition of New Phase Factor

Form Eq. (6), $\tilde{\mathbf{x}}$ is an $M \times N$ matrix. The i-th row of $\tilde{\mathbf{x}}$ is the i-th sub-block after passing IFFT, where $\tilde{x}_{i,k}$ means the k-th sample value of the i-th sub-block after IFFT, $i = 1, 2, \ldots, M$ and $k = 0, 1, \ldots, N-1$, and each $\tilde{x}_i$ is $1 \times N$ matrix.

The output signal can be written as

$$S = IFFT\{X\} = \left[\sum_{i=1}^{M} \tilde{x}_{i,0} \quad \sum_{i=1}^{M} \tilde{x}_{i,1} \quad \cdots \quad \sum_{i=1}^{M} \tilde{x}_{i,N-1} \right], \tag{12}$$

If we can't consider each sub-block multiply phase factor, the element of $1 \times N$ output matrix is the k-th sample output, S is output signal without pass PAPR reduction scheme. For all samples, let the index of the sample which has maximum value be $\hat{k}$ as

$$\hat{k} = \arg \max_{0 \leq k \leq N-1} \left\{ \left| \sum_{i=1}^{M} \tilde{x}_{i,k} \right| \right\} \tag{13}$$

The original PAPR can write as

$$PAPR_{original} = \frac{\left| \sum_{i=1}^{M} \tilde{x}_{i,\hat{k}} \right|^2}{\frac{1}{N} \sum_{k=0}^{N-1} \left| \sum_{i=1}^{M} \tilde{x}_{i,k} \right|^2} \tag{14}$$

For all sub-blocks of the $\hat{k}$-th sample, let the index of the sub-block which has the maximum value be $\hat{i}$.

$$\hat{i} = \arg \max_{0 \leq i \leq M} \left\{ \left| \sum_{i=1}^{M} \tilde{x}_{i,\hat{k}} \right| \right\} \tag{15}$$

The maximum sample $\sum_{i=1}^{M} \tilde{x}_{i,\hat{k}}$, we can be re-written as

$$\begin{aligned} \sum_{i=1}^{M} \tilde{x}_{i,\hat{k}} &= \tilde{x}_{1,\hat{k}} + \tilde{x}_{2,\hat{k}} + \cdots + \tilde{x}_{M,\hat{k}} \\ &= \left| \tilde{x}_{1,\hat{k}} \right| e^{j\angle \tilde{x}_{1,\hat{k}}} + \left| \tilde{x}_{2,\hat{k}} \right| e^{j\angle \tilde{x}_{2,\hat{k}}} + \cdots + \left| \tilde{x}_{M,\hat{k}} \right| e^{j\angle \tilde{x}_{M,\hat{k}}}, \end{aligned} \tag{16}$$

We define the phase set as

$$\theta_{\hat{k}} = \left\{ \angle \tilde{x}_{i,\hat{k}} : i = 1, 2, \ldots, \hat{i} - 1, \hat{i} + 1, \ldots, M \right\}, \tag{17}$$

Let

$$\theta_{d_t} = \left\{ \angle \tilde{x}_{i,\hat{k}} - \angle \tilde{x}_{\hat{i},\hat{k}} : i = 1, 2, \ldots, \hat{i} - 1, \hat{i} + 1, \ldots, M \right\}, \tag{18}$$

where t is the decreasing order that arranges the index of the sample values, so $t = 1$ is the 1-st sample. We simulate the PDF of θ_d in Fig. 2 shows the PDF of θ_{d_t} for difference orders of sample [8].

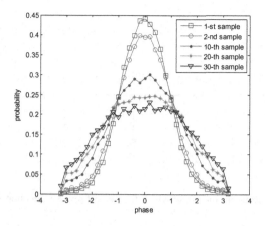

Fig. 2. PDF of θ_{d_i} for difference orders of sample.

In Fig. 2, we observe that the phases of $\tilde{x}_{i,\hat{k}}$, $i = 1, 2, \ldots, M$, are very close and it is why the maximum amplitude value is on the $\hat{k}$-th sample value of original signal after passing IFFT. Because the phases of $\hat{k}$-th sample value of each sub-block after IFFT are very close, we want to us this property and the amplitudes of $\tilde{x}_{i,\hat{k}}$, $i = 1, 2, \ldots, M$, $i \neq \hat{i}$ to reduce the amplitude of $\tilde{x}_{\hat{i},\hat{k}}$. Now, we need to choose proper phase factor to reduce high PAPR. Recall the property that $\angle \tilde{x}_{i,\hat{k}}$ is very near $\angle \tilde{x}_{\hat{i},\hat{k}}$ for $i \neq \hat{i}$, we define a new phase factor.

We define each $\angle \tilde{x}_{i,\hat{k}}$ that rotates the phase to $\{0, \frac{\pi}{2}, \pi, \frac{3\pi}{2}\}$, respectively, for $i \neq \hat{i}$. Then we can get four phase factor for some i:

$$\left\{ \angle \tilde{x}_{i,\hat{k}} \quad \angle \tilde{x}_{i,\hat{k}} + \tfrac{\pi}{2} \quad \angle \tilde{x}_{i,\hat{k}} + \pi \quad \angle \tilde{x}_{i,\hat{k}} + \tfrac{3\pi}{2} \right\}, \tag{19}$$

let

$$\phi_j = \angle \tilde{x}_{i,\hat{k}} + j\frac{\pi}{2}, j = 0, 1, 2, 3 \tag{20}$$

then, we select one of ϕ_j which is the nearest reverse direction of $\angle \tilde{x}_{\hat{i},\hat{k}}$ to rotate. Let can write as

$$\phi_i = \underset{0 \leq j \leq 3}{\arg\min}\left(\angle \tilde{x}_{\hat{i},\hat{k}} + \pi - \phi_j \right). \tag{21}$$

We gave an example as shown in Fig. 3.

Form Eq. (19), each sub-block has been calculated phase vector, except for the $\hat{i}$-th sub-block.

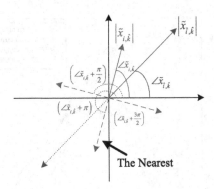

Fig. 3. Rotating the phase which the nearest reverse direction of $\angle \tilde{x}_{\hat{i},\hat{k}}$

3.2 A Sub-optimal Search Algorithm for PTS Phase Selection

Although $\sum_{i=1}^{4} \tilde{x}_{i,\hat{k}}$ can be reduced, but more number of peak value are generated than the number of original maximum peak value. We should consider that not all sub-blocks need to be multiplied by the corresponding calculated phase vectors.

Thus, the data of the i-th sub-block after passing IFFT can be multiplied by $e^{j\phi_i}$ or $e^{j0}(=1)$ for $i \neq \hat{i}$, the $\hat{i}$-th sub-block after passing IFFT can't be multiplied any phase, means unchanged. θ_i can be redefined as

$$\theta_i = \left\{ \begin{array}{l} \phi_i, \ i \neq \hat{i}; \ \theta_i = 0, \ i = \hat{i}. \\ 0 \end{array} \right. \tag{22}$$

Finally, we calculate all results of PAPR and select the suitable phase vectors such that the transmitted signal has minimum PAPR. Each sub-block of $\tilde{x}$ has a new phase factor which was calculated by Eq. (22), see new structure in Fig. 4.

Then, we have an algorithm as follows:

1. Input signal in frequency domain needs to be partitioned into M disjoint sub-blocks,
   $$\mathbf{X} = \sum_{i=1}^{M} \tilde{X}_i.$$
2. Each $\tilde{X}_i$ passes IFFT, we can show the equation in (12).
3. Let $\hat{k} = \arg \max_{0 \leq k \leq N-1} \left\{ \left| \sum_{i=1}^{M} \tilde{x}_{i,k} \right| \right\}$.
4. Let $\hat{i} = \arg \max_{0 \leq i \leq M} \left\{ \left| \sum_{i=1}^{M} \tilde{x}_{i,\hat{k}} \right| \right\}$.
5. Keep $\hat{i}$-th sub-block unchanged. Each of the other $M - 1$ sub-blocks has two selection: unchanged or rotating to the nearest reverse direction of $\tilde{x}_{i,\hat{k}}$. So, there are totally 2^{M-1} possible candidates.
6. Calculate the PAPR for each candidate, select signal with minimum PAPR. The concert illustrated is shown in Fig. 4.

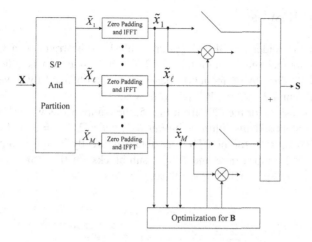

Fig. 4. The modified PTS structure.

With the new minimum PAPR signal, we can repeat step 3 to step 6 for pre-defined times until can't find the minimum PAPR.

3.3 A Modified Sub-optimal Search Algorithm for PTS Phase Selections

We can from the simulations of section B algorithm, the PAPR reduction with original and the PAPR reduction of we proposed algorithm, although the efficient is not good compared to the original, but that can be reduced the search complexity. When $iter = 3$, we can't find the minimum PAPR value. Then we proposed a modified sub-optimal search algorithm for PTS phase selection.

The algorithm is as follows:

1. Input signal in frequency domain needs to be partitioned into M disjoint sub-blocks,
   $$\mathbf{X} = \sum_{i=1}^{M} \tilde{X}_i.$$
2. Each $\tilde{X}_i$ passes IFFT, we can show the equation in (12).
3. Let $\hat{k} = \arg \max_{0 \le k \le N-1} \left\{ \left| \sum_{i=1}^{M} \tilde{x}_{i,k} \right| \right\}$.
4. Let $\hat{i} = \arg \max_{0 \le i \le M} \left\{ \left| \sum_{i=1}^{M} \tilde{x}_{i,\hat{k}} \right| \right\}$.
5. Keep $\hat{i}$-th sub-block unchanged. Each of the other $M - 1$ sub-blocks has two selection: unchanged or rotating to the nearest reverse direction of $\tilde{x}_{i,\hat{k}}$. So, there are totally 2^{M-1} possible candidates.
6. Calculate the PAPR for each candidate, select signal with minimum PAPR. The concert illustrated is shown in Fig. 4.

Instead of considering the sample with the largest magnitude only we can consider the samples 1st–kth largest magnitude.

4   Numerical Results

In this study, we consider an OFDM system with 128subcarriers with QPSK data symbols. A sub-optimal search algorithm for PTS phase selection is called the proposed Algorithm I. The PAPR reduction performance is obtained by a Monte Carlo search with a full enumeration of W^M phase factors.

In the CCDFs results for the PTS from Fig. 5, the comparisons were shown for the ESA method, the proposed algorithm I with $iter = 1$, $iter = 2$, $iter = 3$, and the original OFDM. The CCDFs results for the PTS were obtained directly from the output of IFFT operation for $k = 128$ subcarriers and $M = 8$ sub-blocks. In the ESA, four allowed phase factors $+1, -1, +j, -j$ ($W = 4$) are used.

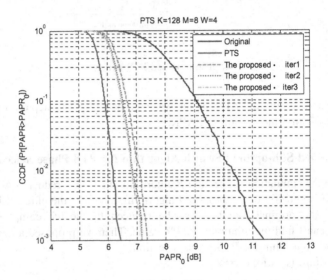

Fig. 5. The CCDFs results of the PAPR for PTS methods, with $M = 8$, and 4 times oversampling, algorithm I.

In Fig. 5, it is observed that the 10^{-3} PAPR of the OFDM signal is 11.36 dB, The 10^{-3} PAPR of the ESA is 6.43 dB. It is evident that the ESA algorithm obtains the better PAPR reduction. However, when the proposed algorithm I with iteration value $iter = 1$, $iter = 2$ and $iter = 3$ when $M = 8$, the 10^{-3} PAPRs reduce to 7.36 dB, 7.162 dB, 7.162 dB, respectively. Form Fig. 5, it can be easily seen that the performance of our proposed algorithm I is much closer to that of the ESA. However, the search complexity is reduced significantly. We compare the search complexity in Table 1.

In this paper, a modified sub-optimal search algorithm for PTS phase selection that be called the proposed Algorithm II. In Fig. 6, the 10^{-2} PAPR of the OFDM signal is 9.982 dB. The 10^{-3} PAPR of the ESA is 6.244 dB, it is evident that the ESA algorithm can provide the better PAPR reduction. However, when the proposed algorithm II with the sample value consider the 1st sample, the 1st-2nd, 1st-3rd, 1st-4th and 1st-5th,

Table 1. Search complexity of ALGORITHM I with $M = 8$

Algorithm I	Search complexity	$M = 8$, $W = 4$	10^{-3} PAPR
ESA	W^M	65536	6.428 dB
$iter = 1$	2^{M-1}	128	7.355 dB
$iter = 2$	$2 \times 2^{M-1}$	256	7.162 dB
$iter = 3$	$3 \times 2^{M-1}$	384	7.162 dB

the 10^{-3} PAPRs reduce to 7.704 dB, 6.928 dB, 6.839 dB, 6.734 dB, 6.701 dB, respectively. Form Fig. 6, it can be easily seen that the performance of our proposed algorithm II is much closer to that of the ESA. However, the search complexity is reduced significantly. We compare the search complexity in Table 2.

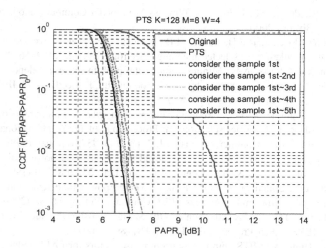

Fig. 6. Performance comparisons of CCDFs results of PAPR for PTS methods, with $M = 8$, and 4 times oversampling, algorithm II.

Table 2. Search complexity of Algorithm II with $M = 8$.

Algorithm II	Search complexity	$M = 8$, $W = 4$	10^{-2} PAPR
ESA	W^M	65536	6.244 dB
1st	2^{M-1}	128	7.704 dB
$1^{st}-2^{nd}$	$2 \times 2^{M-1}$	256	6.928 dB
$1^{st}-3^{rd}$	$3 \times 2^{M-1}$	384	6.839 dB
$1^{st}-4^{th}$	$4 \times 2^{M-1}$	512	6.734 dB
$1^{st}-5^{th}$	$5 \times 2^{M-1}$	640	6.701 dB

5 Conclusions

This paper presented two algorithms that was obtain the optimal phase factor for the PTS method to reduce the PAPR of OFDM signals. The simulation results show that all the proposed schemes can lower the PAPR. Our proposed method reduces the search complexity while keeping good PAPR performance.

Acknowledgment. This work was funded in part by Ministry of Science and Technology of Taiwan under Grant MOST 106-2632-E-468-003, MOST 106-2632-E-468-003 and MOST 106-2221-E-324-020.

References

1. Van Nee, R., Prasad, R.: OFDM for Wireless Multimedia Communication. Artech House Publishers, Boston (2000)
2. Bauml, R.W., Fischer, R.F.H., Huber, J.B.: Reducing the peak-to-average power ratio of multicarrier modulation by selected mapping. Electron. Lett. **32**(22), 2056–2057 (1996)
3. Wilkinson, T.A., Jones, A.E.: Minimization of the peak-to mean envelope power ratio of multicarrier transmission schemes by block coding. In: Proceedings of IEEE Vehicular Technology Conference, Chicago, pp. 825–829, July 1995
4. Schmidt, H., Kammeyer, K.D.: Reducing the peak to average power ratio of multicarrier signals by adaptive subcarrier selection. In: Proceedings of IEEE International Conference on Universal Personal Communications, vol. 2, pp. 933–937, October 1998
5. Muller, S.H., Huber, J.B.: OFDM with reduced peak-to-average power ratio by optimum combination of partial transmit sequences. Electron. Lett. **33**, 368–369 (1997)
6. Cimiini Jr., L.J., Sollenberger, N.R.: Peak-to-average power ratio reduction of an OFDM signal using partial transmit sequences. IEEE Commun. Lett. **4**, 86–88 (2000)
7. Han, S.H., Lee, J.H.: PAPR reduction of OFDM signals using a reduced complexity PTS technique. IEEE Signal Process. Lett. **11**(11), 887–890 (2004)
8. Tsai, Y.R., Hung, S.J.: PTS with non-uniform phase factors for PAPR reduction in OFDM Systems. IEEE Comm. Lett. **12**(1), 20–22 (2008)
9. He, Q., Dong, Q., Zhao, B., Wang, Y., Qiang, B.: P2P traffic optimization based on congestion distance and DHT. J. Internet Serv. Inf. Secur. (JISIS) **6**(2), 53–69 (2016)
10. Taqieddin, E., Awad, F., Ahmad, H.: Location-aware and mobility-based performance optimization for wireless sensor networks. J. Wirel. Mob. Netw. Ubiquitous Comput. Dependable Appl. (JoWUA) **8**(4), 37–59 (2017)
11. Majeed, A., Zia, T.: Multi-layer network architecture for supporting multiple applications in wireless sensor networks. J. Wirel. Mob. Netw. Ubiquitous Comput. Dependable Appl. (JoWUA) **8**(3), 36–56 (2017)
12. Kitana, A., Traore, I., Woungang, I.: Impact study of a mobile botnet over LTE networks. J. Internet Serv. Inf. Secur. (JISIS) **6**(2), 1–22 (2016)
13. Chen, H.-C.: TCABRP: a trust-based cooperation authentication bit-map routing protocol against insider security threats in wireless ad hoc networks. IEEE Syst. J. **11**(2), 449–459 (2017)

A Frame-Based Approach to Generating Insider Threat Test Suite on Cloud File-Sharing

Tsung-Ju Lee[1], Shian-Shyong Tseng[2(✉)], Hsing-Chung Chen[2],
Sung-Chiang Lin[3], and Chiun-How Kao[4]

[1] National Penghu University of Science and Technology,
Magong, Penghu, Taiwan
freeman.tj.lee@gms.npu.edu.tw
[2] Asia University, Taichung, Taiwan
{sstseng, cdma2000}@asia.edu.tw
[3] National Taipei University of Education, Taipei, Taiwan
lschiang@tea.ntue.edu.tw
[4] National Taiwan University of Science and Technology, Taipei, Taiwan
maokao25@gmail.com

Abstract. Insider threat has attracted considerable attention in security industry. It is difficult to detect insiders, because they know organization's security
countermeasures and usually hide their tracks in their normal activities. For
evaluating insider detection algorithm on specific organization, it is important to
generate a test suite with the corresponding normal activities. However, it is
costly and time consuming to generate tailor-made test suite. Due to the complexity of combining different insider attack technique with different organization's audit data, the insider attack scenario modeling issue arises when
adaptively generate test suite for insider threat detection. In this paper, we
propose the insider attack frame hierarchy to describe stereotype features of
insider attack scenario. The proposed frame-based approach has been combined
with the RBAC technologies, and its instantiation property allow us generate the
customized insider attack test suite with full test coverage. The evaluation results
show that most of experts satisfy with our proposed system.

Keywords: Frame-based approach · Insider threat

1 Introduction

Insider threat has become most critical security threat, and causes huge harm to
organizations. This kind of information security threats is that insiders use their permissions to view, download or delete valuable data. It is difficult to detect insiders,
because they know organization's security countermeasures well and in most of time
they act as normal as usual. Many insider detection systems are based on different
indicator [1–9]. The identified indicators of an insider usually are: logical or physical
location, authorization, expected behavior, motivation, and trust. However, each
organization has its own countermeasures and hence may has distinct indicators.

© Springer Nature Singapore Pte Ltd. 2019
I. You et al. (Eds.): MobiSec 2017, CCIS 971, pp. 151–156, 2019.
https://doi.org/10.1007/978-981-13-3732-1_12

Furthermore, insiders would intend to hide their tracks in their routine activities. Therefore, how to generate a tailor-made test suite of insider threat for specific organization becomes an important issue.

For evaluating insider detection algorithm, it is important to develop a test suite adapted to each organization's normal activities. With our observation, the insider threat test items are composed by the attack step called Attack Action and the context information called Attack Environment. For example, the case "The insider made unauthorized copies of confidential information on google drive and moved the information to a laptop" is composed by the Attack Actions "copy confident information and download it" and the Attack environment about "the audit data of google drive". For a given insider threat case with Attack Action and Attack Environment, our goal is to generate different test items from different environment [10–13].

In this paper, the typical insider threat case of "unauthorized copy" is analyzed to design the model. Since the attack actions and attack environment can be simply described by stereotyped attributes, the frame-based knowledge representation is used to model these cases. Besides, the instantiation property of our proposed frame-based knowledge representation can further extend the original insider threat case. For given a new attack action, Instantiation property can be used to apply different environment to the attack action; thus a tailor-made insider threat case can be generated.

The remainder of the article is organized as follows. Section 2 introduces the Insider Threat Frame model and the properties of the model. Section 3 describes the system implementation of test suite generation. Finally, Sect. 4 gives the conclusion and future work.

2   Insider Threat Frame Model

Attack scenario of an insider's malicious activities can be described by stereotype attributes such as characters, time, location, target files and actions. Therefore, frame model can be applied to represent the knowledge structure of insider threat.

According, from the above observations of insider threat, we can decompose an attack scenario into several attack actions. Each attack action can be further decomposed into several scenario slots. Different attack actions and scenario slots has its own types. Hence, it needs attack actions and scenario slots to represent the structure of the insider attack scenario. Below is an example of Insider Attack Action Frame.

Figure 1 shows the slot attributes of insider attack action frame which is a "unauthorized copy case" frame. Actor login at Time from IP and downloaded Target.doc owned by Owner. There are three additional rules of insider attack action frame describing the insider attack techniques. Role attack rule describes that insider may use coworker's account to implement the attack. Temporal attack rule describes that insider may implement the attacks in the rush hours or in a long time period. Spatial attack rule describes that insider could launch attacks from inside or outside network. Insider attack frame model can also be extended to represent a series of attack actions, attack scenario. Below is an example of attack scenario.

Figure 2 shows an insider attack scenario example represented by Insider Attack Action Frame.

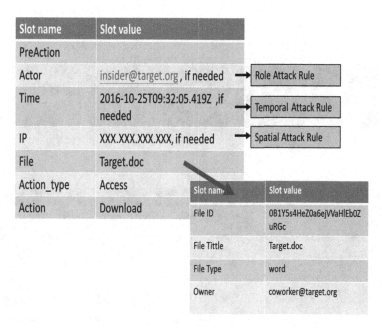

Fig. 1. Slot attributes of Insider Attack Action Frame.

Insider login google drive using insider@target.org, and then searched files with keyword "LinTech". Insider randomly preview searched files, and view and downloaded the target file. Three attack rules can also be applied to generate advanced attacks. For example, insider may know only two months of audit data are stored and hence perform each attacks over two months to avoid possible detection.

3 Insider Threat Test Suite Generation

According to the frame model defined above, the system architecture of the insider threat test suite generation system is shown in Fig. 3. The experts edit the attack actions of insider threat case with the insider attack decomposer. Next, the insider attack action frame and environment are maintained in the separate repository referred to the frame structured defined in the attack action (AA) ontology and attack environment (AE) ontology. When generating a tailor-made test suite, the insider attack composer applies the frame inference process to generate the test suite based on their queries. Besides, the question composer allows experts to extend the original insider threat cases to generate the new ones for target organization.

Experts can also use implemented user interface to trigger different attack rules. Parameters include: attack scenarios, insider (email account), time period (short period and long period), locations (local network and outside network), and performing time (on-duty and off-duty). The screen shot of user interface is shown in Fig. 4.

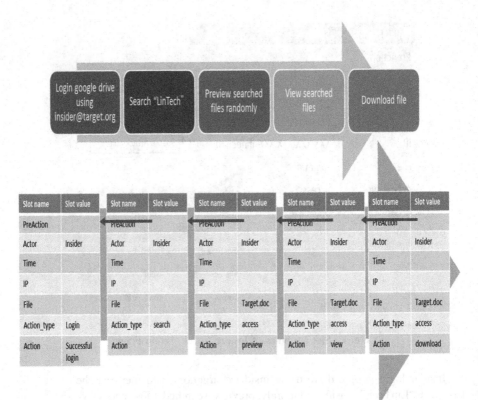

Fig. 2. Attack scenario represented by Insider Attack Action Frame

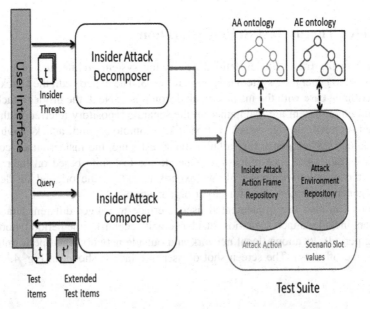

Fig. 3. System architecture of Insider Threat Test Suite Generation

Reinjecting Attack Sehaviors

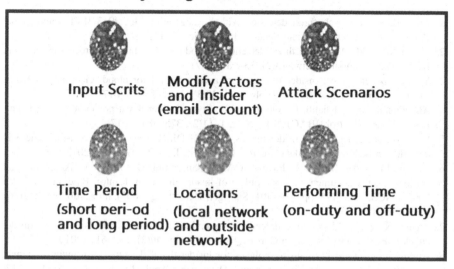

Fig. 4. Screen shot of user interface

4 Conclusion

The main contributions of this paper is to model the knowledge of insider threat, together with a systematical approach to generate test suite of insider threat detection. Several modeling features are proposed in this paper. The first, the composition of an insider threat case, attack action and attack environment, to model the insider threat case by the Insider Attack Action Frame. The second, the relations between attack action and attack environment can be modeled by the Instantiation property. From our usability evaluation, the results showed that the frame-based test suite is effective for maintenance and extension of test suite. In the near future, the adaptive test suite generation approaches can apply to generate tailor-made test suite according to routine behaviors within target organization.

Acknowledgement. This study is conducted under the "III Innovative and Prospective Technologies Project (1/1)" of the Institute for Information Industry which is subsidized by the Ministry of Economic Affairs of the Republic of China. This work was partially supported by National Science Council of the Republic of China under contracts 106-2511-S-468-002-MY3 and 106-2511-S-468-004-MY2.

References

1. Kitts, B., et al.: Click fraud detection with bot signatures. In: 2013 IEEE International Conference on Intelligence and Security Informatics (2013)
2. Zhu, T.M., et al.: An insider threat detection method based on business process mining. Int. J. Bus. Data Commun. Netw. **13**(2), 83–98 (2017)
3. Yaseen, Q., et al.: An insider threat aware access control for cloud relational databases. Clust. Comput. J. Netw. Softw. Tools Appl. **20**(3), 2669–2685 (2017)
4. Almehmadi, A., El-Khatib, K.: On the possibility of insider threat prevention using Intent-Based Access Control (IBAC). IEEE Syst. J. **11**(2), 373–384 (2017)
5. Bose, B., et al.: Detecting insider threats using RADISH: a system for real-time anomaly detection in heterogeneous data streams. IEEE Syst. J. **11**(2), 471–482 (2017)
6. Aleman-Meza, B., Burns, P., Eavenson, M., Palaniswami, D., Sheth, A.: An ontological approach to the document access problem of insider threat. In: Kantor, P., et al. (eds.) ISI 2005. LNCS, vol. 3495, pp. 486–491. Springer, Heidelberg (2005). https://doi.org/10.1007/11427995_47
7. Zhang, N., et al.: Maintaining defender's reputation in anomaly detection against insider attacks. IEEE Trans. Syst. Man Cybern. Part B-Cybern. **40**(3), 597–611 (2010)
8. Agrafiotis, I., et al.: Formalising policies for insider-threat detection: a tripwire grammar. J. Wirel. Mob. Netw. Ubiquitous Comput. Dependable Appl. (JoWUA) **8**(1), 26–43 (2017)
9. Kammüller, F., et al.: Insider threats and auctions: formalization, mechanized proof, and code generation. J. Wirel. Mob. Netw. Ubiquitous Comput. Dependable Appl. (JoWUA) **8**(1), 26–43 (2017)
10. Kammüller, F., et al.: Enhancing video surveillance with usage control and privacy-preserving solutions. J. Wirel. Mob. Netw. Ubiquitous Comput. Dependable Appl. (JoWUA) **7**(4), 20–40 (2016)
11. Pandit, T., et al.: Attribute-based signcryption: signer privacy, strong unforgeability and IND-CCA security in adaptive-predicates model (extended version). J. Internet Serv. Inf. Secur. (JISIS) **6**(3), 61–113 (2016)
12. Guerar, M., et al.: ClickPattern: a pattern lock system resilient to smudge and side-channel attacks. J. Wirel. Mob. Netw. Ubiquitous Comput. Dependable Appl. (JoWUA) **8**(2), 64–78 (2017)
13. Ishida, T., et al.: Implementation of an integrated disaster information cloud system for disaster control. J. Internet Serv. Inf. Secur. (JISIS) **7**(4), 1–20 (2017)

User Keystroke Authentication Based on Convolutional Neural Network

Mengxin Liu and Jianfeng Guan$^{(\boxtimes)}$ (ID)

State Key Laboratory of Networking and Switching Technology,
Beijing University of Posts and Telecommunications, Beijing 100876, China
{mxliu,jfguan}@bupt.edu.cn

Abstract. Biometric authentication technology has become an important measure to protect user information security. Among them, keystroke authentication technology has attracted the attention of many researchers because of its low cost and high benefit. In recent years, various methods such as statistical methods and integrated models have been increasingly used in user keystroke authentication and have achieved relatively good results. However, few people try to convert keystroke data into images and tap spatial information between keystroke data. In this paper, we used a new way to convert keystroke data into images, then we use a binary model based on a Convolutional Neural Network (CNN) for each genuine user and try to import the transformed images into the CNN model. In this way, we can dig out the "spatial information" of keystroke features, which is the advantage over other models, and this method is first proposed for keystroke behavior authentication. In addition, we have also tried data augmentation, relu activation functions and dropout methods to reduce overfitting. In the end, we got an accuracy of 96.8%, which is about 10% higher than the previous work.

Keywords: Keystroke authentication · Convolutional neural network
Information security · Overfitting

1 Introduction

The development of social information and network led to the explosion of data, more and more people are aware of the importance of data to the enterprise. According to the statistics of China Internet Network Information Center on the development of China's Internet, in June 2017, the number of Chinese Internet users has reached 751 million with an increase of 19.9 million in six months and an Internet penetration rate of 54.3% [15]. The rapid development of computer technology not only makes people's quality of life improved, but also brings

Supported in part by the National Basic Research Program of China (973) under Grant No. 2013CB329102, and in part by the Natural Science Foundation of China (NSFC) under Grant No. 61003283.

opportunities and challenges to computer information security. Whether individuals or businesses want to ensure that their personal privacy or trade secrets are secure and reliable. How to protect these massive information, especially for the malicious use or theft [3], has gradually become the core issue of our time [7].

User authentication systems, as an effective access control tool, have become an integral part of any system requiring security controls [16]. As we all know, user authentication methods can be roughly divided into the following three kinds. First, through user memory, such as static passwords, static passwords are mutually exclusive in terms of usability and security. Simple and easy-to-remember passwords are weak and complex static passwords are highly secure but not easy to memorize and maintain [12]. Second, through the user owned items, such as smart cards, SMS passwords and dynamic passwords. Thirdly, Biometric identification, using the inherent physiological features of the human body (such as fingerprints, face, etc.) and behavioral characteristics (such as gait, keystrokes, etc.) for personal identification [5,6,13].

An endless stream of cyber attacks exacerbates the possibility of misappropriation of user information (including passwords), while the first and second types of authentication can only identify authentication information such as passwords, verification codes, etc., and can not identify the users themselves. Once the password is stolen or the phone used to receive the verification code was stolen, the identity of the user is very easy to be posing as others. This obviously can no longer meet the needs of contemporary information security, on the contrary, Keystroke authentication technology has the characteristics of low cost, high availability, easy popularization, good user interactivity, is a good choice.

At present, the main biometric identification methods are mainly fingerprinting, face recognition and iris authentication, but such identification technologies usually require expensive biosensors. The keystroke authentication technology does not require any special equipment to collect the required data. Therefore, from the aspects of security, low cost and universality, it is an inevitable trend to study the keystroke authentication technology. Although free text research is now available, static identification when a user logs in is always the first line of defence to ensure safety and needs to be as accurate as possible. So this paper is mainly focused on the study of user login authentication based on keystroke dynamics.

The rest of the paper will be introduced in the following order. In Sect. 2, we provide a state of the art on user login authentication systems based on keystroke dynamics. In Sect. 3, we introduce the basic background support used in this paper. In Sect. 4, we describe the processing of data. In Sect. 5, we introduce the contributed algorithm. In Sect. 6, we show the results of the experiment and summarize it in Sect. 7.

2   Related Work

Keystroke authentication technology is mainly divided into the following two categories: one is based on static text, mainly used for implicit authentication in user login module. The other one is based on dynamic text, mainly used for continuous authentication of users using the system. As mentioned in the first section, we mainly focus on the one based on static text.

The use of keystroke dynamics to identify user identities was first proposed by R. Gaines, a British scientist, in 1980, which first to the study of keystroke recognition based on static text. In 1990, Joyce and Gupta introduced the absolute distance method into the keystroke kinematics for the first time, obtaining a false acceptance rate (FAR) of 0.25% and a false rejection rate (FRR) of 16.36% [10]. In the same year, Slivinsky et al. used Bayesian statistical classification to study the user's keystroke behavior, resulting in 2.8% FAR and 8.1% FRR. In the 1990s, Brown et al. [2] introduced neural networks and other methods to improve the recognition rate. By 2007, Azevedo et al. [1] adopted a combination of support vector machine (SVM), genetic algorithm (GA) and particle swarm optimization (PSO) to reduce the average error rate (AER) to 5.18%. In 2009, Killourhy et al. [11] contributed Carnegie Mellon University (CMU) benchmark dataset, provided a standard dataset for keystroke research, making comparison of keystroke domain research possible. At the same time, the best score they got was the use of Manhattan (scaled) which obtained a equal error rate (EER) of 9.6%. Later, a large number of researchers used this dataset. In 2015, Pisani [17] used the M2005IDB which is a statistical method to achieve a 79.7% accuracy in this dataset. In the same year, ensemble methods such as random forests were also widely used in the field of keystrokes, and they all reached close to 80% accuracy [18]. In 2017, Ceker et al. [4] used CNN to achieve 96.7% accuracy on the CMU dataset, although CNN is also used in this paper, the difference is that them used a multi-classification model, and we used multiple binary models, and there are two distinct methods in the input data construction.

In the field of keystrokes, the evaluation methodology used by each are different. The above-mentioned FAR, FRR, and Accuracy are the most commonly used indicators, and their meaning will be described in Sect. 6.2. The EER refers to the value of the FAR when the FAR and the FRR are the same, and the AER refers to the ratio of the number of errors to the total number.

3   Background Knowledge

3.1   Convolutional Neural Network

Due to the excellent performance of convolutional neural network (CNN) in various image competitions, it has been rapidly developed in recent years. As an effective recognition method, it has attracted a wide range of researchers. CNN is a feed-forward neural network with excellent performance in large-scale image processing. When using CNN, we can implicitly extract features from the training data, thereby avoiding explicit feature extraction, especially when training images that require multi-dimensional input vectors, this advantage can reduce the step of feature extraction. In addition, the neurons on the same feature map have the same weight, so they can be calculated in parallel, that is, the weight is shared, which reduces the complexity of the network. This is also a great advantage of the convolutional network over the ordinary neural network. CNN can share the local information while weight sharing, which makes it has great advantage in image processing and speech recognition [14].

CNN is mainly composed of three structures. The first is the convolutional layer, the second is the pooling layer, and the last is the fully-connected layer.

1. Convolutional layer: Each convolution layer in the CNN consists of multiple convolution kernels. The parameters of each convolution kernel are optimized by a back-propagation algorithm. Finally, different features can be extracted according to different parameters, such as certain convolutions. The nuclear extracted horizontal lines, and some extracted vertical lines. However, a convolutional layer can only extract some low-level features, while a network with more convolutional layers can iteratively extract more complex features.
2. Pooling layer: Usually after the convolution layer will get a large dimension of the feature, in the pooling layer, the feature cut into several areas, whichever is the maximum or average, get a new, smaller dimension features.
3. Fully-Connected layer: In the fully-connected layer, all local features are combined into global features, which is used to calculate the score of each class in the last.

3.2   Dropout

Methods to reduce overfitting are prematurely terminated (when the effect on the validation set is poor), L1 and L2 regularization weights, dropouts, etc., where we choose to use dropout. Dropout that is in the process of deep learning network training, for the neural network unit, according to a certain probability to be discarded from the network.

3.3   Relu

It is well known that if there is no nonlinear join, the neural network can be linearly represented. At this time, there is no difference between a layer of neural network or a multi-layer neural network, and the result is that it cannot solve more complicated problems, so it is necessary to add an activation function. Rectified Linear Unit (ReLU), also known as modified linear unit, can alleviate over-fitting while adding nonlinearity. It is the most commonly used activation function. So here we use Relu as the activation function.

4   Dataset Description and Data Processing

4.1   Dataset Description and Feature Extraction

Today there are very few public datasets on keystroke dynamics, mainly CMU benchmark dataset and GREYC web-based keystroke dynamics dataset. To facilitate comparison with others, we chose the earliest CMU datasets.

CMU benchmark dataset has used '.tie5Roanl' as the password. There are 51 subjects, each subject needs to be divided into eight sessions, each session contains 50 events. Therefore, the dataset consists of 20,400 events. This dataset contains three types of features: The first category is Hold (H), which means the time duration of pressing a key, usually called a dwell time. The second category is Up-Down (UD), which means the time duration between the first key bounced and the second key pressed, usually called a flight time. The last category is Down-Down (DD), said the time duration between the first key pressed and the second key pressed. And DDan = Ha + UDan [9].

At present, most papers choose to use one of dwell time and flight time as the input data, while we choose to combine dwell time, flight time and DD as the input data to better represent a person's typing habits.

4.2   Data Separation

During the training phase, we chose one of the subjects as a genuine user, while the rest of the subjects were set as impostors. From the selected subject, we use 70% of the data as a positive sample of the training data, and the remaining 30% of the data as a positive sample of the testing data. At the same time, we extract the data of other users and construct a negative sample of the training data and the testing data according to the positive sample ratio [8].

5   Contributed Algorithms

5.1   Preprocessing Phase

Before we can classify, we need to convert the data into images first. When the password has n characters, the width and height of the converted image are n, and the row name and column name are key names. For example, the password is ".tie5Roaln", then the converted image is as shown in the Fig. 1, so that we convert the problem into an image problem. Obviously, everybody's keystroke rules for fixed passwords (H, UD, DD's general convention) are hidden in the image, and then we can use CNN to dig out the unique keystroke convention for everyone.

5.2 Data Augmentation

Data augmentation is creating a batch of "new" data from existing data by methods such as panning, flipping, and noise. This is a good way to reduce overfitting when the number of dataset is small, this is in line with our keystroke research on the CMU benchmark dataset. This paper uses the following two data augmentation methods:

1. In this paper we do the same as Çeker and Upadhyaya [4] did, borrow a keystroke augmentation method from a study in which the digraphs are synthetically generated to launch a forgery attack [19]. As these study did, the keystroke datas are assumed to show a Gaussian distribution in each feature. First of all, we get the mean and the standard deviation from each feature separately in the CMU benchmark dataset. Then the data of augmentation is generated and the values fall in the range of $\mu - \alpha \times \delta$ to $\mu + \alpha \times \delta$. Unlike previous papers, here we fix $\delta = 0.6$ after multiple attempts. At last, we get four times synthetic data.
2. After augmentation data by adding noise, we also use flipping which is the most common data enhancement method for images. After flipping all the images horizontally, this will double the size of the dataset.

	.	t	i	e	5	R	o	a	l	n
.	H	DD								
t	UD	H	DD							
i		UD	H	DD						
e			UD	H	DD					
5				UD	H	DD				
R					UD	H	DD			
o						UD	H	DD		
a							UD	H	DD	
l								UD	H	DD
n									UD	H

Fig. 1. Converted data

6 Experimental Results

6.1 Model

Some papers use a model to classify multiple users, but this paper always insists on using different parameters to make the model suitable for each user. This is the most suitable method in the private laptop scenario. After all, a laptop does not have so many users, even if it does, it cannot determine how many users it should be divided into. In addition, each laptop only needs single user authentication. So we only need to train each user with the same CNN model, and can create a personalized model for each user. In this paper we mainly focus on improving the average accuracy of models for different users. Such as Fig. 2, Model_n is the model of user_n, so there are 51 CNN models in this dataset.

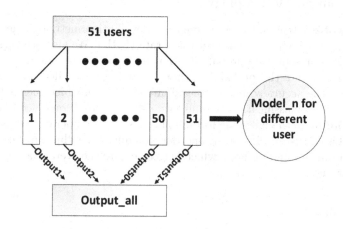

Fig. 2. Global model

After data preprocessing and data augmentation, we put the dataset into the CNN model in Fig. 3. This paper use only one convolution layer, one pooling layer, and one fully-connected layer. In the convolution layer, we use a filter with height and width both of 3, the number of channels is 32, and the horizontal and vertical strides are set to 1, padding selects 'SAME'. The output of convolution layer is added relu activation function, this will not only add the nonlinear feature, but also to reduce overfitting to a certain extent, and can reduce part of the calculation. In the pooling layer, we use the maximum pooling, setting both

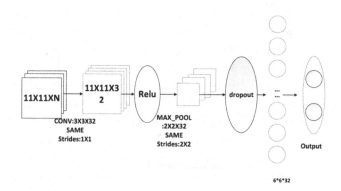

Fig. 3. CNN model

the size and the strides to 2. We added dropout after the pooling layer, which is one of the ways to reduce overfitting. We set the dropout probability to 0.7. Finally, the results are flattened and output through the full-connected layer. Throughout the process, we set the batch-size to 64.

6.2 Evaluation Methodology

In the field of keystrokes, the commonly used evaluation methodologies are false acceptance rate (FAR) and false rejection rate (FRR). We also use these in this paper. FAR represents the probability that an impostor passes authentication, and FRR represents the probability that a genuine user failed authentication. Also, we use the accuracy metric to evaluate our model which means the probability of correct classification. Usually we can get the average accuracy of the model according to the following formula, because the number of test sets of each user model is consistent. However, in order to reduce the influence of outliers, we use the trimmean function here, which is to calculate the average after removing the highest and lowest values.

6.3 Results

We set model_n to refer to the model of the nth user (i.e. user_n). The indicators of model_1 and model_2 are shown in the Fig. 4 and the Fig. 5 which include FAR, FRR, and accuracy. The trend of each model is basically the same, it can be seen that the accuracy of our model will eventually converge to 1 as the epoch increases.

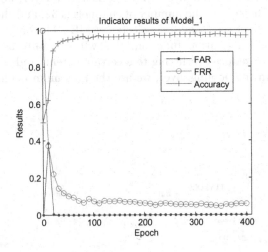

Fig. 4. Indicator results of model_1

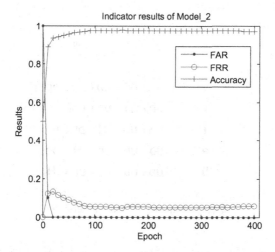

Fig. 5. Indicator results of model_2

Table 1. Compare Results

	Previous research	Decision tree	Convolutional neural network
CMU	79.7%	94.3%	96.8%

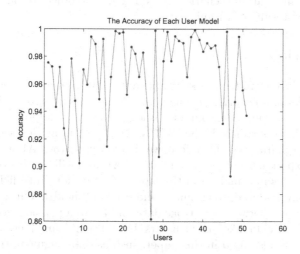

Fig. 6. The accuracy of each user model

	.	t	i	e	5
.	H.	DD.t	DD.i	DD.e	DD.5
t	UD.t	Ht	DDti	DDte	DDts
i	UD.i	UDti	Hi	DDie	DDi5
e	UD.e	UDte	UDie	He	DDt.
5	UD.5	UDt5	UDi5	UDe5	H5

Fig. 7. Improved data conversion

The Fig. 6 shows the accuracy of each user model. Here we get the average accuracy of the model by the trimmean function is 96.8%. Also get an average FAR of 0.04% and an average FRR of 6.5%. This means that imposters have little chance of stealing information from the laptop, and this is a good guarantee for user information security. As shown in Table 1, we also used the decision tree classifier of sklearn's library, and obtained 94.3% accuracy under the same dataset, data partitioning, and evaluation methods. It can be seen that our accuracy rate is nearly 3% points higher than that. Although Ceker et al. [4] got an accuracy of 96.7%, but because of the differences in dataset, evaluation methods, and application scenarios, it cannot be the object of our comparison, so we chose the results of Pisani [17].

7   Conclusion

This paper mainly introduces a keystroke authentication model that is applicable to private laptop scenarios, in which a CNN model is used for each user. In the private laptop scenario, if the computer is logged on by the impostor, all resources in the laptop may be stolen. If the FAR is high, the information security for the user will not be guaranteed. Therefore, we should reduce the FAR as much as possible. In our experiment, we achieved 0.04% FAR and will be able to protect the safety of the user's information in the laptop. In this keystroke field, almost no one tries to convert data into an image and use CNN model. This method mines spatial information between keystroke data and forms a personalized image that belongs to the individual keystroke habits. In addition, many methods for reducing overfitting are also used in this paper, such as data augmentation, relu, and dropout. The dataset used in this paper is a public dataset, which is convenient for comparison with other researchers. According to the experimental results, the accuracy of this paper is at the forefront when using the same dataset, achieving an accuracy of 96.8%. We plan to further study the application of the CNN model in keystroke dynamics and adopt more ways to make the performance better, so that the model can be applied to various fields.

8 Future

In the future work, the following aspects will be improved:

1. First of all, data construction will be improved in the next work to enhance data utilization. Obviously, in the current work, our data reorganization has a large blank space. When performing convolution operations, these places are wasteful. At the same time, some information is not reflected in the adjacent data, it may be a certain habit between playing a few consecutive letters, this time requires the relationship between non-adjacent data. So we must come up with a way to make full use of these blank places. The improvement is to fill the blanks. For example, the time when the second button is pressed until the fourth button is pressed is equal to the DD of the second key plus the DD of the third key. As the Fig. 7 shows, there is a numerical relationship between any two keys.
2. The second job to be done in the future is to conduct free-text-based identity authentication research. Nowadays, many people do not have the habit of locking screens when they leave for a short time, which makes the criminals have a chance. It is the future trend to study the free text-based identity authentication and combine the two authentication methods to form a more stable and applicable identity authentication method.
3. The third direction is to make full use of other tools like mouse to assist the verification, which will more fully form a person's behavior habits, and greatly help the identity authentication.

References

1. Azevedo, G.L.F.B.G., Cavalcanti, G.D.C., Filho, E.C.B.C.: Hybrid solution for the feature selection in personal identification problems through keystroke dynamics. In: International Joint Conference on Neural Networks, pp. 1947–1952 (2007). http://dx.doi.org/10.1109/IJCNN.2007.4371256. ISSN 2161-4393
2. Brown, M., Rogers, S.J.: User identification via keystroke characteristics of typed names using neural networks. Int. J. Man Mach. Stud. **39**(6), 999–1014 (1993). https://doi.org/10.1006/imms.1993.1092
3. Casey, W., Morales, J.A., Mishra, B.: Threats from inside: dynamic utility (mis)alignments in an agent based model. J. Wirel. Mob. Netw. Ubiquitous Comput. Dependable Appl. (JoWUA) **7**(1), 97–117 (2016). https://doi.org/10.22667/JOWUA.2016.03.31.097
4. Çeker, H., Upadhyaya, S.: Sensitivity analysis in keystroke dynamics using convolutional neural networks. In: IEEE Workshop on Information Forensics and Security (WIFS), pp. 1–6, December 2017. http://dx.doi.org/10.1109/WIFS.2017.8267667
5. Chen, C., Anada, H., Kawamoto, J., Sakurai, K.: A hybrid encryption scheme with key-cloning protection: user/terminal double authentication via attributes and fingerprints. J. Internet Serv. Inf. Secur. (JISIS) **6**(2), 23–36 (2016). https://doi.org/10.22667/JISIS.2016.05.31.023
6. Conti, V., Rundo, L., Militello, C., Mauri, G., Vitabile, S.: Resource-efficient hardware implementation of a neural-based node for automatic fingerprint classification. J. Wirel. Mob. Netw. Ubiquitous Comput. Dependable Appl. (JoWUA) **8**(4), 19–36 (2017). http://isyou.info/jowua/papers/jowua-v8n4-2.pdf

7. Harilal, A., et al.: The wolf of SUTD (TWOS): a dataset of malicious insider threat behavior based on a gamified competition. J. Wirel. Mob. Netw. Ubiquitous Comput. Dependable Appl. (JoWUA) **9**(1), 54–85 (2018). https://doi.org/10.22667/JOWUA.2018.03.31.054

8. Ho, J., Kang, D.K.: Mini-batch bagging and attribute ranking for accurate user authentication in keystroke dynamics. Pattern Recognit. **70**, 139–151 (2017). https://doi.org/10.1016/j.patcog.2017.05.002

9. Ho, J., Kang, D.: One-class naïve Bayes with duration feature ranking for accurate user authentication using keystroke dynamics. Appl. Intell. 1–18 (2017). https://doi.org/10.1007/s10489-017-1020-2

10. Joyce, R., Gupta, G.K.: Identity authentication based on keystroke latencies. Commun. ACM **33**(2), 168–176 (1990). https://doi.org/10.1145/75577.75582

11. Killourhy, K.S., Maxion, R.A.: Comparing anomaly-detection algorithms for keystroke dynamics. In: IEEE/IFIP International Conference on Dependable Systems & Networks, pp. 125–134 (2009). https://doi.org/10.1109/DSN.2009.5270346

12. Kim, A., Han, G., Seo, S.H.: Secure and usable bio-passwords based on confidence interval. J. Internet Serv. Inf. Secur. (JISIS) **7**(1), 14–27 (2017). http://isyou.info/jisis/vol7/no1/jisis-2017-vol7-no1-02.pdf

13. Kim, J.S., Pan, S.B.: A study on EMG-based biometrics. J. Internet Serv. Inf. Secur. (JISIS) **7**(2), 19–31 (2017). http://isyou.info/jisis/vol7/no1/jisis-2017-vol7-no2-02.pdf

14. Kuang, P., Cao, W., Wu, Q.: Preview on structures and algorithms of deep learning. In: International Computer Conference on Wavelet Active Media Technology and Information Processing, pp. 176–179 (2014). http://dx.doi.org/10.1109/ICCWAMTIP.2014.7073385

15. Li, X., Qin, Y.: Research on criminal jurisdiction of computer cybercrime. Procedia Comput. Sci. **131**, 793–799 (2018). https://doi.org/10.1016/j.procs.2018.04.263

16. Park, M., Seo, J., Han, J., Oh, H., Lee, K.: Situational awareness framework for threat intelligence measurement of android malware. J. Wirel. Mob. Netw. Ubiquitous Comput. Dependable Appl. (JoWUA) **9**(3), 25–38 (2018). https://doi.org/10.22667/JOWUA.2018.09.30.025

17. Pisani, P.H., Lorena, A.C., de Carvalho, A.C.P.L.F: Adaptive approaches for keystroke dynamics. In: International Joint Conference on Neural Networks, pp. 1–8 (2015). http://dx.doi.org/10.1109/IJCNN.2015.7280467

18. Pisani, P.H., Lorena, A.C., De Carvalho, A.C.P.L.F.: Ensemble of adaptive algorithms for keystroke dynamics. In: Brazilian Conference on Intelligent Systems (BRACIS), pp. 310–315, November 2015. http://dx.doi.org/10.1109/BRACIS.2015.29

19. Stefan, D., Shu, X., Yao, D.: Robustness of keystroke-dynamics based biometrics against synthetic forgeries. Comput. Secur. **31**(1), 109–121 (2012). https://doi.org/10.1016/j.cose.2011.10.001

An SDN-Based Secure Mobility Model for UAV-Ground Communications

Rajesh Kumar[1]([✉]), Mohd. Abuzar Sayeed[1], Vishal Sharma[2], and Ilsun You[2]

[1] Computer Science and Engineering Department,
Thapar Institute of Engineering and Technology (TIET),
Patiala 147004, Punjab, India
rakumar@thapar.edu, abuzar.sayeed@gmail.com
[2] Department of Information Security Engineering, Soonchunhyang University,
Asan-si 31538, Republic of Korea
vishal_sharma2012@hotmail.com, ilsunu@gmail.com

Abstract. Multi-UAV collaborative networks provide with the opportunity to exploit civil, chemical, biological, radiological, nuclear and geographical reconnaissance, survey, management, and control. For the collaborative network formation, coverage is of prime paramountcy. Alongside coverage, possession of information and communication security is withal a major challenge. The coverage quandary can be resolved by a perspicacious selection of UAV waypoints. But the security paradigm which can be an effect of faulty node, intrusion or even choice of erroneous communication channels needs to be taken care of through efficacious strategies. Consequently, both a specialized UAV mobility model and a security mechanism are required in order to establish prosperous collaborative networks. In this article, an SDN-based secure mobility model is proposed which takes into account the topological density and restricts the UAV and ground node (Wireless Sensor Networks (WSNs)) transmissions to authenticity. Significant gains are observed for throughput, coverage, and latency by establishing a simulated network between multiple UAVs and WSN motes.

Keywords: UAVs · Mobility model · SDN · Security · WSNs

1 Introduction

Unmanned Aerial Vehicles (UAVs) are autonomous flying nodes which are either pre-programmed or controlled via a ground station. UAVs have found application in scientific, research, civilian and military applications as a result of the flexibility and ease of deployment [1–4]. UAVs have taken the cooperative networks to a new level. The cooperation between ground and aerial nodes has resulted in significant gains in data dissemination, monitoring, and control over strategic locations [5–8]. UAVs also prove significant when it comes to data gathering from

© Springer Nature Singapore Pte Ltd. 2019
I. You et al. (Eds.): MobiSec 2017, CCIS 971, pp. 169–179, 2019.
https://doi.org/10.1007/978-981-13-3732-1_14

inaccessible locations. One such case is autonomous networking where UAVs help uplifting the problem of coverage, failures, limiting guidance and dead nodes by acting as supervisors [9–14]. Efficient and intelligent surveying is one of the key aspects of UAV networks.

Nature-based algorithms like Hill Myna and Desert Sparrow optimizations (HMADSO) performs cooperative rendezvous and efficient task allocation [15]. Cooperative ground and air surveillance mechanisms utilize UAVs for a broad coverage and ground nodes for a detailed zoom in picture of the area surveillance as studied in [16–18]. In [19], the multi-hop characteristics of WSN data transmission were replaced by direct communication between UAV and sensor nodes where UAVs served as sinks. Efficient deployment of available resources can help improve the coverage and reduce the number of hops for boosting the overall throughput [20, 21].

Wireless Sensor Networks (WSNs) are spatially dispersed energy concentric dedicated sensor nodes largely deployed in inaccessible locations [22]. WSNs are energy sensitive devices and suffer from a constant depletion. Together with path selection, the multi-hopping produces un-necessary traffic, delays and packet drops. With a general deployment in sensitive areas the transmission carried to or from UAV is of prime importance for UAVs-WSNs communications. These collaborative networks involve threats in the form of UAVs communicating with non-authentic ground nodes [23–25]. Such a problem becomes gross when ground and aerial nodes are allowed to communicate without coordination and authentication. Another scenario involves UAVs communicating with a faulty aerial node. These types of issues can be resolved through efficient mobility model and novel routing schemes [26, 27].

Mobility model defines a movement scheme which mimics the real world movements, traffic and response scenarios. One key characteristic of a good mobility model is its ability to adapt to the dynamically changing network behavior [28]. The coordination between WSN and UAV nodes is characterized by the erratic and dynamic behavior of the networks. Vehicular models like Synthetic, Survey and Simulation-based approaches do not suffice as the inherent inconsistencies of the erratic network behavior hinder the overall mathematical formulation of the scenario as well as the survey and simulation of every single scenario is not feasible. Trace-based models don't suffice under disaster condition, military applications, unforeseen events and even under extreme security requirements [29, 30].

In this paper, a Software Defined Network (SDN) [31] controller based mobility model for communication between Multi-UAV and WSNs is introduced. SDN is effectively a new paradigm in the field of computer networks which separates data forwarding from the control logic thus facilitating better flexibility, scalability, and dynamic adaptability. The SDN controller provides with the opportunity to update flows on the move, thus, adapting to the dynamic topology, and also updates the legal moves as well as node authentication by means of pre-installed flow tables [31].

Mobility model for multi-UAV WSN networks is proposed which takes into account the attraction factor for setting up the waypoints for UAV movements. The authentication is performed on the basis of pre-installed flows. The pre-installed flow table of the UAV is constantly updated with the changing topology. The controller-generated dynamic waypoints prevent UAV from erratic movements as well as any unidentified transmission is discarded based on the flow action rules. The proposed approach is compared against the traditional Clustered Hierarchical WSN layout [32] with UAVs as sinks and against a technique where UAV maneuvers are statically fixed before the flight.

The rest of the paper is organized as follows: Sect. 2 presents system model and the proposed approach. Section 3 evaluates the performance and finally, Sect. 4 concludes the paper.

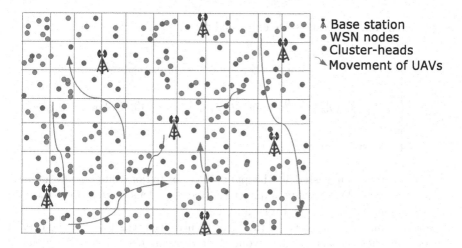

Fig. 1. An exemplary illustration of the network model.

2 Proposed Approach

This article presents a secure SDN-based mobility model for Multi-UAV coordinated WSN networks. The complete geography is divided into a matrix, as shown in Fig. 1. The WSN nodes falling into a particular sector (block of the matrix) are default considered into the same cluster. In the given model, the selection of controller and cluster head is done as

$$\min(D_m) \text{ and } \max(\mathcal{L}), \forall \mathcal{N}, \tag{1}$$

s.t.

$$\mathcal{L}_A > 0,$$
$$\tau_s \geq Mean(\tau_\mathcal{N}), \tag{2}$$

where $\mathcal{L}$ refers to the set containing the total connections for nodes, $\mathcal{L}_A$ is the number of connections active on a node, τ_s is the mean life time of the selected node, and $\tau_{\mathcal{N}}$ refers to the mean life time of $|\mathcal{N}|$ nodes, D_m is the average one hop distance for nodes represented with a set $\mathcal{N}$, which is given as the distance metric, such that,

$$D_{m_i} = \frac{\sum_{i=1}^{S_n} \mathcal{H}}{S_n}, S_n \leq |\mathcal{N}|, \tag{3}$$

D_{m_i} is the node under consideration, $\mathcal{H}$ is one hop distances from the node under consideration with S_n being the active nodes, given that the node coordinates lie within the same sector as that of the base station. For the model to proceed further,

$$0 \leq D_{m_i} \leq \frac{S_n (S_n - 1)}{2\mathcal{N}}, \tag{4}$$

where the extreme values are expressed as:

$$D_{m_i} = \begin{cases} 0, D_m^{(selected)} = \text{infinite}, \mathcal{L} = \min, \tau_s = \max, \text{Isolated} = True \\ \frac{S_n(S_n-1)}{2\mathcal{N}}, D_m^{(selected)} = \max, \mathcal{L} = \max, \tau_s = \min, \text{Isolated} = False \\ \text{Otherwise, Select.} \end{cases}$$
$$\tag{5}$$

The controller suggested in the paper has six major components namely; Mission control, UAV topology map, active topology, Density Function for Route Establishment (DFRE), flow Table, and logs.

Mission control component of the UAV Controller keeps track of the overall mission statistics and conceptual layout of the system. The information includes cell structure, information about the geography. The main function is to provide preliminary information to the UAV topology map. Active topology component stores the current UAV movement statistics and functions which dictate the overall movement criterion and geometric characteristics of the flight path. Active topology also forwards the overall sensed statistics of the geographical area to the UAV topology map. The UAV topology map component serves as data storage for mission control and active topology components.

DFRE works on the stored statistics to find an efficient and viable route for the UAVs. Once the complete area is surveyed, the component starts with calculating the density component of respective areas. Figure 2 presents the block diagram of the SDN controller used by the proposed model for coordinating UAVs with WSNs over a defined geographical area.

The transfer between UAV and sensor nodes always happens through the cluster-head. When UAV is in range of the cluster head the Head Swap are performed for inter-changing the cluster heads. UAV becomes the cluster head of the sector to facilitate transfer not only from the designated cluster head but also allows the cluster members to send data directly towards the UAV.

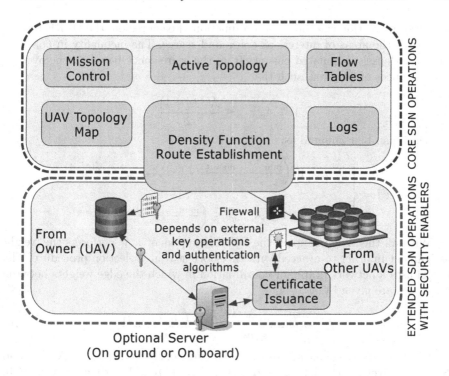

Fig. 2. A component diagram of the considered SDN controller for UAV-WSN coordinations.

The UAV waypoints are set in a way that it moves from head of one densely populated cluster towards the head of another densely populated cluster. UAV waypoints are decided on the basis of topological density and distance. The transmissions are facilitated by coordination function, which is calculated by means of topological density as follows:

$$A_f = \frac{S_a}{\mathcal{A}} \times \frac{S_n}{\mathcal{N}} \left(\sqrt{\frac{1}{|\mathcal{N}|} \left(T_{psys} - \overline{T_{psys}}\right)^2} - \sqrt{\frac{1}{S_n} \left(T_p - \overline{T_p}\right)^2} \right) \qquad (6)$$

where T_p is the number of transmissions per unit time in a sector, S_a denotes the sector area, and T_{psys} is the number of transmissions per unit time in the entire system.

Similarly, this model can be extended to calculate the coordination of each sector as well as the entire zone while fixating the number of transmissions permissible to each node, each sector and each area under the control of a single base station.

After estimating the coordination function of each region, the DFRE further prioritizes the areas of interest as dense and scarce. The inequality in (7) identifies the densely populated clusters from the scares ones based on the average hop distances of the area, such that,

$$1 \leq \mathcal{A}_{range} \leq \frac{\mathcal{N}(\mathcal{N}-1)}{2}, \tag{7}$$

which can be evaluated as:

$$Area = \begin{cases} \text{Dense, if,} \left(\frac{\min(S_n) - mean(S_n)}{2} \right) < \mathcal{A}_{range} \leq \frac{\mathcal{N}(\mathcal{N}-1)}{2} \\ \\ \text{Sparse, if,} 1 \leq \mathcal{A}_{range} \leq \left(\frac{\min(S_n) - mean(S_n)}{2} \right) \end{cases} \tag{8}$$

With all the areas mapped, the DFRE component now performs the weight assignment in order to proceed with the shortest route selection procedure. The model uses a network graph for coordination in which the edge weights between the nodes are given by:

$$E_w = \frac{T_{psys}\eta_1 + |\mathcal{N}|\eta_2}{\eta_1\eta_2} - \frac{T_p\eta_3 + S_n\eta_4}{\eta_3\eta_4}, \tag{9}$$

where η_1, η_2, η_3, and η_4 are the balancing constants for T_{psys}, $\mathcal{N}$, T_p, and S_n, respectively, such that $\eta_1 + \eta_2 = 1$ and $\eta_3 + \eta_4 = 1$ with $\eta_1 \neq 0$, $\eta_2 \neq 0$, $\eta_3 \neq 0$, and $\eta_4 \neq 0$.

The densely populated sectors are serviced by UAV maneuvers directly along with the sectors which fall in line to two consecutive UAVs. The scarce sectors which don't fall in the path of UAV are the designated as isolated zones. These isolated zones fixate on sensors, which send hello packets towards nearby dense regions and the base station when the network is initialized. The purpose of the hello packets is to determine the number of active nodes in the region and number of hops required to reach the dense sector and the base station.

The proposed model considers that the Flow table component of the controller is pre-installed with the specific information of the available sensor nodes. The data transmission is controlled by the flow table match action rules. The DFRE component keeps tracks of the overall topology and updates the flow tables accordingly. In addition, it interacts with the security module to authenticate the waypoints and maintain the legitimacy of incoming connections. Further, to verify the connectivity between the UAVs and the WSNs, DFRE checks for previously calculated waypoints and matches with the next possible waypoints. In such a way, the movement of UAVs is authenticated and verified before transmissions[1]. The details of security considerations and requirements are provided below:

- The system maintains the check on the certificates generated by the controller for other UAVs in the form a centralized corpus on the controller. It also maintains the details of keys to be used for securing the communications.
- The channel security is based on the network architecture and depends on the initial phases of mutual authentication, which are not covered at the moment and is marked as an assumption.
- The keys for securing the location as well as the system conditions are generated by the owner UAV, which can relay with an optional server to check for freshness and prevent any replay attacks.
- Once the keys are initiated, the DFRE module improvises the availability of waypoints and allocate it to the topology generator, which helps to fixate the points for maneuverability. Any violation in the waypoints is tracked through crypto-mechanisms based on keys generated in the initial phase.
- The certificate issuance helps to re-verify the UAVs and the waypoints and avoids overheads associated with re-verification. However, the requirement of verification of waypoints depends on the type of network layout and the environment in which the UAVs are deployed.

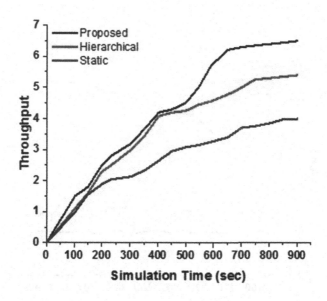

Fig. 3. Throughput vs. Simulation time.

---

[1] The detailed procedure for authentication and verification will be presented in our future reports.

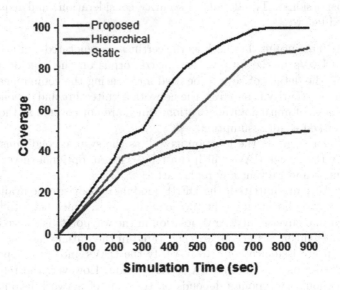

Fig. 4. Coverage vs. Simulation time.

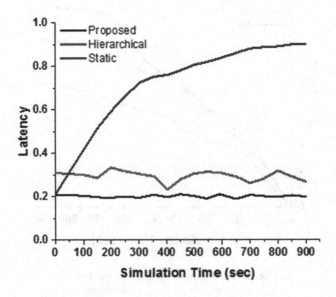

Fig. 5. Latency vs. Simulation time.

At the moment, the major security requisites are discussed as an abstracted aspect by following the layout in Fig. 2. However, the future reports will present the detailed working as well as detailed security analysis of the proposed system.

3 Performance Evaluations

The proposed technique relies on exploits the movement characteristics of UAV in order to achieve significant gains over the already existing models. The evaluation and testing of the approach are done on a model consisting of the base station, WSN motes and the UAVs serving as relays by using NS-3 and Matlab^{TM}. The testing is performed on a $1200 \times 1200\,m^2$ area. The number of UAVs is varied between 1 and 10 with WSN nodes equaling 100.

The average packet size is varied between 512 bytes to 1024 bytes and the value of balancing constants (η) are kept fixed at 0.5. The connections are generated through the modeling without overlapping and the proposed approach is compared with hierarchical WSN layout and Statically Maneuvered UAV approaches. The approaches are compared on the basis of throughput, coverage, and latency. At the moment only performance-based evaluations are presented and the security evaluations will be covered in upcoming reports.

The proposed approach performs at the maximum throughput level of 95.7% as compared to 77.1% and 57.1% throughput levels of hierarchical WSN approach and static deployment of UAVs respectively. Figure 3 gives the throughput compassion of the considered approaches against the proposed approach. Initially, three approaches have comparable throughput but with time the static approach starts degrading. The traditional hierarchical approach initially performs in close proximity to the proposed approach but cannot match the steep ascent as the proposed approach performs uniformly throughout the simulation tests.

The proposed approach provides the maximum coverage of around 99% in comparison to 84% and 49% coverage of hierarchical and static deployment. The approach also provides a faster and efficient coverage against the other two solutions. Figure 4 gives the coverage relationship between the existing and the proposed approaches. The latency of the proposed approach is approximately constant at 20% gains. The hierarchical approach works with a varying latency between 19% and 34%. The latency levels always stay in close proximity to the proposed approach but with consistent fluctuation. The static UAV approach possesses inconsistent latency measures with a maximum of 84% and average latency of around 65%, as shown in Fig. 5.

4 Conclusion

In this article, a novel mobility scheme based on the transmission density of the WSN nodes is proposed which is capable of including waypoint-security of UAVs. The UAVs perform successive shifts towards dense regions thus resulting in high coverage and throughput. The proposed approach incorporates a simple flow based technique through SDN controller for authentication and coordination of WSN as well as aerial nodes. Significant gains are observed for metrics like throughput, coverage, and latency. The details on authentication procedures and verification mechanisms will be presented in our future reports.

Acknowledgement. This paper was presented at the Workshop associated with the 12th International Conference on Provable Security, 25–28 October, 2018, Jeju, Rep. of Korea.

References

1. Bunse, C., Plotz, S.: Security analysis of drone communication protocols. In: Payer, M., Rashid, A., Such, J.M. (eds.) ESSoS 2018. LNCS, vol. 10953, pp. 96–107. Springer, Cham (2018). https://doi.org/10.1007/978-3-319-94496-8_7
2. Wu, Q., Zeng, Y., Zhang, R.: Joint trajectory and communication design for multi-UAV enabled wireless networks. IEEE Trans. Wirel. Commun. **17**(3), 2109–2121 (2018)
3. Shi, W., Zhou, H., Li, J., Xu, W., Zhang, N., Shen, X.: Drone assisted vehicular networks: architecture, challenges and opportunities. IEEE Network (2018)
4. Naqvi, S.A.R., Hassan, S.A., Pervaiz, H., Ni, Q.: Drone-aided communication as a key enabler for 5G and resilient public safety networks. IEEE Commun. Mag. **56**(1), 36–42 (2018)
5. Sharma, V., Kumar, R.: A cooperative network framework for multi-UAV guided ground ad hoc networks. J. Intell. Robot. Syst. **77**(3–4), 629–652 (2015)
6. Sekander, S., Tabassum, H., Hossain, E.: Multi-tier drone architecture for 5G/B5G cellular networks: challenges, trends, and prospects. IEEE Commun. Mag. **56**(3), 96–103 (2018)
7. Dey, V., Pudi, V., Chattopadhyay, A., Elovici, Y.: Security vulnerabilities of unmanned aerial vehicles and countermeasures: an experimental study. In: VLSI Design, pp. 398–403. IEEE (2018)
8. Wu, Q., Liu, L., Zhang, R.: Fundamental tradeoffs in communication and trajectory design for UAV-enabled wireless network, arXiv preprint arXiv:1805.07038 (2018)
9. Wang, W., Guan, X., Wang, B., Wang, Y.: A novel mobility model based on semi-random circular movement in mobile ad hoc networks. Inf. Sci. **180**(3), 399–413 (2010)
10. Zhao, J., Gao, F., Kuang, L., Wu, Q., Jia, W.: Channel tracking with flight control system for UAV mmWave MIMO communications. IEEE Commun. Lett. **22**, 1224–1227 (2018)
11. Liu, L., Zhang, S., Zhang, R.: CoMP in the sky: UAV placement and movement optimization for multi-user communications, arXiv preprint arXiv:1802.10371 (2018)
12. Yang, D., Wu, Q., Zeng, Y., Zhang, R.: Energy trade-off in ground-to-UAV communication via trajectory design. IEEE Trans. Veh. Technol. **67**, 6721–6726 (2018)
13. Sharma, V., You, I., Kumar, R., Chauhan, V.: OFFRP: optimised fruit fly based routing protocol with congestion control for UAVs guided ad hoc networks. Int. J. Ad Hoc Ubiquit. Comput. **27**(4), 233–255 (2018)
14. Sharma, V., Bennis, M., Kumar, R.: UAV-assisted heterogeneous networks for capacity enhancement. IEEE Commun. Lett. **20**(6), 1207–1210 (2016)
15. Sharma, V., Reina, D., Kumar, R.: HMADSO: a novel hill Myna and desert sparrow optimization algorithm for cooperative rendezvous and task allocation in FANETS. Soft Comput. **22**(18), 6191–6214 (2018)

16. Grocholsky, B., Keller, J., Kumar, V., Pappas, G.: Cooperative air and ground surveillance. IEEE Robot. Autom. Mag. **13**(3), 16–25 (2006)
17. Ciobanu, R.-I., Reina, D., Dobre, C., Toral, S., Johnson, P.: JDER: a history-based forwarding scheme for delay tolerant networks using Jaccard distance and encountered ration. J. Netw. Comput. Appl. **40**, 279–291 (2014)
18. Chandhar, P., Danev, D., Larsson, E.G.: Massive MIMO as enabler for communications with drone swarms. In: Unmanned Aircraft Systems, pp. 347–354. IEEE (2016)
19. Ho, D.-T., Shimamoto, S.: Highly reliable communication protocol for WSN-UAV system employing TDMA and PFS scheme. In: 2011 IEEE GLOBECOM Workshops (GC Wkshps), pp. 1320–1324. IEEE (2011)
20. Han, Z., Swindlehurst, A.L., Liu, K.R.: Optimization of MANET connectivity via smart deployment/movement of unmanned air vehicles. IEEE Trans. Veh. Technol. **58**(7), 3533–3546 (2009)
21. Han, Z., Swindlehurst, A.L., Liu, K.R.: Smart deployment/movement of unmanned air vehicle to improve connectivity in MANET. In: 2006 IEEE Wireless Communications and Networking Conference, WCNC 2006, vol. 1, pp. 252–257. IEEE (2006)
22. Taqieddin, E., Awad, F., Ahmad, H.: Location-aware and mobility-based performance optimization for wireless sensor networks. JoWUA **8**(4), 37–59 (2017)
23. Azari, M.M., Rosas, F., Chen, K.-C., Pollin, S.: Ultra reliable UAV communication using altitude and cooperation diversity. IEEE Trans. Commun. **66**(1), 330–344 (2018)
24. Nguyen, M.-N., Nguyen, L.D., Duong, T.Q., Tuan, H.D.: Real-time optimal resource allocation for embedded UAV communication systems. IEEE Wirel. Commun. Lett. (2018). https://doi.org/10.1109/LWC.2018.2867775
25. Liu, D., et al.: Self-organizing relay selection in UAV communication networks: A matching game perspective, arXiv preprint arXiv:1805.09257 (2018)
26. Sharma, V., Kumar, R., Kumar, N.: DPTR: distributed priority tree-based routing protocol for FANETs. Comput. Commun. **122**, 129–151 (2018)
27. Sharma, V., Kumar, R.: Three-tier neural model for service provisioning over collaborative flying ad hoc networks. Neural Comput. Appl. **29**(10), 837–856 (2018)
28. Harri, J., Filali, F., Bonnet, C.: Mobility models for vehicular ad hoc networks: a survey and taxonomy. IEEE Commun. Surv. Tutor. **11**(4), 19–41 (2009)
29. Valenza, F., Su, T., Spinoso, S., Lioy, A., Sisto, R., Vallini, M.: A formal approach for network security policy validation. J. Wirel. Mob. Netw. Ubiquit. Comput. Dependable Appl. (JoWUA) **8**(1), 79–100 (2017)
30. Bhargava, B.K., Johnson, A.M., Munyengabe, G.I., Angin, P.: A systematic approach for attack analysis and mitigation in V2V networks. JoWUA **7**(1), 79–96 (2016)
31. Secinti, G., Darian, P.B., Canberk, B., Chowdhury, K.R.: SDNs in the sky: robust end-to-end connectivity for aerial vehicular networks. IEEE Commun. Mag. **56**, 16–21 (2018)
32. Abbasi, A.A., Younis, M.: A survey on clustering algorithms for wireless sensor networks. Comput. Commun. **30**(14–15), 2826–2841 (2007)

Author Index

Printed in the United States
By Bookmasters